The European Drivers Handbook

AA

REYKJAVÍK
ICELAND
Norwegian Sea
0 200 400 600 800 km
0 100 200 300 400 500 miles
ATLANTIC OCEAN
NORWAY
OSLO
Inverness
Aberdeen
NORTHERN IRELAND
Glasgow
Londonderry
Edinburgh
Belfast
North Sea
Galway
Newcastle upon Tyne
REPUBLIC OF IRELAND
Killarney
DUBLIN
York
Liverpool
Manchester
Cork
BRITAIN
Birmingham
Bristol
Oxford
LONDON
Plymouth
Southampton
English Channel
Gothenburg
Aalborg
DENMARK
Esbjerg
Malmö
Odense
Hamburg
BERLIN
NETHERLANDS
AMSTERDAM
The Hague
Bruges
Calais
Ghent
BRUSSELS
BELGIUM
Cologne
GERMANY
Le Havre
Brest
Frankfurt-am-Main
PRAGUE
LUXEMBOURG
PARIS
Nantes
Strasbourg
Stuttgart
Bay of Biscay
FRANCE
Munich
Salzburg
BERN
Zürich
Innsbruck
AUSTRIA
Geneva
SWITZERLAND
La Coruña-A Coruna
Bordeaux
Clermont-Ferrand
Lyon
Santiago de Compostela
Santander
Milan
Trieste
SLOVENIA
Venice
Biarritz
Toulouse
Genoa
Porto
Bologna
ANDORRA
Marseille
Nice
Florence
Zaragoza
PORTUGAL
LISBON
MADRID
ITALY
Corsica
Pescara
Barcelona
Ajaccio
ROME
SPAIN
Olbia
Foggia
Valencia
Naples
Sardinia
Seville
Balearic Islands
Cádiz
Málaga
Murcia
Tyrrhenian Sea
Cagliari
Algeciras
Mediterranean Sea
Messina
Palermo
Sicily
MOROCCO
ALGERIA
TUNISIA
MALTA

Barents Sea
FINLAND
RUSSIA
HELSINKI
TALLINN
ESTONIA
MOSKOW
LATVIA
RĪGA
LITHUANIA
VILNIUS
RUSSIA
MINSK
BELARUS
KIEV
UKRAINE
MOLDOVA
CHIȘINĂU
ROMANIA
BELGRADE
BUCHAREST
Black Sea
TBILISI
GEORGIA
AZERBAIJAN
ARMENIA
YERAVAN
BULGARIA
SKOPJE
SOFIA
MACEDONIA
ANKARA
TURKEY
GREECE
Aegean Sea
ATHENS
SYRIA
IRAQ
CYPRUS
LEBANON
Crete

Contents

First published 2008

Managed and designed by Bookwork Creative Associates Ltd
Driving in... motoring information supplied by AA International Motoring Services

Published by AA Publishing, a trading name of Automobile Association Developments Limited, whose registered office is Fanum House, Basing View, Basingstoke, Hampshire RG21 4EA. Registered number 1878835.

ISBN: 978-0-7495-5643-3

A CIP catalogue record for this book is available from the British Library.

Printed and bound by Leo Paper Products, China

Find out more about AA Publishing and the wide range of services the AA provides by visiting our website at **www.theAA.com**

A03334

Cover picture credits – front cover: (main) AA/C Sawyer (Provence, France); (inset) AA/J Smith (Istria, Croatia); back cover: (i & iii) AA/S Day (Brittany, France); (ii) AA/M Chaplow (Costa Brava, Spain).

Introduction

This essential handbook, covering 35 European countries, has been put together to ensure you are well prepared for motoring in Europe, whether you are an experienced motorist or adventuring abroad with your car for the first time.

We have included information on requirements by country – from Austria to Turkey – with local rules for drivers, including seatbelt and drink/driving laws, speed limits and headlight requirements. There are also details of the documents you should take, equipment to carry in your car and what toll charges you will encounter. Useful quick-reference charts detail compulsory requirements, winter motoring information and distances. Principal mountain passes are also included. Easy-to-read maps, showing both toll and toll-free motorways, will help with route planning and budgeting.

A selection of scenic tours, each with an accompanying route map, will guide you through the best places of interest the region has to offer.

The words and phrases section is tailored to assist if you encounter difficulties on the road, from asking directions to reading traffic signs.

With all this information at your fingertips, the AA's European Drivers Handbook is your passport to a safe and enjoyable trip.

The car tours featured in this handbook were taken from The AA Best Drives series of top-selling tour guides for the motorist to all the best driving destinations. The words and phrases were taken from the AA Phrase Books, which contain everything you'd expect from a comprehensive language series. For information on the full range of the AA's guides, maps and atlases visit – **www.theAA.com/travel**

Part 1
Before you go

Before you go

Documents and insurance

Documents you should take with you

- A valid full driving licence (not provisional), with paper counterpart if you have a photocard licence.
- An International Driving Permit where necessary (see individual country sections).
- The original vehicle registration document.
- Your motor insurance certificate.
- Your passport.
- You may need a visa for certain countries if you hold a UK passport that was not issued in the UK or a foreign passport that was issued outside Europe.
- If you're travelling in a vehicle other than a motor car or motorcycle or taking a boat, make sure you have any additional documentation that may be required.
  If the vehicle you're driving is borrowed, hired or leased, contact the AA for guidance.

Breakdown cover

Make sure that you have adequate cover. AA European Breakdown Cover provides cover for many European countries, **tel: 0800 072 3279** or visit **www.theAA.com** and follow the link **European Breakdown Cover**.

Car insurance

Contact your insurer for advice at least a month before taking a vehicle overseas. Ensure that you're adequately covered and have the necessary documents to prove it. A Green Card (proof of insurance cover while using your vehicle abroad) is compulsory in Bosnia.

Credit cards

Occasionally we hear that UK issued credit cards are not accepted at stores or petrol stations in other countries. If you're going to rely on a particular credit card while away we recommend that you check with your card company to confirm that it can be used in the countries you are visiting.

Driving licence

You must always carry your full UK driving licence and other qualified drivers in your party should take their licences in case of an emergency. All valid UK licences should be accepted in the countries listed in this book. However, this cannot be guaranteed for older all green style UK licences (in Northern Ireland older paper style with photographic counterpart). Drivers may wish to voluntarily update them before travelling abroad, if time permits. Alternatively, older licences may be accompanied by an International Driving Permit (IDP).

Passports

Each person (including children and babies) must hold or be named on an up-to-date passport. Some countries require a passport to remain valid for a minimum period (usually at least six months) beyond the date of entry

– check before you travel. Application forms are available from main post offices and from Passport Offices or you can apply for an application form online at **www.passport.gov.uk**. Allow at least 10 working days for your application to be processed. Holders of passports from outside the UK should check regarding any visa requirements with the appropriate embassy or consulate. Note down your passport number and the date of issue and keep this information in a safe place, separate from your passport. Carry your passport at all times as proof of identity and take one other form of photo ID with you.

Note: children visiting Bulgaria must have their own passport. Children included in parent's passports will only be allowed in if the passport also has their photograph.

Personal insurance

It is essential that you are fully covered by travel insurance. Make sure you have at least the minimum cover for medical expenses, theft and losses abroad.

European Health Insurance Card

National Health treatment is not available outside the UK but you may be able to get free or reduced cost treatment within the EU with the European Health Insurance Card (EHIC). The EHIC (which replaced the E111) entitles UK residents who are travelling in Europe to reduced cost, sometimes free, state provided emergency healthcare when visiting a European Union (EU) country, Iceland, Liechtenstein, Norway or Switzerland. The card is available free of charge and is valid for up to five years. Apply online at **www.dh.gov.uk/travellers**, or by phoning the EHIC Application Line on **0845 606 2030**. Postal application packs are available from post offices. The EHIC may not cover you for all medical costs incurred (the cost of bringing a person back to the UK in the event of illness or death is never covered) so you are strongly advised to also arrange travel insurance to ensure that you are covered for all possible eventualities.

Pets

If you intend to take your pet abroad contact the Pet Travel Scheme (PETS) helpline **tel: 0870 241 1710** or visit the PETS website **www.defra.gov.uk/animalh/quarantine/pets/index.htm**

Travel advice

For up-to-date travel advice from the Foreign & Commonwealth Office **tel: 0845 850 2829** or visit **www.fco.gov.uk/travel**

Your documents

You may be asked to produce your documents at any time. To avoid a police fine and/or confiscation of your vehicle, be sure that they are in order and readily available for inspection.

Preparing your car

Child restraints

Never fit a rear-facing car seat in any seat with an active airbag. Use only an approved restraint suitable for the child's weight and height, visit **www.childcarseats.org.uk** for further information.

Fire extinguisher/first aid kit

In some countries it is compulsory to equip your vehicle with these items (see individual country sections). A fire extinguisher is not required for two-wheeled vehicles.

Headlights

If you're driving to the Continent you must adjust the headlamp beam pattern to suit driving on the right so that the dipped beam doesn't dazzle oncoming drivers (this is a compulsory requirement in most countries). Headlamp beam converter kits are widely available but don't leave headlamp conversion to the last minute, as a dealer may need to make the adjustment especially if your car has high-intensity discharge (HID), halogen-type or xenon headlamps – check the car's handbook. Remember to remove the converters as soon as you return to the UK. We also recommend that you take a set of replacement bulbs even when it is not a compulsory requirement.

Keys

Many modern cars have a 'transponder' key to prevent theft. If you lose the key, recovery to an authorised dealer is usually the only answer. Even a dealer may take several days to obtain a replacement, so always carry a spare set of keys.

Mirrors

It is essential to have clear all-round vision. External rear-view mirrors should be fitted to both sides of your vehicle.

Nationality plate

Vehicles must display a nationality plate of the approved pattern, design and size. UK registration plates displaying the GB Euro

symbol (Euro plates) make display of a conventional sticker unnecessary when driving within the EU. In some countries outside the EU a conventional sticker is required even if you have Euro plates, so it is always safer to display one.

Overloading

Don't overload the car as, safety risks apart, this can incur fines and possibly invalidate your insurance.

Reflective jacket/waistcoat

Reflective jackets/waistcoats are compulsory in Andorra, Austria, Belgium, Croatia, Italy, Slovakia and Spain. We recommend that that you carry at least two jackets/waistcoats in the passenger compartment – one for the driver and one for a passenger who may assist in changing a wheel. If you intend to hire a car in one of the countries that require reflective jackets be aware that not all rental firms provide jackets with their cars. Check with the hire company before you travel.

Preparing your car continued

Seat belts
If seat belts are fitted to your vehicle it is compulsory to wear them.

Servicing
Service your car well in advance of your journey to reduce the chance of expensive breakdowns when abroad.

Speed-trap detection devices
The use or possession of devices to detect police radar is illegal in most European countries. Penalties can include a fine, driving ban and even imprisonment.

Toolkit
Check the handbook for the location of the basic toolkit for the car which should contain at least a jack and wheel removal tools. If locking wheel nuts are fitted make sure that the toolkit includes the key or removal tool.

Tyres
Most countries require a minimum tread depth of 1.6mm over the central three-quarters of the tread and around the whole circumference. We recommend a minimum of 2mm but consider changing tyres if the tread is down to 3mm before you go. Tyres wear out quickly after they get down to 3mm.

Warning triangle
The use of a warning triangle is compulsory in most European countries in the event of accident or breakdown (not always required for two-wheeled vehicles). In certain circumstances two triangles are required.

Wheel chains
Wheel chains are important for any winter motoring and compulsory in some countries even when using winter tyres (see the

individual country sections). Snow chains are available from the AA's Dover and Folkestone shops (Dover **tel: 01304 208122**; Folkestone **tel: 01303 273576**).The Folkestone shop is beyond the customs point. Telephone ahead to check availability, you will be asked for the vehicle make and model and the tyre size read from the sidewall of the tyre.

A selection of travel and emergency kits are available from accessory stores and the AA Travelshops at Folkestone (Eurotunnel) and Dover.

Part 2

On the road

General motoring information

Accidents

If you are involved in an accident you must stop, switch on your hazard warning lights and place a warning triangle on the road at a suitable distance. If the accident necessitates calling the police, leave the vehicle in position and phone the police, also obtain medical assistance if needed. Notify your insurance company (by letter) within 24 hours, making sure all the essential particulars are noted. If you can, take photographs of the scene of the accident. (See the individual country sections for emergency telephone numbers.)

Blue Badge users

The Blue Badge is recognised in most European countries. When displayed on the dashboard of a car, it allows you to make use of the same parking concessions allowed for the country's own citizens with a disability.

The concessions do differ from country to country so it's important to know where, when and for how long you can park in each country. Visit **www.theaa.com/motoring_advice/overseas/blue-badge-users.html** to download a leaflet giving details of parking concessions in 29 countries. It's a good idea to print off the information you need for each country along with a copy of the multilingual notice towards the back of the leaflet. Leave this notice next to your Blue Badge when you park to tell the police and parking officers about your rights in their own language. **Remember, if you are in any doubt about your rights, don't park.**

Breakdown

Try to move your car to the side of the road so that it does not obstruct traffic flow. Switch on your hazard warning lights and place a warning triangle to the rear of the vehicle at a suitable distance. Find the nearest telephone to call for assistance. On motorways, emergency telephones are generally located every 2km (1.25 miles) and automatically connect you to the official motorway breakdown service.

Car crime

Never leave handbags and other attractive items in obvious view even when you are in the car, and never leave anything in an unattended car. For advice on car crime or personal safety in specific countries, contact the Foreign Office Travel Advice Unit on **0845 850 2829** or visit **www.fco.gov.uk**

Crash or safety helmets

The wearing of crash or safety helmets by motorcyclists and their passengers is compulsory in all countries.

Delays and diversions

Roadworks and major events mean roads are sometimes closed completely, in which case follow locally signed detours. There may be delays at peak travel periods, delays on some main routes and at frontier crossing points. Mountain passes and alpine roads may be closed during the winter months (see pages 206–217).

Drinking and driving

There is only one safe rule – if you drink, don't drive. Laws are strict and the penalties are severe.

Fines

Some countries impose on-the-spot fines for minor traffic offences. Fines are generally paid in the currency of the country concerned. You must obtain a receipt as proof of payment.

General motoring information continued

Journey times

Volume of traffic, road and weather conditions will all affect calculations when estimating how long a journey will take. On motorways the average speed will be about 37kph (60mph), on all-purpose roads out of town the average can be about 28kph (45mph), and in urban areas it may be as low as 9–12kph (15–20mph). Make allowances for refreshments, petrol and toilet stops, and if travelling to a port or airport add extra time for checking in and unforeseen delays.

Leaded petrol

Leaded petrol is no longer generally available in northern European countries and Lead Replacement Petrol (LRP) is getting more difficult to find. If LRP is not on sale, an anti-wear additive (for treating unleaded petrol) can be bought from the filling station shop.

Mobile phones

The use of hand-held mobile phones while driving is prohibited in many countries.

Overloading

Don't overload your car as, safety risks apart, this can incur fines and possibly invalidate insurance. Overloading can damage the suspension, burn out the clutch and cause punctures or uneven wear on tyres.

Priority including roundabouts

In mainland Europe in built-up areas, you must give way to traffic coming from the right – *priorité à droite*. However, at roundabouts with signs bearing the words *'Vous n'avez pas la priorité'* or *'Cédez le passage'* traffic on the roundabout has priority. Where no such sign exists, traffic entering the roundabout has priority. Outside built-up areas, all main roads of any importance have right of way. This is indicated by a red-bordered triangle showing a black cross on a white background with the words *'Passage Protégé'* underneath; or a red-bordered triangle showing a pointed

black upright with horizontal bar on a white background; or a yellow square within a white square with points vertical.

Rule of the road

In all countries covered in this guide, apart from Cyprus (north and south), Malta, Great Britain and Ireland, the rule of the road is to drive on the right and overtake on the left. For UK drivers it's easy to forget to drive on the right, particularly after doing something familiar, such as leaving a petrol station or car park.

Signposting

Signposting between major towns and along main roads is generally efficient, but on some secondary roads and in open country advance direction signs may be less frequent. Signs are often of the pointer type and placed on walls or railings on the far side of the turn; they tend to point across the road they indicate which can be confusing at first. Difficulties may arise with spellings when crossing frontiers, and place names may not be so easily recognised when written in a different language. Extra difficulties may arise in countries with two or more official languages or dialects, although some towns may have both spellings, e.g. San Sebastian – Donostia in Spain, Antwerpen – Anvers in Belgium, Basel – Bâle in Switzerland.

Size restrictions

Check with your national camping or caravanning club that your vehicle and/or trailer complies with the weight and size legislation in the countries that you intend to visit.

Spectacles

Take a spare pair of spectacles if you wear them – especially if you are the sole driver. This is a compulsory requirement for Spain.

Speed limits

Speed limits for individual countries are listed in the appropriate country sections. Lower limits will apply to motorcycles in some countries and also generally when towing a trailer unless indicated otherwise. Visiting drivers who have held a full licence for under two years may also have to adhere to lower speed limits.

How far in miles – conversion table: kilometres – miles

kms	1	2	3	4	5	10	15	20	25	30	35	40	45	50
miles	0.62	1.24	1.86	2.49	3.11	6.21	9.32	12.43	15.53	18.64	21.75	24.85	27.96	31.07

DRIVING REQUIREMENTS	Austria	Belgium	Croatia	Denmark	Fra
Minimum age/UK licence holders **(1)**	**18**	**18**	**18**	**17**	**18**
International Driving Permit required for UK licence holders (IDP)	**No (2)**	**No**	**No**	**No**	**N**
Original registration document	**C**	**C**	**C**	**C**	**C**
Motor vehicle insurance **(4)**	**C**	**C**	**C**	**C**	**C**
Motorway tax	**C & Tolls**	**No**	**Tolls**	**Tolls**	**To**
GB sticker (5)	**C**	**C**	**C**	**C**	**C**
Warning triangle	**C (6)**	**C (6)**	**C (8)**	**C**	**R**
Reflective jacket/waistcoat	**C (6)**	**C (11)**	**C**	**n/a**	**n/**
First-aid kit	**C**	**R (17)**	**C**	**R**	**No**
Fire extinguisher (6)	**No**	**R (17)**	**No**	**R**	**N**
Headlamp adjustment (12)	**C**	**C**	**C**	**C**	**C**
On-the-spot fines	**Yes**	**Yes**	**Yes (13)**	**Yes**	**Ye**
Radar dectectors	**F**	**F**	**F**	**F**	**F**
Daytime headlights/passing lights: cars	**R**	**No (16)**	**C**	**C**	**R**
Daytime headlights/passing lights: m/cycles	**R**	**C**	**C**	**C**	**C**

C = Compulsory **R** = Recommended by AA/respective country **F** = Forbidden **n/a** = Not applicable. The above chart covers some of the most popular countries featured in this book. It must be read in conjunction with the Driving in... information for the relevant country. The numbers in brackets refer to the notes below. Items highlighted in **bold** above can be purchased from the AA Travelshop (**www.AAtravelshop.co.uk**) – the one-stop shop for all your motoring accessories.

NOTES

(1) Minimum age at which a visitor may drive a car.

(2) UK driving licences which do not incorporate a photograph are recognised but, drivers must be able to produce photographic proof of identity (e.g. passport).

(3) All valid UK licences should be accepted. However, this cannot be guaranteed on older all green style UK licences. Drivers may wish to voluntarily update them before travelling abroad, if time permits. Alternatively, older licences may be accompanied by an IDP.

(4) Before taking a vehicle abroad contact your motor insurer or broker to notify them of your intentions, and ask their advice. It is important to know what level of cover you will have and what documents you need to prove it.

(5) GB Stickers are compulsory within the EU unless your UK registration plates display the GB Euro-symbol (Euro plates) which became a legal option from 21 March 2001. The Euro plate must comply with the new British Standard (BS AU 145d). The Euro plate is only legally recognised in the EU; it is still a requirement to display a GB sticker when travelling outside the EU.

(6) Not required for two-wheeled vehicles.

(7) Although it is not compulsory for visiting motorists to carry a warning triangle, its use is compulsory in an accident/breakdown situation.

(8) Spain: One warning triangle is compulsory fo non-Spanish registered vehicles; two for Spanish registered vehicles. **Note:** Drivers of non-Spanish registered vehicles should consider carrying two triangles as, regardless of regulations, local officials may impose an on-the-spot fine if only one is available. **Croatia:** Two triangles are compulsory for vehicles towing a trailer.

(9) The use of hazard warning lights or a warning triangle is compulsory in an accident/breakdown situation. However, a warning triangle should always be carried as hazard warning lights have no effect at bends or rises in the road, or may become damaged or inoperative.

(10) Compulsory for vehicles with an unladen weight exceeding 1524kg.

ermany	Ireland	Italy	Netherlands	Norway	Portugal	Spain	Sweden	Switzerland
8	17	18	18	18	17 (14)	18	18	18
o	No	No (3)	No	No	No (3)	No (3)	No (2)	No
;	C	C	C	C	C	C	C	C
:	C	C	C	C	C	C	C	C
lo	Tolls	Tolls	No	Tolls	Tolls	Tolls	Tolls	C & Tolls
;	C	C	C	C	C	C	C	C
(7)	C (10)	C (6)	R (9&6)	C (6)	R (9)	C (8&6)	R	C (6)
/a	n/a	C (11&6)	n/a	R (11)	R (11)	C (11&6)	n/a	n/a
(17)	No	No	No	R	No	No	R	No
lo	No	No	No	R	No	No	R	No
;	No	C	C	C	C	C	C	C
'es	Yes (13)	Yes (13)	Yes	Yes	Yes	Yes	Yes (13)	Yes
	F	F	F	F	F	F	F	F
(16)	No (16)	C (15)	R	C	No (16)	No	C	R
;	R	C	R	C	C	C	C	R

11) It is compulsory for driver and/or assenger(s) to wear a reflective jacket/waistcoat vhen exiting a vehicle immobilised on the arriageway; in **Italy** at night or in poor visibility; n **Spain** on all motorways and busy roads. In **roatia** wearing a jacket is compulsory whenever ou have to get out of the vehicle at the roadside n an emergency. In **Portugal** and **Norway** the ctual law applies to residents; however, egardless of the regulations local officials may mpose an on-the-spot fine. In **Belgium** the vearing of a reflective jacket only applies to the river, it must be worn should you be stranded on Belgian motorway or on a major road or should ou stop at a place where parking is not allowed.

12) Headlamp adjustment for older vehicles can e done by using simple adhesive masks on the eadlamp glass. For newer vehicles with HID, enon or many halogen headlamps it is not so asy. Check out what you must do well before our departure by contacting a dealer for your nake of vehicle. Without adjustment the dipped eam will dazzle oncoming drivers and this could esult in a fine. In some countries it is compulsory o use dipped headlights at all times when driving luring the day. **Note:** This adjustment is not equired for two-wheeled vehicles as the beam attern is more symmetrical, but check that any xtra loading has not affected the beam height.

On some cars it is inadvisable or impossible for anyone other than a qualified technician to change a headlamp bulb unit e.g. high intensity discharge (HID) headlamps and carrying spares is not an option. However, it is recommended that spare bulbs are carried for any lights that may be easily and/or safely replaced by the owner/driver. Spare bulbs are compulsory for **Spain** and **Croatia** and the tools to change them are still a requirement for **Spain**.

(13) Sweden: Police are not authorised to actually collect fines, which must be paid in accordance with notice instructions. **Italy:** Police will collect a quarter of the maximum fine amount from drivers of foreign registered vehicles. Ireland: Police are not authorised to actually collect fines, they will issue a notice which must be paid within 21 days. **Croatia:** The fine does not have to be paid on the spot; however it does need to be paid within 8 days.

(14) Portugal: Visiting drivers of 17 years of age may encounter problems even though they hold a valid driving licence in the UK.

(15) Outside built-up areas, during snow/rain/poor visability.

(16) Compulsory during daylight hours if visibility is poor.

(17) Recommended as their carriage is compulsory for vehicles registered in that country.

WINTER TYRE/SNOW CHAIN REQUIREMENT CHART

	Andorra	Austria	Denmark	Finland
Winter tyres	**R**	**R**	**–**	**M (1)**
Snow chains **(3)**	**C**	**C**	**R**	**–**

P = Permitted
C = Should be carried and must be used as dictated by local signs or road conditions. Reduced speed limits may apply.
R = Recommended
M = Mandatory

This information is purely for vehicles not exceeding 3,500kg.
This chart only displays Winter Requirements, these are in addition to the 'standard' compulsory items that should be carried.
The above chart should be read in conjunction with the Driving in... information.
Snow chains may be purchased from the **AA Travelshop** at Dover and Eurotunnel (Folkestone) – the one-stop shop for all your motoring accessories.

NOTES
(1) From the 1 December to the end of February, unless otherwise indicated by road signs.
Tyres must be marked M&S on the side wall. Spiked tyres may be used from 1 November to the first Monday after Easter.

France	Germany	Great Britain	Italy	Norway	Sweden	Switzerland
–	R (2)	–	R	R	R	–
C	C	P	C	C	C	C

(2) Winter tyres (or 'all-year' tyres) must bear the mark M&S or the snowflake symbol on the side wall.

(3) Snow chains must be fitted on at least two drive wheels. In any country, snow chains may only be used where there is sufficient snow covering to avoid any possibility of damage to the road surfaces. A fine may be imposed if damage is caused.

General advice

In any country the driver is responsible for equipping and controlling their vehicle correctly. Drivers may be liable to a fine if they impede the normal flow of traffic or cause an accident as a consequence of not adapting their vehicle (tyres/snow chains) to the prevailing weather conditions. Road conditions in winter in many resorts will be much more severe than anything encountered in the United Kingdom. The AA only recommends driving in extreme winter conditions if the driver is confident and the vehicle suitably equipped.

Driving in Austria (Central Europe)

The regulations below should be read in conjunction with the General motoring information on pages 18–21.

Drinking and driving

The maximum permitted level of alcohol in the bloodstream is 0.049. If it is between 0.05 per cent and 0.079 per cent a fine will be imposed, 0.08 per cent or more a severe fine and/or a driving ban for Austria imposed.

Driving licence

The minimum age at which a UK licence holder may drive a temporarily imported car is 18, motorcycle (up to 50cc) with a maximum design speed of 45km/h (27mph) 16 and motorcycle (over 50cc) 18. Note: UK Driving licences that do not incorporate a photograph are only valid when accompanied by photographic proof of identity, e.g. passport.

Fines

On-the-spot fines of up to €36, can be imposed. The officer collecting the fine should issue an official receipt. For higher fines the driver will be asked to pay a deposit and the remainder of the fine within two weeks. Parked vehicles obstructing traffic may be towed away.

Fuel

Unleaded petrol (95 and 98 octane) and diesel available, limited LPG available. Leaded petrol is not sold, although a lead substitute additive is available. Petrol in a can is permitted. Credit cards are accepted by larger filling stations; check with your card issuer for usage in Austria before you travel.

Lights

Passing lights (dipped headlights or daytime running lights) are recommended at all times, for all vehicles.

Motorcycles

It is recommended to use dipped headlights during the day. It is compulsory for the driver and passenger to wear a crash helmet.

Motor Insurance

Third-party insurance is compulsory, including cover for trailers.

Passengers/children in cars

Children under 14 and less than 1.5m (4ft 11in) in height cannot travel as a front/rear seat passenger unless using suitable restraint system for their height/weight. Vehicles without such protection (e.g. two-seater sports cars or vans/lorries) may not carry children under 14 years. Children under 14 but over 1.5m (4ft 11in) in height must use the adult seat belt. Children 14 or over and over 1.35m (4ft 5in) in height are allowed to use a *Dreipunktgurt* (three-point seat belt) without a special child seat, if the belt does not cover the child's throat/neck.

Seat belts

It is compulsory for front- and rear-seat occupants to wear seat belts, if fitted. If you do not comply there is a fine of €35.

Speed limits

The standard legal limits, which may be varied by signs, for **private vehicles without trailers** are: In built-up areas up to 50km/h (31mph), outside built-up areas 100km/h (62mph) and motorways up to 130km/h (80mph). Lower limits apply to a **car towing a caravan (not over 750kg):** In built-up areas areas 50km/h (31mph), outside built-up areas and motorways 100km/h (62mph). For a **car towing a caravan over 750kg** when the weight of the trailer does not exceed that of the vehicle and the maximum weight of both vehicles does not exceed 3,500kg the standard legal limits are: In built-up areas 50km/h (31mph), outside built-up areas 80km/h (49mph), motorways 100km/h (62mph).

Vehicles not capable of sustaining minimum speed of 60km/h (37mph) are not permitted on motorways. Mopeds must not exceed 45km/h (28mph). The maximum recommended speed limit for vehicles with snow chains is 40km/h (24mph). Vehicles with spiked tyres must not exceed 100km/h (62mph) on motorways and 80km/h (49mph) on other roads.

Additional information

- It is compulsory to carry a warning triangle that conforms to EC regulation 27 (for vehicles with more than two wheels) and a first-aid kit in a strong dirt-proof box.
- All vehicles using Austrian motorways (see map on page 68) and expressways must display a motorway tax sticker (*vignette*). The stickers, valid for one calendar year, two months or 10 days, may be purchased at some petrol stations located close to the border in neighbouring countries and in Austria, at the frontier, at post offices or in ÖAMTC offices. Tolls are also payable when passing through certain motorway tunnels (see page 28). The fine for driving without a motorway sticker can be severe.
- The use of the horn is generally prohibited in Vienna and in the vicinity of hospitals.
- When a school bus has stopped to let children on and off, indicated by a yellow flashing light, drivers travelling in the same direction are not permitted to overtake.
- Every car driver has to carry a reflective jacket/waistcoat (compliant with European regulation EN471) which must be used in case of breakdown or accident and even when setting up a warning triangle on the road.
- In winter months, fitting winter tyres is highly recommended and, in extreme conditions, cars should be fitted with snow chains. The international sign for the compulsory use of snow chains is then used. Spiked tyres may be used from 1 October to 31 May, local regulations may extend this period.
- It is prohibited to use radar detectors.

Travel facts and tolls: Austria

Austrian National Tourist Office
9–11 Richmond Buildings
London W1D 3HF
Tel: 020 7440 3830
Holiday Information Line: **0845 101 1818**
www.austria.info

Banking hours
Banks are generally open Monday to Friday 8am to 3pm and up to 5.30pm on Thursday.

Credit/debit cards
Visa, MasterCard and Diners Club are accepted by the larger hotels, restaurants and some garages, but smaller establishments prefer cash.

Currency
The Euro (€) is the currency of Austria. Euro coins are issued in denominations of 1, 2, 5, 10, 20 and 50 cents and €1 and €2. Banknotes are issued in denominations of €5, €10, €20, €50, €100, €200 and €500.

Electricity
Electric current is 220 volts AC and appliances need two-round-pin continental plugs.

Health care
Free or reduced-cost medical treatment is available in Austria to European visitors on production of a valid European Health Insurance Card (EHIC). See page 11. Comprehensive travel insurance is still advised and is essential for all other visitors.

Pharmacies
Pharmacies (*Apotheken*) are the only places that sell over-the-counter medicines. Take all prescription medicines with you.

Post offices
Postage stamps are sold at post offices and from tobacco kiosks. Post boxes are yellow. Post Office (*Postamt*) opening times are generally Monday to Friday 8 to 12 and 2 to 6. In major cities, hours extend through lunch time and into Saturday morning and at least one office will be open 24 hours.

Safe water
Tap water throughout Austria is safe to drink. Bottled mineral water from local springs is available – look out for well-known brands *Vöslauer* and *Römerquelle.*

Telephones
Austrian phone booths are generally dark green with yellow roofs. All boxes display the post horn symbol. Most boxes will only accept phone cards which are sold by post offices and tobacconists. The country code for Austria is 43. To call home from Austria dial the international code (00) followed by the country code. To call the UK from Austria dial 00 44.

Time
Austria is on Central European Time, one hour ahead of GMT (GMT + 1). Daylight Savings Time comes into effect from the end of March to the end of October (GMT + 2).

Emergency telephone numbers
Police **133**
Fire **122**
Ambulance **144**

Toll charges in Euros
For details of where to buy the motorway tax sticker (*vignette*) see page 27.

General		**Car**	**Car towing caravan/ trailer**
10 day vignette		7.60	7.60
2 month vignette		21.80	21.80
Annual vignette		72.60	72.60
Road			
A10	Tauern Autobahn	9.50	9.50
A13	Innsbruck – Brenner pass	8.00	8.00
Bridges and tunnels			
Bosruck Tunnel on **A9**		4.50	4.50
Gleinalm Tunnel on **A9**		7.50	7.50
Karawanken Tunnel on **A11**		6.50	6.50

Driving in Belgium (Western Europe)

The regulations below should be read in conjunction with the General motoring information on pages 18–21.

Drinking and driving

The maximum permitted level of alcohol in the bloodstream is 0.049 per cent. If the level of alcohol in the bloodstream is between 0.05 and 0.08 per cent you will be banned from driving for a minimum of three hours and issued an on-the-spot fine of €137.50. If you refuse to pay the fine the public prosecutor will prosecute and impose a fine up to €2,750; 0.08 per cent or more an on-the-spot fine of up to €550 and a ban from driving for at least six hours; if prosecuted (more than 0.15 per cent) fine up to €11,000 and licence suspened for up to five years.

Driving licence

The minimum age at which a UK driving licence holder may drive a temporarily imported car and/or motorcycle is 18.

Fines

The officer collecting the on-the-spot fine must issue an official receipt showing the amount of the fine. Motorists can refuse to pay an on-the-spot fine; a foreign motorist refusing to do so may be invited to make a *consignation* (deposit). If he does not, his vehicle will be impounded by the police and permanently confiscated if the deposit is not paid within 96 hours. The deposit payment is €110 higher than the amount of the on-the-spot fine. Fines can be paid in cash Euros or by debit/credit card.

Fuel

Unleaded petrol (95 and 98 octane), diesel and LPG are available. Leaded petrol is not sold, although an anti-wear additive is available. Petrol in a can is permitted, but forbidden aboard ferries/Eurotunnel. Credit cards are accepted at filling stations; check with your card issuer for usage in Belgium before you travel.

Lights

Dipped headlights should be used in poor daytime visibility.

Motorcycles

The use of dipped headlights during the day compulsory. The wearing of crash helmets is compulsory for both driver and passenger.

Motor insurance

Third-party insurance is compulsory. The police can impound an uninsured vehicle.

Motorways

Motorways are toll-free. See map page 31.

Passengers/children in cars

Children under 18 and less than 1.35m (4ft 5in) must use a suitable child-restraint system whether seated in the front or rear seat of a vehicle. When two child-restraint systems are used on the rear seats and there isn't adequate room for a third child-restraint system, then the third child may travel on the back seat protected by the

adult seat belt. It is prohibited to use a rear-facing child seat on a front seat with a front airbag unless it is deactivated.

Seat belts

It is compulsory for front/rear-seat occupants to wear seat belts, if fitted.

Speed limits

The standard legal limits, which may be varied by signs, for **private vehicles with or without trailers** are: In built-up areas up to 50km/h (31mph), outside built-up areas 90km/h (55mph) and on motorways and dual carriageways separated by a central reservation 120km/h (74mph). The minimum speed on motorways is 70km/h (43mph). A limit of 30km/h (19mph) may be indicated at the entrance to a built-up area. Vehicles with spiked tyres must not exceed 60km/h (37mph) on normal roads and 90km/h (55mph) on motorways/dual carriageways.

Additional information

- Drivers stranded on a Belgian motorway or on a major road (high-speed, usually four-lane roads, called *route pour automobiles* – sign E17), stopping at places where parking is not allowed, must wear a reflective safety jacket as soon as they leave their vehicle. The fine for non-compliance is €50 but the amount can be much higher (€55–€1,375) if the driver refuses to pay or when he must go to court (e.g. in the event of an accident).
- A warning triangle is compulsory for vehicles with more than two wheels. A first-aid kit and fire extinguisher are recommended as their carriage is compulsory for Belgian-registered vehicles.
- Traffic on a roundabout must give way to traffic coming from the right, unless indicated otherwise by road signs.
- A road sign has been introduced banning the use of cruise control on congested motorways and can also appear during motorway roadworks. Some signs will apply to vehicles over a certain weight, which will be specified on the sign should this be relevant. A fine will be imposed for non-compliance.
- Any vehicle standing must have its engine switched off, unless absolutely necessary.
- A white disc bordered in red, bearing the word *Peage* in black indicates that drivers must stop. The Dutch word *Tol* sometimes replaces *Peage*.
- The use of radar detectors is prohibited.
- The police can impound a vehicle with an unsafe load.
- Spiked tyres are permitted from 1 November until 31 March.
- Snow chains are only permitted on snow or ice covered roads.
- Winter tyres are permitted from 1 October until 30 April, a lower speed limit needs to be adhered to and the maximum design speed for the tyres displayed on a sticker on the dashboard.

BELGIUM, NETHERLANDS & LUXEMBOURG

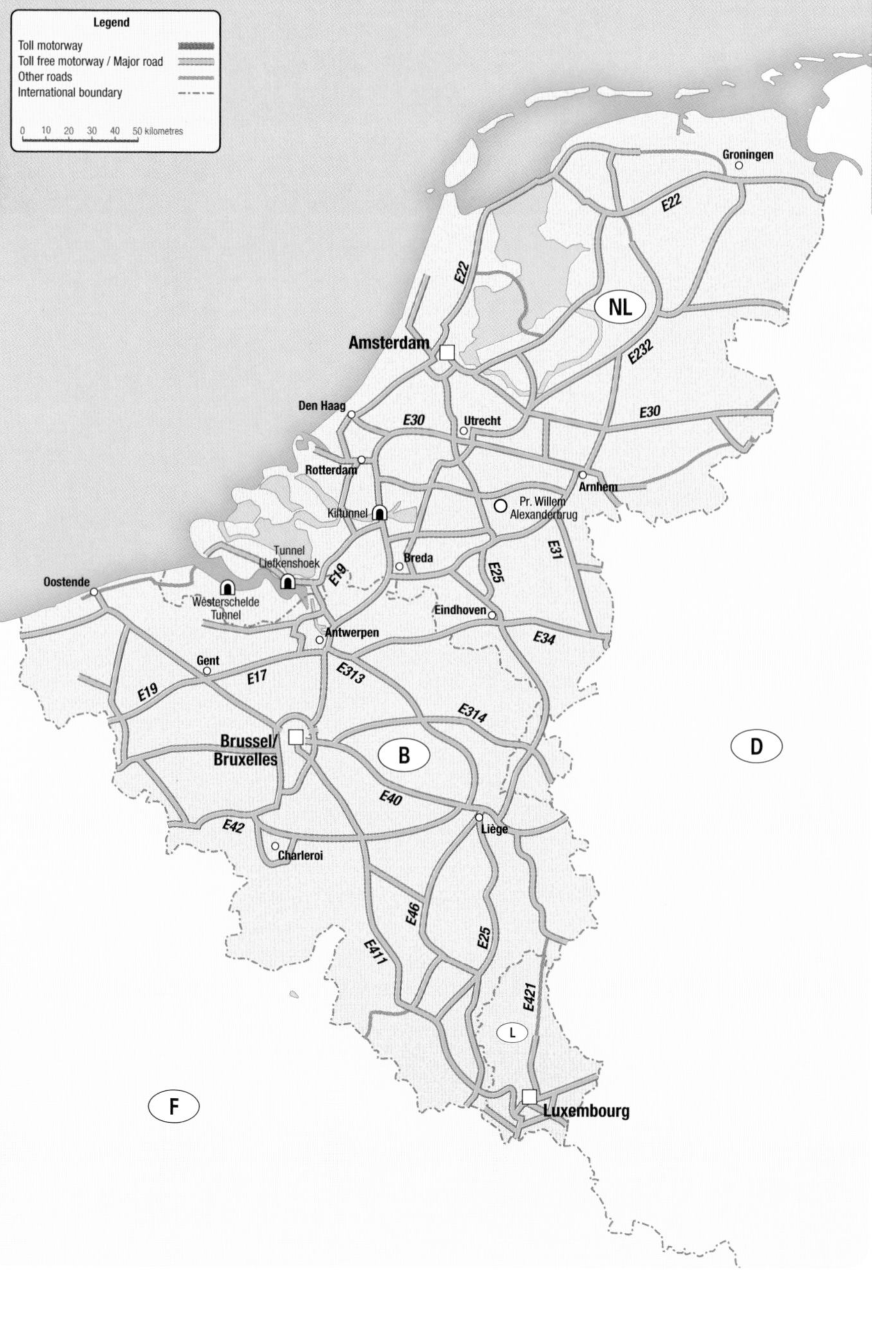

Legend
Toll motorway
Toll free motorway / Major road
Other roads
International boundary
0 10 20 30 40 50 kilometres
Groningen
E22
E22
NL
Amsterdam
E232
Den Haag
E30
Utrecht
E30
Rotterdam
Arnhem
Kiltunnel
Pr. Willem Alexanderbrug
Tunnel Liefkenshoek
Breda
E31
Oostende
E19
E25
Westerschelde Tunnel
Eindhoven
Antwerpen
E34
Gent
E17
E313
E19
E314
Brussel/ Bruxelles
B
D
E40
Liège
E42
Charleroi
E46
E25
E411
E421
L
F
Luxembourg

Travel facts: Belgium

Tourism Flanders – Brussels
Flanders House
1a Cavendish Square
London W1G 0LD
Tel: 020 7307 7739
Brochure order: **0800 954 5245**
www.visitflanders.co.uk

Belgian Tourist Office Brussels – Wallonia
217 Marsh Wall
London E14 9FJ
Tel: 0800 9545 245
www.belgiumtheplaceto.be

Banking hours
Banks are generally open Monday to Friday 9am to 4pm.

Credit/debit cards
Most major credit cards are accepted by larger hotels, restaurants and some garages but smaller establishments prefer cash. ATMs for cash advances can be found outside banks in all the major towns.

Currency
The unit of currency in Belgium is the Euro (€). Euro coins are issued in denominations of 1, 2, 5, 10, 20 and 50 cents and €1 and €2. Banknotes are issued in denominations of €5, €10, €20, €50, €100, €200 and €500.

Electricity
In Belgium the power supply is 220 volts. Plugs are round with two pins. British appliances will need an adaptor. For most non-European equipment you will also need a transformer to 100–120 volts AC.

Health care
Free or reduced-cost medical treatment is available in Belgium to European visitors on production of a valid European Health Insurance Card (EHIC). See page 11. Comprehensive travel insurance is still advised and is essential for all other visitors.

Pharmacies
Belgian pharmacies have many medicines available. Nevertheless, it is handy to take a supply of the medicines which you regularly need. It is also advisable to take a leaflet or list of active components, so that the pharmacy can find an alternative under a different product name, if necessary.

Post offices
Stamps can be bought at the post office or from a machine. Letters under 20g have a fixed rate within the EU; the weight and measurements of the envelope determines the price for destinations outside the EU. Most post offices are open Monday to Saturday 9am to 5pm.

Safe water
It is safe to drink tap water, but sometimes bottled water may taste better. Café-restaurants usually offer still or sparkling mineral water.

Telephones
For most public telephones you need a phone card, available from post offices, kiosks and some supermarkets. The country code for Belgium is 32. To call home from Belgium dial the international code (00) followed by the country code. To call the UK from Belgium dial 00 44.

Time
Belgium is on Central European Time, one hour ahead of GMT (GMT + 1). Daylight Savings Time comes into effect from the end of March to the end of October (GMT + 2).

Emergency telephone numbers
Police **101** Fire and Ambulance **100**

Toll charges in Euros

Bridges and tunnels	**Car**	**Car towing caravan/ trailer**
Liefkenshoek Tunnel on **R2**	5.00	16.00

(charges are subject to change and should only be used as a guide)

Driving in Bosnia and Herzegovina (South East Europe)

The regulations below should be read in conjunction with the General motoring information on pages 18–21.

Drinking and driving

If the level of alcohol in the bloodstream is 0.031 per cent or more, severe penalties include a fine, imprisonment and/or suspension of driving licence.

Driving licence

The minimum age at which a UK licence holder may drive a temporarily imported car and/or motorcycle (exceeding 125cc) is 18. We recommend that you obtain an International Driving Permit to accompany your UK driving licence.

Fines

On-the-spot fines can be imposed or, for more serious violations, sentence by a local court. An official receipt should be obtained.

Fuel

Leaded petrol (98 octane), unleaded petrol (95 and 98 octane) and diesel (*dizel*) is available. LPG is available at approximately 60 filling stations throughout the country. Petrol in a can is permitted. Credit cards are accepted at a few filling stations in the Sarajevo area; check with your card issuer for usage in Bosnia and Herzegovina before you travel.

Lights

The use of dipped headlights during the day is compulsory throughout Bosnia and Herzegovina.

The tranquil River Neretva can be explored by canoe at Mostar

Motorcycles

The use of dipped headlights during the day is compulsory throughout Bosnia and Herzegovina. The wearing of crash helmets is compulsory for both driver and passenger.

Driving in Bosnia and Herzegovina continued

Sarajevo's old Turkish Quarter

Motor insurance

A Green Card is compulsory.

Passengers/children in cars

A person visibly under the influence of alcohol is not permitted to travel in a vehicle as a front seat passenger. Children under 12 cannot travel as front seat passengers. Children under five must use a suitable child-restraint system.

Seat belts

It is compulsory for front/rear-seat occupants to wear seat belts, if fitted.

Speed limits

The standard legal limits, which may be varied by signs, for **private vehicles without trailers** are: In built-up areas 60km/h (37mph), outside built-up areas 80km/h (49mph) but 100km/h (62mph) on dual carriageways and 130km/h (80mph) on motorways.

Additional information

- It is compulsory for visitors to equip their vehicle with a set of replacement bulbs. A first-aid kit and a warning triangle are also compulsory, two triangles are required if towing a trailer.
- The authorities at the frontier must certify any visible damage to a vehicle entering Bosnia and Herzegovina and a certificate obtained; this must be produced when leaving.
- Winter tyres or M&S tyres are compulsory between 15 November and 15 April. It is recommended that snow chains are carried as their use is compulsory if the relevant road sign is displayed or the snow covering is over 5cm (2.5in) deep. Spiked tyres are forbidden.

Travel facts: Bosnia and Herzegovina

Tourism Association of Bosnia & Herzegovina
Branilaca Sarajeva st 21/II
71000 Sarajevo
Bosnia & Herzegovina
Tel: 33 252 924
www.bhtourism.ba

Embassy of Bosnia & Herzegovina
5–7 Lexham Gardens
London W8 5JJ
Tel: **020 7373 0867**

Visitors from the UK should check **www.fco.gov.uk** for the latest travel advice.

Banking hours
Banks are generally open Monday to Friday 8am to 7pm.

Credit/debit cards/travellers' cheques
Most transactions are in cash. The acceptance of major credit and debit cards outside of Sarajevo is becoming more widespread (check with your card provider), but it is advisable to carry enough cash when travelling outside major cities. Cashing traveller's cheques is possible at some banks. ATMs are available in increasing numbers in the larger cities.

Currency
The official currency is the Convertible Mark (Konvertibilna Maraka or KM), abbreviated as BAM. It is linked to the Euro (1.95KM = 1 Euro). Notes are in denominations of BAM200, 100, 50, 20, 10, 5 and 1 and 50 pfenings. Coins are in denominations of BAM2 and 1, and 50, 20 and 10 pfenings. Some Euro notes (but not coins) are widely accepted. Expect your change in KM.

Electricity
The power supply is 220 volts AC, 50Hz. Two-pin plugs are in use.

Health care
Comprehensive travel insurance is essential for all visitors.

Language
The official languages are Bosnian, Serbian and Croatian. The Croats and Bosniaks use the Latin alphabet, whereas the Serbs use the Cyrillic. Most young people will know some English.

Pharmacies
To find a pharmacy, ask for *apoteka.* In major cities they will generally have regular prescription drugs readily available; there is usually at least one that is open 24 hours a day. Not all villages and smaller towns have a pharmacy. Contact your embassy if you need medical attention, as they will be able to recommend a doctor.

Post offices
You have to go to a post office to buy stamps and to send letters or postcards abroad.

Safe water
The water is generally considered safe to drink, although bottled water is recommended.

Telephones
Phone booths, at bus stations and post offices, accept 10KM and 20KM phone cards which can be bought from post offices or small newspaper kiosks. Different phone companies provide services in different parts of the country and a phone card may not be valid once you leave the town you bought it in. It is cheaper to phone after 7pm. The country code for Bosnia and Herzegovina is 387. To call home from here dial the international code (00) followed by the country code. To call the UK from Bosnia and Herzegovina dial 00 44.

Time
Bosnia is on Central European Time, one hour ahead of GMT (GMT + 1). Daylight Savings Time comes into effect from the end of March to the end of October (GMT + 2).

Emergency telephone numbers
Police **122** Fire **123**
Medical emergency **124**

Driving in Bulgaria (South East Europe)

The regulations below should be read in conjunction with the General motoring information on pages 18–21.

A sea of golden sunflowers in the Bulgarian countryside around Bozhentsi

Drinking and driving

If the level of alcohol in the bloodstream is 0.05 per cent or more the driver will be prosecuted.

Driving licence

The minimum age at which a UK driving licence holder may drive a temporarily imported car and/or motorcycle is 18. An International Driving Permit (IDP) must accompany UK driving licences that do not incorporate a photograph, and it is also recommended for photocard licence holders.

Fines

On-the-spot fines are issued. An official receipt should be obtained.

Fuel

Leaded petrol is no longer available in Bulgaria. Unleaded petrol (95 and 98 octane), diesel and LPG are available. It is forbidden to carry petrol in a can. Credit cards are accepted at most filling stations but not all local stations in small towns accept international cards; check with your card issuer for usage in Bulgaria before travel. Motorists should not use the 'red' pumps at petrol stations as these are for service vehicles only.

Lights

The use of dipped headlights during daylight hours throughout the year is recommended, however their use is compulsory from 1 November to 1 March.

Motorcycles
The wearing of crash helmets is compulsory for both driver and passenger. Motorcyclists must have their lights on at all times.

Motor insurance
Green Cards are recognised. A motorist who does not hold a Green Card must take out short-term insurance at the border, this is payable in BGL only.

Passengers/children in cars
A child under 12 cannot travel as a front seat passenger.

Seat belts
It is compulsory, for front seat occupants to wear seat belts, if fitted.

Speed limits
The standard legal limits, which may be varied by signs, for **private vehicles without trailers** are: In built-up areas 50km/h (31mph), outside built-up areas 90km/h (55mph) and motorways: 130km/h (80mph). Lower limits apply to **cars towing a caravan or trailer:** Outside built-up areas 70km/h (43mph), motorways 100km/h (62mph).

Additional information
- A fire extinguisher, a first-aid kit and a warning triangle are compulsory.
- In built-up areas it is prohibited to use the horn between 10pm and 6am (9am on public holidays), and between midday and 4pm.
- Visiting motorists are required to pay a sanitary tax, €4 (approx) on entry, and also purchase a *vignette* (road tax). The *vignette* is available at the border, UAB offices, some petrol stations and offices of the DZI Bank, weekly, monthly or annually. Heavy fines are imposed for non-compliance.
- Snow chains are permitted. Their use can become compulsory according to road conditions, in which case this is indicated by the international road sign.
- Spiked tyres are forbidden.
- Drivers are advised to drive during daylight hours only.
- Drivers of luxury or 4 x 4 vehicles are advised to use guarded car parks.

Road signs (a selection of standard and non-standard)

Recommended maximum speed

U-turn allowed

Travel facts: Bulgaria

Embassy of the Republic of Bulgaria
Commercial Section
186–188 Queen's Gate
London SW7 5HL

Information for UK-based residents planning a trip to Bulgaria:
Tel: 020 7589 8402
Email: tourism@bulgarianembassy.org.uk
www.bulgariatravel.org

Banking hours
Banks are generally open Monday to Friday 9am to 4pm.

Credit/debit cards
Major international credit cards (Visa, MasterCard or American Express) are accepted in larger hotels and car hire offices, and in some restaurants and shops, mainly in Sofia. Check with your provider for details. Bulgaria is still a country that operates mainly on cash rather than credit cards.

Currency
Bulgarian Lev (Lv) = 100 stotinki. Notes are in denominations of Lv50, 20, 10, 5, 2 and 1. Coins are in denominations of 50, 20, 10, 5, 2 and 1 stotinki. The Lev is pegged to the Euro. 1 Euro = 1.955 BGN. Many banks will cash Euro cheques.

Electricity
The power supply is 220 volts, 50 Hz. Appliances need two-round-pin continental plugs.

Health care
Comprehensive travel insurance is essential for all visitors.

Pharmacies
Many pharmacies are not as widely stocked as at home. Minor complaints can be solved at a pharmacy (*Apteka*), but if you need a doctor (*lekar*) or dentist (*zâbolekar*) visit the nearest health centre (*Poliklinika*), where staff might speak English, German or French, and will almost certainly understand Russian.

Post offices
Post offices are open 8am to 6pm. Postage stamps and postcards are sold in post offices and at newspaper kiosks.

Safe water
Drinking water in major towns is generally safe to drink, though you may prefer to buy bottled mineral water.

Telephones
Public phones on the streets operate with tokens (0.20 leva) and phone cards which are available from post offices and newspaper kiosks. The country code for Bulgaria is 359. To call home from here dial the international code (00) followed by the country code. To call the UK from Bulgaria dial 00 44.

Time
Bulgaria is on Eastern European Time. It is two hours ahead of Greenwich Mean Time (GMT + 2) and from late March to late October it is three hours ahead of Greenwich Mean Time (GMT + 3).

Emergency telephone numbers
Police **166**
Fire **160**
First aid **150**
Road assistance **146**
Traffic police (accidents) **2982 72 823** or **2866 50 60**

Driving in Croatia (South East Europe)

The regulations below should be read in conjunction with the General motoring information on pages 18–21.

A quiet road winds past the outskirts of the village of Motovun in central Croatia

Drinking and driving

Drinking and driving is strictly forbidden. Nil percentage of alcohol is allowed in the driver's blood. Tests for narcotics may be performed; if proved positive severe consequences include confiscation of vehicle, severe fine and licence removal.

Driving licence

The minimum age at which a UK licence holder may drive a temporarily imported car and/or motorcycle (exceeding 125cc) is 18.

Fines

The police officer will impose a fine on the spot; the fine must be paid within eight days at a post office or bank. The police may hold your passport until evidence of payment is produced.

Fuel

Unleaded petrol (95 and 98 octane) is sold at filling stations. It is forbidden to carry petrol in a can. Diesel (*dizel*) is available and LPG is available at most filling stations located on motorways. Credit cards are generally accepted at filling stations – check with your card issuer for use in Croatia before you travel.

Lights

Driving with dipped headlights during the day is compulsory, a fine is imposed for non-compliance.

Motorcycles

The use of dipped headlights during the day is compulsory. The wearing of crash helmets is compulsory for both the driver and passenger. A child under 12 cannot travel as passenger. A fine will be imposed if the passenger on a motorcycle is found to be under the influence of alcohol or narcotics.

Motor insurance

Third-party insurance is compulsory.

Passengers/children in cars

A child under 12 cannot travel as front seat passenger.

Seat belts

It is compulsory for front/rear-seat occupants to wear seat belts, if fitted.

Speed limits

The standard legal limits, which may be varied by signs, for **private vehicles without trailers** are: In built-up areas 50km/h (31mph), outside built-up areas 90km/h (55mph) but 110km/h (68mph) on expressways and 130km/h (80mph) on motorways, unless otherwise indicated by road signs. All motorists who have held a driving licence for less than two years must not exceed 80km/h (49mph) on normal roads outside built-up areas, 100km/h (62mph) on expressways and 110km/h (68mph) on motorways.

Additional information

- It is compulsory for visitors to equip their vehicle with a set of replacement bulbs and a tow rope or pole. A first-aid kit and a warning triangle are compulsory, two triangles are required if towing trailer.
- During the winter months, especially in the Gorski Kotar and Lika regions, the use of snow chains is compulsory. The use of spiked tyres is prohibited.
- It is generally prudent to have winter equipment ready between November and the end of April. This may consist of snow tyres on all wheels or snow chains for the driving wheels.
- The authorities at the frontier must certify any visible damage to a vehicle entering Croatia and a certificate obtained; this must be produced when leaving the country.
- All drivers of motor vehicles (except motorcycles with sidecars and mopeds under 50cc) must have a reflective safety jacket in the vehicle and wear it whenever they have to get out of the vehicle at the roadside, in an emergency. Car hire companies may not supply them to persons hiring vehicles.

Travel facts: Croatia

Croatian National Tourist Office
2 The Lanchesters
162–164 Fulham Palace Road
London W6 9ER
Tel: 020 8563 7979
www.visit-croatia.co.uk

Banking hours
Banks are generally open Monday to Friday 7am to 4 or 7pm, Saturday until 1pm. In the larger cities some banks open on Sundays.

Credit/debit cards
All major credit cards are accepted in hotels, larger shops and restaurants. Large cities, towns and resorts have ATM facilities in banks, supermarkets, airports and elsewhere.

Currency
The currency in Croatia is Kuna (1 Kuna = 100 Lipa). There are 1, 2, 5, 10, 20, 50 Lipa coins; 1, 2, 5 and 25 Kuna coins and 5, 10, 20, 50, 100, 200, 500 and 1,000 Kuna banknotes.

Electricity
Electric current is 220 volts, 50Hz. Appliances need two-round-pin continental plugs.

Health care
Comprehensive travel insurance is essential for all visitors.

Pharmacies
Pharmacies sell over-the-counter medicines, most have English speaking staff.

Post offices
Post offices are open from 7am to 7pm, Saturday until 1pm. In larger cities some are open until 10pm in summer. Postage stamps (*marke*) are sold in post offices and at news-stands.

Safe water
The tap water in Croatia is chlorinated and safe to drink, however, it is advisable to drink bottled water throughout your stay.

Telephones
Public telephones are operated by phone cards, available from post offices, and news-stands and in hotel and tourist complexes. The country code for Croatia is 385. To call the UK from Croaia dial the international code (00) followed by the country code. To call the UK from Croatia dial 00 44.

Time
Croatia is on Central European Time, one hour ahead of GMT (GMT + 1). Daylight Savings Time comes into effect from the end of March to the end of October (GMT + 2 hours).

Emergency telephone numbers
Police **92**
Fire **93**
Ambulance **94**

Toll charges in kunas

Road		**Car**	**Car towing caravan/ trailer**
E59	Zagreb – Macelj	35.00	53.00
E65	Zagreb – Split – Dubrovnik	171.00	265.00
	Zagreb – Rijeka	56.00	101.00
E70	Zagreb – Lipovac (Slovenian frontier)	105.00	160.00
	Zagreb – Bregana	5.00	7.00
E71	Zagreb – Gorican	36.00	54.00

Bridges and tunnels		
Krk Bridge	30.00	40.00

Driving in Republic of Cyprus (Eastern Mediterranean)

The regulations below should be read in conjunction with the General motoring information on pages 18–21.

Fishing boats in the harbour at Agia Napa (Ayia Napa), on the east coast of southern Cyprus

Drinking and driving

The maximum legal level of alcohol in the blood is 0.049 per cent. Persons suspected of driving under the influence of alcohol may be subject to a blood test.

Driving licence

All national driving licences are accepted. The minimum age for driving a temporarily imported car and/or motorcycle is 18.

Fines

The Cyprus traffic police are empowered to impose on-the-spot fines for traffic offences.

Fuel

Unleaded petrol (95 and 98 octane) and diesel are available. No LPG or leaded petrol available, but can buy lead substitute additive. It is forbidden to carry petrol in a can. Credit cards are accepted at most filling stations, check with your card issuer for use in Cyprus before you travel.

Lights

Vehicle lights must be used between half an hour after sunset and half an hour before sunrise. Spotlights are prohibited.

Motorcycles

The wearing of crash helmets are compulsory, for the rider and passenger.

Motor insurance

Third-party insurance is compulsory.

Passengers/children in cars

Children under five cannot travel as a front-seat passenger. Children over five and under ten must use a suitable child-restraint system.

Seat belts

It is compulsory for front/rear-seat occupants to wear seat belts, if fitted.

Speed limits

The standard legal limits, which may be varied by signs, for **private vehicles with or without trailers** are: In built-up areas 50km/h (31mph) or 65km/h (40mph) depending on the road, outside built-up areas 80km/h (49mph) and 100km/h (62mph) on motorways. The minimum speed on motorways is 65km/h (40mph).

A bird's-eye view of the whitewashed houses in the mountain village of Pedoulas

Additional information

- The rule of the road is drive on the left, overtake on the right.
- Two warning triangles are compulsory.
- The use of the vehicle horn is prohibited between 10pm and 6am, and in the vicinity of hospitals.
- Spiked tyres and snow chains are permitted on mountain roads in winter.

Travel facts: Republic of Cyprus

Cyprus Tourism Organisation
17 Hanover Street
London W1R 0AA
Tel: 020 7569 8800
www.visitcyprus.com

Banking hours
May to September, Monday to Friday 8:15am to 1:30pm. October to April, Monday to Friday 8:30am to 1pm; also Monday 3:15pm to 4:45pm. May to August, Monday to Friday 8:15am to 1pm.

Credit/debit cards
Hotels, large shops and restaurants normally accept major credit cards and traveller's cheques.

Currency
The currency of the Republic of Cyprus is the Euro (€) introduced 1 January 2008, which is divided into 100 cents. Notes are issued in denominations of €5, €10, €20, €50, €100, €200 and €500; coins in 1, 2, 5, 10, 20 and 50 cents, and €1 and €2.

Electricity
The power supply is 240 volts 50Hz. In most buildings sockets take three-square-pin plugs (as UK). In older buildings, round two-pin sockets take two-round-pin Continental-style plugs.

Health care
Free or reduced-cost medical treatment is available in Cyprus to European visitors on production of a valid European Health Insurance Card (EHIC). See page 11. Comprehensive travel insurance is still advised and is essential for all other visitors.

Language
The official language is Greek. English is widely spoken and French and German are spoken within the tourism industry.

Pharmacies
Minor ailments can be dealt with at pharmacies (*farmakio*), which sell most branded medicines. Local newspapers list pharmacies which are open at night and on weekends/holidays, as well as the names of doctors who are on call on weekends/holidays.

Post offices
There are main post offices in main towns and sub-post offices in the suburbs. Post offices are open Monday to Friday 7:30am to 1:30pm (Thursday also 3–6). Post boxes are painted yellow.

Safe water
Tap water in hotels, restaurants and public places is generally safe to drink in Cyprus. Bottled mineral water is inexpensive and widely available.

Telephones
There are public telephones in all towns and villages as well as at International airports, harbours and other locations. Coin phones take 2, 5, 10 and 20 cent coins; card phones are operated by telecards which can be purchased in denominations of CY£3, CY£5 and CY£10 from post offices, banks, souvenir shops etc. The country code for Cyprus is 357. To call home from here dial the international code (00) followed by the country code. To call the UK from Cyprus dial 00 44.

Time
Cyprus is on Eastern European Time. It is two hours ahead of Greenwich Mean Time (GMT + 2) and from late March to late October it is three hours ahead of Greenwich Mean Time (GMR + 3).

Emergency telephone numbers
Police **199, 112**
Fire **199, 112**
Ambulance **199, 112**

Driving in Turkish Republic of Northern Cyprus (Eastern Mediterranean)

The regulations below should be read in conjunction with the General motoring information on pages 18–21.

Pleasure boats tied up by the quayside cafés in the harbour at Kyrenia

Drinking and driving

Drivers are permitted to have 80 milligrams of alcohol in 100 millilitres of their blood, provided they are capable to drive.

Driving licence

A UK licence is acceptable. The minimum age for driving a temporarily imported car and/or motorcycle is 17.

Fines

There are no on-the-spot fines.

Fuel

Leaded (98 octane), unleaded petrol (95 and 97 octane), diesel (*mazot*) and Euro-diesel are available but not LPG. It is permitted to carry petrol in a can, but not aboard ferries. Credit cards are accepted at most filling stations; check with your card issuer for use in Cyprus before you travel.

Driving in Turkish Republic of Northern Cyprus continued

The picturesque ruins of the Church of St George of the Latins in Famagusta

Lights
Vehicle lights must be used between half an hour after sunset and half an hour before sunrise.

Motorcycles
The wearing of crash helmets is compulsory.

Motor insurance
Third-party insurance is compulsory. A Green Card is not accepted. Short term insurance may be purchased at the port of arrival.

Passengers/children in cars
A child under five cannot travel as a front seat passenger; children over five and under ten must use a suitable child restraint system.

Seat belts
It is compulsory for front seat occupants to wear seat belts.

Speed limits
The standard legal limits, which may be varied by signs, for **private vehicles without trailers** are: In built-up areas 50km/h (31mph), outside built-up areas 70km/h (43mph) or 80km/h (49mph).

Additional information
- The rule of the road is drive on the left, overtake on the right.
- Two warning triangles are compulsory.
- Road signs are predominately in English.

Travel facts: Northern Cyprus

Northern Cyprus Tourism Centre
29 Bedford Square
London
WC1B 3ED
Tel: 0207 631 1930
www.cypnet.co.uk/ncyprus

Banking hours
In North Cyprus banks are open Monday to Saturday 8.30am to 12 noon throughout the year. Afternoon times vary depending on the bank. Most major banks have ATMs which accept main credit and debit cards.

Credit/debit cards
Most major credit and debit cards are accepted by hotels, restaurants and shops.

Currency
The unit of currency in North Cyprus is Turkish Lira (TL). Coins are TL100, 500, 1,000, 5,000, 10,000, 25,000 and 50,000; notes TL10,000, 20,000, 50,000, 100,000, 250,000, 500,000, 1,00,000 and 5,00,00. Most businesses will accept the Euro, Pound Sterling, US Dollars and Cyprus Pounds.

Electricity
The power supply is 240 volts 50Hz. In most buildings sockets take three-square-pin plugs (as UK). In older buildings, round two-pin sockets take two-round-pin plugs.

Health care
Comprehensive travel insurance is essential for all visitors.

Language
Turkish is the official language, English is widely spoken and understood.

Pharmacies
Pharmacies sell many prescription drugs over the counter. Many pharmacists, provided they speak English, will advise you which medicine to take for your condition

Post offices
There are main post offices in large towns and sub-post offices in the suburbs. Post offices are open Monday to Friday 8am to 1pm and 2 to 5pm; Saturday 8.30am to 12.30. Post boxes are painted yellow. Mail posted in Northern Cyprus has to travel via Turkey.

Telephones
There are few public phones in North Cyprus, these accept phone cards which cost 1, 1.5 and 2TL. The country code for Cyprus is 357. To call home from here dial the international code (00) followed by the country code. To call the UK from Cyprus dial 00 44.

Time
Cyprus is on Eastern European Time. It is two hours ahead of Greenwich Mean Time (GMT + 2) and from late March to late October it is three hours ahead of Greenwich Mean Time (GMT + 3).

Emergency telephone numbers
Police **155**
Fire **119**
Ambulance **112**

Driving in Czech Republic (Central Europe)

The regulations below should be read in conjunction with the General motoring information on pages 18–21.

Drinking and driving

Drinking and driving is strictly forbidden. Nil percentage of alcohol is allowed in the drivers' blood. A fine between 25,000 and 50,000CZK (Czech crown) will be imposed and the withdrawal of the driving licence for up to two years. Driving under the influence of alcohol or drugs is considered a criminal offence.

Driving licence

The minimum age at which a UK licence holder may drive a temporarily imported car is 18, motorcycle up to 125cc 17 years, over 125cc 18 years. Photocard licences are accepted, licences that do not incorporate a photo must be accompanied by an International Driving Permit (IDP).

Fines

On-the-spot fines of up to 3,000CZK can be imposed, the maximum fine for a traffic offence 100,000CZK. An official receipt should be obtained. The police are empowered to retain the driving licence when a serious traffic offence has been committed. Illegally parked vehicles may be clamped or towed away.

Fuel

Unleaded petrol (*natural*), (95 and 98 octane), diesel (*nafta*) and LPG (*autoplyn* or *plyn*) are available. It is permitted to carry up to 10 litres of petrol in a can. Credit cards are accepted at filling stations, check with your card issuer for usage in Czech Republic before you travel.

Lights

You must use dipped headlights during the day throughout the year. The fine for non-compliance is approximately 2,000CZK. Any vehicle warning lights, other than those supplied with the vehicle as original equipment, must be made inoperative.

Motorcycles

The use of dipped headlights during the day is compulsory throughout the year. The wearing of crash helmets is compulsory for the driver and passenger of motorcycles. It is forbidden for motorcyclists to smoke while riding their machine.

Motor insurance

Third-party insurance is compulsory.

Passengers/children in cars

All passengers must use seat belts. Child passengers (persons with a weight under 36kg/79lbs and under 150cm/4ft 11in in height) are not permitted to travel in a vehicle unless using a suitable restraint

system. A child in the front seat of a vehicle using a suitable child-restraint system where the airbag is activated must travel facing forward.

Seat belts

It is compulsory for front/rear-seat occupants to wear seat belts, if fitted.

Speed limits

The standard legal limits, which may be varied by signs, for **private vehicles without trailers** are: In built-up areas: 50km/h (31mph), outside built-up areas 90km/h (55mph) and motorways (for vehicles not exceeding 3500kg and buses) 130km/h (80mph). On expressways that pass through built-up areas 80km/h (50mph). Maximum speed with snow chains 50km/h (31mph). At railway crossings drivers must not exceed 30km/h (18mph) for 50 metres before the crossing. If white lights are flashing the maximum speed for 50 metres before the crossing is 50km/h (31mph) and 30km/h (18mph) and you may cross. The arrival of a train is indicated by red flashing lights/red or yellow flag. Vehicles that are constructed with a maximum speed of 80km/h (49mph) or under are not permitted to travel on motorways.

Additional information

- A first-aid kit and a warning triangle are compulsory. Visitors must also equip their vehicle with a set of replacement bulbs.
- Motorway tax is payable for the use of motorways and express roads.
  A windscreen sticker must be displayed on all four-wheeled vehicles as evidence of payment. The sticker can be purchased at the Czech frontier, UAMK branch offices, petrol stations or post offices for periods of one year, one month or seven days. Fines are imposed for non-display.
- The authorities at the frontier must certify any visible damage to a vehicle entering the Czech Republic. If any damage occurs inside the country a police report must be obtained at the scene of the accident. Damaged vehicles may only be taken out of the country on production of this evidence.
- The use of an audible warning device is only permitted in built-up areas to avoid imminent danger, they are prohibited between 8pm and 6am, and in Prague.
- Winter tyres are strongly recommended during the winter months.
- The use of spiked tyres and radar detectors are prohibited.
- Snow chains may be used but only when there is enough snow cover to prevent road damage. The authorities can require cars to be fitted with snow chains on the driving wheels, the international road sign is used.

Travel facts: Czech Republic

Czech Tourist Authority
13 Harley Street,
London W1G 9QG
Tel: 020 7631 0427
www.czechtourism.com
www.pis.cz

Banking hours
Banks are normally open Monday to Friday from 8am to 5pm. Some open Saturday morning.

Credit/debit cards
Payment by credit/debit card in the Czech Republic is not as widespread as it is in other European countries. There are plenty of ATMs throughout the country.

Currency
The local currency is the Czech koruna, or Czech Crown, (Kč) which is divided into 100 heller. Notes are issued in denominations of Kč 20, 50, 100, 200, 500, 1000, 2000, 5000; coins in hellers 50 and Kč 1, 2, 5, 10, 20, 50.

Electricity
The electrical supply is 220V, as in the rest of Europe. Czech plugs have two round pins.

Health care
Free or reduced-cost medical treatment is available in Czech Republic to European visitors on production of a valid European Health Insurance Card (EHIC). See page 11. Comprehensive travel insurance is still advised and is essential for all other visitors.

Pharmacies
Pharmacies (*lékánat* or *apothéka*) are the only places to sell over-the-counter medicines. They also dispense many drugs (*leky*) normally available only on prescription in other Western countries. Take a supply of your own prescription medicines with you as you may not be able to find exactly the same in Czech Republic.

Post offices
Post offices have distinctive orange *Posta* signs outside. They are normally open Monday to Friday 8am to 7pm and Saturday until noon.

Safe water
It is not advisable to drink tap water as it is loaded with toxins and is heavily chlorinated. Bottled mineral water is available everywhere.

Telephones
There are public telephones on the street and near metro stations. Older orange phones accepting only Kc coins are solely for local calls. Grey phones take Kc1, 2, 5 and 10 coins. In Prague there are an increasing number of phonecard (*Telefonní karta*) booths. Phonecards are available from tobacconists, newsagents and post offices. The country code for Czech Republic is 420. To call home from here dial the international code (00) followed by the country code. To call the UK dial 00 44.

Time
The Czech Republic is on Central European Time (GMT + 1), but from late March, when clocks are put forward one hour, until late October, Czech Summer Time (GMT + 2) operates.

Emergency telephone numbers
General **112** Police **158**
Fire **150** Ambulance **155**

Toll charges in Czech koruna
For details of where to buy the motorway tax see page 49. You may be charged more if your vehicle is over 3,500kg.

General	Car (with or without trailer)
1 week	200.00
1 month	300.00
1 year	900.00

Driving in Denmark (Northern Europe)

The regulations below should be read in conjunction with the General motoring information on pages 18–21.

Driving in Denmark

Drinking and driving

If the level of alcohol in the bloodstream is 0.05 per cent or more severe penalties include licence suspension, fines or imprisonment will be imposed depending on the amount of excess.

Driving licence

The minimum age at which a UK licence holder may drive a temporarily imported car and/or motorcycle is 17.

Fines

Visitors who infringe traffic regulations can be fined on the spot. If you do not accept the fine, the police will take the matter to court to be settled by a judge. The police may retain the vehicle until such time. Vehicles parked against regulations will be taken away by the police at the owner's expense.

Fuel

Unleaded petrol (95 and 98 octane) and diesel are available. Leaded petrol is no longer available, a leaded petrol substitute (*Millennium*) is available. There is limited availability of LPG. It is permitted to carry petrol in a can, but not aboard ferries or in the Eurotunnel. Petrol stations/pumps are not situated on motorways. Credit cards are accepted at most filling stations; check with your card issuer for use in Denmark before travel.

Fishing boats beached at Noerre Vorupor in northwest Jutland

Lights

The use of dipped headlights is compulsory during the day.

Motorcycles

The use of dipped headlights is compulsory during the day. The wearing of crash helmets with straps is compulsory for both driver and passenger.

Driving in Denmark continued

Motor insurance
Third-party insurance is compulsory.

Passengers/children in cars
Children under three years must be seated in a child-restraint system adapted to their size. Children over three and less than 1.35m (4ft 5in) must be seated in a child restraint system suitable for their height and weight. A child must not be placed in the front seat with their back to the road if the vehicle is fitted with an active airbag.

Seat belts
It is compulsory for front/rear-seat occupants to wear seat belts, if fitted.

Speed limits
The standard legal limits, which may be varied by signs, for **private vehicles without trailers** are in built-up areas 50km/h (31mph), outside built-up areas 80km/h (49mph) or 90km/h (55mph), and motorways 110km/h (68mph) or 130km/h (80mph). Lower limits apply to **private cars towing a trailer or caravan:** outside built-up areas 70km/h (43mph) and on motorways 80km/h (49mph).

Additional information
- A red warning triangle is compulsory. It is recommended that visitors equip their vehicle with a fire extinguisher and a first-aid kit.
- Generally there is a duty to give way to traffic approaching from the right.
- A line of white triangles (shark's teeth) painted across the road indicates that you must stop and give way to traffic on the road you are entering.
- When roads are wet or slushy, speed must be reduced as far as possible to prevent other road users from being splashed.
- It is prohibited to use radar detectors.
- Spiked tyres may be used between 1 November and 15 April, they must be fitted to all 4 wheels.
- Right-hand drive vehicles must have wing mirrors on both sides of the vehicle.

Road signs (a selection of standard and non-standard)

Traffic merges

Minimum speed limit

Recommended speed limit

Compulsory slow lane

1 hour parking zone

Place of interest

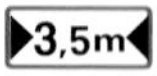

Maximum width

Travel facts: Denmark

Danish Tourist Board
55 Sloane Street
London SW1X 9SY
Tel: 020 7259 5959
www.visitdenmark.com

Banking hours
Banks are normally open Monday to Friday from 10am to 4pm, and until 6pm on Thursday.

Credit/debit cards
Most shops accept major credit cards. The most common are VISA and MasterCard.

Currency
The monetary unit is the Danish Kroner (DKr), which is divided into 100 øre. Bank notes are issued in denominations of DKr50, DKr100, DKr200, DKr500 and DKr1,000. Coins are found in DKr20, DKr10, DKr5, DKr2, DKr1 and 50 øre and 25 øre. Some shops, hotels and restaurants, particularly in larger cities, display prices in both Danish Kroner and Euros and many are likely to accept payment in Euros. It is advisable to ask beforehand if you wish to pay in anything other than Danish Kroner.

Electricty
The elctricity supply in Denmark is 220 volts AC (50 Hz). Appliances need two-round-pin Continental plugs.

Health care
Free or reduced-cost medical treatment is available in Denmark to European visitors on production of a valid European Health Insurance Card (EHIC). See page 11. Comprehensive travel insurance is still advised.

Pharmacies
Only medicine prescribed by Danish or other Scandinavian doctors can be dispensed at a chemist (*Apotek*). Many medicines that can be bought over the counter in the UK can only be obtained with prescriptions in Denmark.

Post offices
Post offices are generally open Monday to Friday from 9 or 10am to 5 or 6pm. Some are closed on Saturdays. Opening hours for those that are open are usually from 9 or 10am to noon or 2pm. You can buy stamps from newsagents and post offices.

Safe water
The tap water in Denmark is safe to drink. Bottled mineral water is widely available.

Telephones
Coin-operated public phones are white and need a minimum of 2DKr (either one 2DKr coin or two 1DKr coins) for a local call and 5 DKr for an international call; cards for the blue cardphones, which come in denominations of 30DKr, 50DKr and 100DKr, are sold in newsagents and post offices. There are no area codes. The country code for Denmark is 45. To call home from Denmark dial the international code (00) followed by the country code. To call the UK dial 00 44.

Time
Denmark follows Central European Time (CET), which is 1 hour ahead of Greenwich Mean Time (GMT + 1). From the last Sunday in March to the last Sunday in October, clocks are put forward one hour.

Emergency telephone numbers
Police **112**
Fire **112**
Ambulance **112**

Toll charges in Danish Kroner

Bridges and tunnels	**Car**	**Car towing caravan/ trailer**
Oresund Bridge (one way)	240.00	480.00
Storebaelt Bridge (one way)	205.00	310.00

Driving in Estonia (Eastern Europe)

The regulations below should be read in conjunction with the General motoring information on pages 18–21.

The domes of Alexander Nevski Cathedral dominate Tallinn's skyline

Drinking and driving
The legal limit is 0.02 per cent in the blood and 0.01 per cent in air exhaled. Breath tests are frequently carried out in Estonia; blood tests can also be taken.

Driving licence
The minimum age at which a UK licence holder may drive a temporarily imported car and/or motorcycle is 18.

Fines
Police can impose fines on the spot. They monitor speeds closely and will give fines for even the smallest speeding offences. Illegally parked cars will be clamped.

Fuel
Unleaded petrol (95 and 98 octane), diesel and LPG are available. Leaded petrol is no longer available. Carrying petrol in a can is permitted, subject to payment of Excise duty at the frontier. Credit cards are accepted at most filling stations; check with your card issuer for use in Estonia before travel.

Lights
The use of dipped headlights during the day is compulsory.

Motorcycles
Use of dipped headlights during the day compulsory. The wearing of crash helmets is compulsory for both the driver and passenger.

Motor insurance
Third-party insurance is compulsory.

Passengers/children in cars
Children too small to wear seat belts must travel in a child seat adapted to their size.

Seat belts

It is compulsory for front-seat occupants to wear seat belts. Rear seat belts must be worn if fitted.

Speed limits

The standard legal limits, which may be varied by signs, for **private vehicles without trailers** are: In built-up areas 50km/h (31mph), outside built-up areas 90km/h (55mph) but up to 110km/h (68mph) on some roads during the summer months. Motorists who have held a driving licence for less than two years must not exceed 90km/h (55mph) outside built-up areas.

Studying the menu at a restaurant in Tallinn's Town Hall Square

Additional information

- A first-aid kit, fire extinguisher, two wheel chocks and a warning triangle are compulsory.
- Winter tyres are compulsory (with a minimum tread depth of 3mm) between 1 December and 1 March, however these dates may vary from October to April according to the weather conditions.
- It is recommended that visitors carry an assortment of spares for their vehicle, such as fan belt, replacement bulbs and spark plugs.
- In addition to the original vehicle registration document it is recommended that an International Certificate for Motor Vehicles (ICMV) is also carried if visiting any Russian speaking areas outside Estonia.
- The border police may ask visitors for proof of sufficient personal insurance cover on entry.
- It is prohibited to overtake a tram which has stopped to let passengers on or off.
- Motorists must pay a toll to enter the city of Tallinn.

Travel facts: Estonia

Estonian Embassy
16 Hyde Park Gate
London SW7 5DG
Tel: **020 7589 3428**

Estonia does not have a Tourist Office in the UK, but the Embassy can help tourists with information. You can collect tourist brochures from the Embassy Monday to Friday 9am to 5pm.
www.estonia.gov.uk
www.visitestonia.com

Banking hours
Banks are generally open from Monday to Friday from 9am to 4pm. Most banks are closed on Saturday and Sunday. Currency exchange offices are open from Monday to Friday from 9am to 6pm; on Saturday from 9am to 3pm. Some are also open on Sunday.

Credit/debit cards
Credit cards such as Visa, Mastercard/Eurocard, Diners Club, American Express are accepted in most of the major hotels, restaurants and shops. Most banks will give cash advances on credit cards supported by a valid passport. Check with the credit card company for further details before travelling.

Currency
The national currency is the Kroon (EEK). The smaller unit is the Sent, 1 Kroon = 100 sents. The Kroon is pegged to the Euro at 1 EUR = 15.65EEK. Foreign currencies can be easily exchanged in banks and exchange offices.

Electricity
The electricity supply in Estonia is 220 volts AC, 50 Hz. Continental-style two-pin plugs are in use.

Health care
Free or reduced-cost medical treatment is available in Estonia to European visitors on production of a valid European Health Insurance Card (EHIC). See page 11. Comprehensive travel insurance is still advised and is essential for all other visitors.

Pharmacies
Over the counter medicaments are available in pharmacies (*Apteek*) which can be found in every town. However, it may be more convenient to bring enough medicines to last throughout your trip.

Post offices
Post offices are generally open during normal shopping hours: Monday to Friday from 9am to 6pm, and Saturday 9.30am to 3pm. The Central Post Office in Tallinn, at Narva mnt, is open Monday to Friday 7.30am to 8pm and from 8am to 6pm on Saturday.

Safe water
The tap water is safe to drink but you may prefer bottled mineral water.

Telephones
Pay phones accept phone cards which can be purchased from hotel reception desks, tourist information offices, post offices, news-stands and some shops. The country code for Estonia is 372. To call home from Estonia dial the international code (00) followed by the country code. To call the UK dial 00 44.

Time
Estonia is on Eastern European Time. It is two hours ahead of Greenwich Mean Time (GMT + 2) and from late March to late October it is three hours ahead of Greenwich Mean Time (GMT + 3).

Emergency telephone numbers
Police **110**
Fire **112**
Ambulance **112**

Driving in Finland (Northern Europe)

The regulations below should be read in conjunction with the General motoring information on pages 18–21.

Drinking and driving

If the level of alcohol in the bloodstream is 0.05 per cent or more the driver will be penalised which could include a daily fine or imprisonment and withdrawal of driving licence. The police test for alcohol, drugs and narcotics.

Driving licence

The minimum age at which a UK licence holder may drive a temporarily imported car is 18, a motorcycle (not exceeding 125cc) 16, exceeding 125cc 18. Motorists banned from driving in an EU or EEA country are not permitted to drive in Finland.

Fines

Police may impose but not collect on-the-spot fines for parking and other minor infringements, up to €115. The fine is payable at a bank within two weeks. For more serious offences there is a system of daily fines with a minimum of €6 per day. The police can remove an illegally parked vehicle, release fee up to €170.

Fuel

Unleaded petrol (95 and 98 octane) and diesel is available. Leaded petrol and LPG is not available. Petrol in a can is permitted. Credit cards are accepted at most filling stations; check with your card issuer for use in Finland before travel.

A sign warns of the likelihood of elk coming out of the dense forest onto the busy road

Lights

All motor vehicles must use their headlights inside and outside built-up areas at all times throughout the year.

Motorcycles

The use of dipped headlights during the day is compulsory. Drivers and passengers of mopeds or motorcycles must wear a crash helmet.

Motor insurance

Third-party insurance is compulsory.

Passengers/children in cars

A child less than 1.5m (4ft 11in) travelling in a car, van or lorry must be seated in a child seat or child-restraint. A child under three

years old may not be transported in a vehicle without a child restraint/seat, except in a taxi. Where a child restraint/seat is not available, a child three years and over must travel in the rear seat of the vehicle using a seat belt or other safety device attached to the seat. It is the responsibility of the driver to ensure that all children are safely restrained.

From 9 May 2008, all child restraints/seats will have to conform with the ECE standard 44/03 or EU directive 77/541EEC.

Seat belts

It is compulsory for front/rear seat occupants to wear seat belts, if fitted.

Speed limits

The standard legal limits, which may be varied by signs, for **private vehicles without trailers** are: inside built-up areas 50km/h (31mph), outside built-up areas 80km/h (49mph) or 100km/h (62mph), according to the quality of road, with 80km/h (49mph) being the upper limit where there are no signs, on motorways 120km/h (74mph). There is no minimum speed on motorways. Temporary speed limits may be enforced on some or all roads by the local road districts. Reduced speed limits apply during the winter months, October to March (generally 20km/h or 12mph less than standard limits). Lower limits apply to **private cars towing a trailer or caravan:** outside built-up areas and on motorways 80km/h (49mph) and for a trailer without brakes 60km/h (37mph).

Additional information

- A warning triangle is compulsory.
- Radar detectors are prohibited. Winter tyres, marked m&s on the sidewall are compulsory between 1 December and end of February.
- Spiked tyres may be used from 1 November to the first Monday after Easter, if used they must be fitted on all wheels.
- Snow chains may be used temporarily when required by conditions, drivers must be careful to avoid damaging the road surface.
- Beware of game (elk, reindeer, etc) as they constitute a very real danger on some roads.
- It is prohibited to sound a horn in towns and villages except in cases of immediate danger.
- It is recommended that should you need to exit your vehicle in the hours of darkness, for example in a breakdown situation, a reflective device is worn for your own safety.

Travel facts: Finland

Finnish Tourist Board
PO Box 33213
London W6 8JX
Tel: 020 7365 2512
www.visitfinland.com/uk

Banking hours
Finnish banks are open Monday to Friday 9am to 4.15pm. ATMs are fairly widespread and marked by the sign OTTO.

Credit/debit cards
Most major credit cards, including Visa, MasterCard and EuroCard can be used for payment in many shops and restaurants.

Currency
The Euro (€) is the official currency of Finland. Banknotes are issued €5, €10, €20, €50, €100, €200 and €500; coins in denominations of €1 and €2 and 1, 2, 5, 10, 20 and 50 cents.

Electricity
The electric current in Finland is 220V (230V), 50 Hz. A two-round-pin plug continental system, is used.

Health care
Free or reduced-cost medical treatment is available in Finland to European visitors on production of a valid European Health Insurance Card (EHIC). See page 11. Comprehensive travel insurance is still advised and is essential for all other visitors.

Pharmacies
Medicines are available over the counter at pharmacies (*Apteekki*). Some have late opening hours. In Helsinki, the pharmacy at Mannerheimintie 96, has 24-hour service.

Post offices
Post offices are open Monday to Friday 9am to 6pm. Post offices in grocery stores and petrol service stations may stay open until 8 or 9pm. Yellow post boxes on walls are for daily collections. Stamps are available at post offices, book and newspaper shops, R-kiosks, stations, and hotels.

Safe water
Tap water is of highest quality and can be consumed throughout the country. Bottled mineral water is available in shops and restaurants.

Telephones
Telephone calls can be made from booths, hotels and post offices. Many public telephones operate using a pre-paid card purchased from R-kiosks, Sonera shops and some post offices. The country code for Finland is 358. To call home from Finland dial the international code (00) followed by the country code. To call the UK dial 00 44.

Time
Finland is on Eastern European Time. It is two hours ahead of Greenwich Mean Time (GMT + 2) and from late March to late October it is three hours ahead of Greenwich Mean Time (GMT + 3).

Emergency telephone numbers
Emergency **112**

Driving in France and Monaco (Western Europe)

The regulations below should be read in conjunction with the General motoring information on pages 18–21.

A masterpiece of design and engineering, the Pont du Gard was built to carry water to Nîmes

Drinking and driving

If the level of alcohol in the bloodstream is 0.05 per cent or more (0.02 per cent for bus/coach drivers), severe penalties include fine, imprisonment and/or confiscation of driving licence. Saliva tests will be used to detect drivers under the influence of drugs – severe penalties are as above.

Driving licence

The minimum age at which a UK licence holders may drive a temporarily imported car is 18, a motorcycle (up to 80cc) is 16, a motorcycle (over 80cc) is 18.

Fines

On-the-spot fines or 'deposits' are severe. An official receipt should be issued. Vehicles parking contrary to regulations may be towed away and impounded.

Fuel

Unleaded petrol (95 and 98 octane), diesel and LPG are available. Leaded petrol is no longer available – lead replacement petrol (*Supercarburant*) is available or a lead substitute additive can be bought. Petrol carried in a can is permitted but forbidden by ferry and Eurotunnel operators. Credit cards are accepted at most filling stations; check with your card issuer for usage in France and Monaco before travel. Many automatic petrol pumps are operated by credit/debit card. However, cards issued outside France are not always accepted by these pumps.

Lights

Dipped headlights must be used in poor daytime visibility. It is highly recommended by the French government that 4 plus-wheeled vehicles use dipped headlights day and night (this is already compulsory for motorcycles).

Motorcycles

The use of dipped headlights during the day is compulsory for motorcycles. The wearing of crash helmets is compulsory for both driver and passenger of any two-wheel motorised vehicle.

Motor insurance

Third-party insurance is compulsory.

Motorways

See motorway map, page 64. To join a motorway follow signs with the international motorway symbol or signs with the words '*par Autoroute*' added. Signs with the words *'péage'* or *'par péage'* lead to toll roads. Motorcycles under 80cc are prohibited. Use green alternative routes to avoid traffic jams on major highways.

Most motorways charge tolls (see page 65) except on certain sections in the immediate vicinity of towns such as Paris, Bordeaux, Lille, Lyon, Marseille and Metz.

On the majority of toll motorways in France a travel ticket is issued on entry and the toll is paid on leaving the motorway and also at occasional intermediate points. The travel ticket gives all relevant information about toll charges, including the toll category of the vehicle. At the exit point the ticket is handed in. On some motorways the toll collection is automatic; ensure you have the correct change ready to throw in the collecting basket. If change is required use the marked separate lane. **Note:** Toll booths will not exchange travellers' cheques – ensure you have sufficient Euros with you to meet the high toll charges (alternatively, credit cards are now accepted at most toll booths).

It is usually possible to obtain 24-hour service for a car and/or occupants every 40km (25 miles). Rest stops, most with toilet facilities, can be found every 15km (9 miles). Free emergency telephones are sited every 2km (1.24 miles) on most motorways.

Passengers/children in cars

Children under the age of 10 are not permitted to travel in the front seats of vehicles, unless there are no rear seats or the rear seats are already occupied with children under 10 or there are no seat belts. In these circumstances a child must not be placed in the front seat with their back to the road if the vehicle is fitted with a passenger airbag, unless it is deactivated. They must travel in an approved child seat or restraint adapted to their size. A baby up to 13kg must be carried in a rear-facing car seat. A child between 9 and 18kg must be seated in a child seat and a child from 15kg up to 10 years can use a booster seat with a seat belt or a harness. It is the driver's responsibility to ensure all passengers under 18 are appropriately restrained.

Seat belts

It is compulsory for front/rear-seat occupants to wear seat belts, if fitted.

Speed limits

The standard legal limits, which may be varied by signs, for **private vehicles without trailers** are: In built-up areas 50km/h (31mph), outside built-up areas 90km/h (55mph), but 110km/h (68mph) on urban motorways and dual-carriageways separated by a central reservation and 130km/h (80mph) on motorways. Lower speed limits of 80km/h (49mph) outside built-up areas, 100km/h (62mph) on dual carriageways and 110km/h (68mph) on motorways apply in wet weather and to visiting motorists who have held a driving licence for less than two years. Additionally, speed limits are reduced on stretches of motorways in built-up areas. The minimum speed limit on motorways is 80km/h (49mph).

Note: Holders of EU driving licences exceeding speed limit by more than 40km/h (25mph) will have their licences confiscated on the spot by the police.

Additional information

- The use of a warning triangle or hazard warning lights is compulsory (it is recommended that a warning triangle is always carried).
- It is recommended that visitors equip their vehicle with a set of replacement bulbs.
- Snow chains must be fitted to vehicles using snow-covered roads in compliance with the relevant road sign.
- In built-up areas give way to traffic coming from the right – *'priorité a droite'*. At signed roundabouts bearing signs *'Vous n'avez pas la priorité'* or *'Cédez le passage'* traffic on the roundabout has priority; where no such sign exists traffic entering the roundabout has priority.
- In built-up areas the use of the horn is prohibited except in cases of immediate danger.
- It is recommended that you wear a reflective jacket when exiting a vehicle which is stopped on the carriageway or on the side of a road outside a built-up area.
- It is absolutely prohibited to carry, transport or use radar detectors. Failure to comply with this regulation involves a fine of up to €1,500, and the vehicle may be confiscated.

Road signs (a selection of standard and non-standard)

Priority road | End of priority road | Traffic on the roundabout has priority | Give way | Continuation of restriction | Alternative holiday routes | Information centre for holiday route

Travel facts: France and Monaco

French Tourist Office
178 Piccadilly
London W1V 0AL
Tel: 09068 244123
www.franceguide.com

Banking hours
Banks are generally open Monday to Friday 9am to 4.30pm. Some open extended hours including Saturday morning, but may close on Monday instead. Banks close at noon on the day before a national holiday, as well as on the holiday itself.

Credit/debit cards
Credit cards are widely accepted in shops, restaurants and hotels. Visa (*Carte Bleue*), MasterCard (*Eurocard*) and Diners Club cards with four-digit PINs can be used in most ATM cash dispensers. Some smaller shops and hotels may not accept credit cards – always check before you book in.

Currency
The currency in France is the Euro (€). Euro coins are issued in denominations of 1, 2, 5, 10, 20 and 50 cents and €1 and €2. Banknotes are issued in denominations of €5, €10, €20, €50, €100, €200 and €500.

Electricity
The power supply in France is 220 volts. Sockets accept two-round-pin (or increasingly three-round-pin) plugs, so an adaptor is needed for most non-Continental appliances. A transformer is needed for appliances operating on 110–120 volts.

Health care
Free or reduced-cost medical treatment is available in France and Monaco to European visitors on production of a valid European Health Insurance Card (EHIC). See page 11. Comprehensive travel insurance is still advised and is essential for all other visitors.

Pharmacies
Pharmacies – recognised by their green cross sign – have highly qualified staff able to offer medical advice, provide first-aid and prescribe a wide range of drugs, although some are available by prescription (*ordonnance*) only.

Post offices
Post offices are identified by a yellow or brown *La Poste* or *PTT* sign, and post boxes are usually square and yellow. Most post offices open from 8am to 7pm, and they usually have an ATM.

Safe water
Tap water is safe to drink, but never drink from a tap marked '*Eau non potable*' (not drinking water). Bottled mineral water is also widely available.

Telephones
All telephone numbers in France comprise ten digits. There are no area codes; simply dial the number. Paris numbers all begin with 01. In addition to coin-operated models, an increasing number of public phones take phone-cards (*télécarte*). These are sold in units of 50 and 120 and can be bought from France Telecom shops, post offices, tobacconists and at railway stations. Cheap call rates generally apply Monday to Friday 7pm to 8am, Saturday and Sunday all day. The country code for France is 33. To call home from France dial the international code (00) followed by the country code. To call the UK from France dial 00 44.

Time
France is on Central European Time, one hour ahead of Greenwich Mean Time (GMT + 1). From late March, when clocks are put forward one hour, until late October, French Summer Time (GMT + 2) operates.

Emergency telephone numbers
Police **17**
Fire **18**
Ambulance **15**

On the road

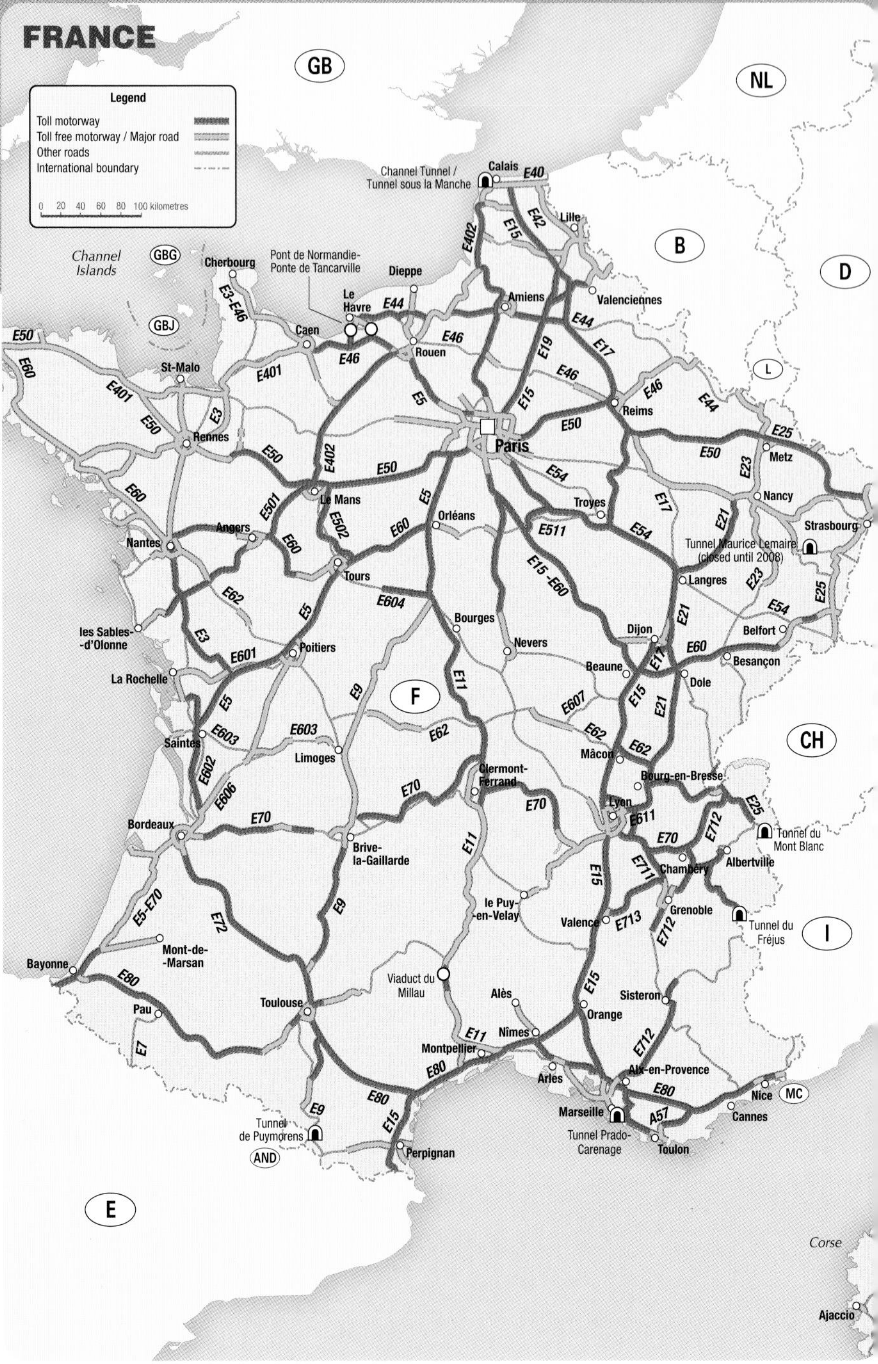
FRANCE
Legend
Toll motorway
Toll free motorway / Major road
Other roads
International boundary
0 20 40 60 80 100 kilometres
GB
NL
B
D
L
F
CH
I
MC
AND
E
Channel Islands
GBG
GBJ
Channel Tunnel / Tunnel sous la Manche
Calais
Lille
Valenciennes
Cherbourg
Pont de Normandie-Ponte de Tancarville
Dieppe
Le Havre
Amiens
Caen
Rouen
St-Malo
Rennes
Reims
Paris
Metz
Nancy
Strasbourg
Troyes
Tunnel Maurice Lemaire (closed until 2008)
Le Mans
Orléans
Angers
Nantes
Tours
Langres
Belfort
Bourges
Nevers
Dijon
Besançon
les Sables-d'Olonne
Poitiers
Beaune
Dole
La Rochelle
Saintes
Limoges
Mâcon
Clermont-Ferrand
Bourg-en-Bresse
Lyon
Tonnel du Mont Blanc
Bordeaux
Brive-la-Gaillarde
Chambéry
Albertville
Grenoble
Tunnel du Fréjus
le Puy-en-Velay
Valence
Mont-de-Marsan
Bayonne
Viaduct du Millau
Alès
Sisteron
Pau
Toulouse
Orange
Nîmes
Montpellier
Arles
Aix-en-Provence
Nice
Cannes
Marseille
Tunnel Prado-Carenage
Toulon
Tunnel de Puymorens
Perpignan
Corse
Ajaccio
E40
E42
E15
E402
E3-E46
E44
E46
E19
E17
E50
E60
E401
E5
E3
E25
E23
E54
E21
E501
E502
E511
E15-E60
E62
E604
E601
E9
E11
E607
E603
E602
E606
E70
E611
E712
E711
E713
E5-E70
E72
E80
E7
A57

Toll charges in Euros

Road		Car	Car towing caravan/ trailer
E3/E5	Nantes – Bordeaux	25.20	38.40
E5	Bordeaux – La Rochelle	11.70	17.90
E5	Bordeaux – Hendaye (Spanish frontier)	6.50	10.10
E5	Paris – Tours	19.80	32.00
	Tours – Bordeaux	28.30	44.60
	Tours – Poitiers	8.90	14.80
	Poitiers – Saintes	10.60	16.50
E5	Rouen – Paris	5.20	8.00
E5/E11	Paris – Clermont-Ferrand	32.30	49.40
E9	Toulouse – Tunnel du Puymorens	4.90	7.30
	Brive – Toulouse	13.00	20.50
E15	Calais – Paris	19.20	29.30
E15	Lille – Paris	13.60	19.90
E15	Lyon – Montpellier	21.50	33.50
E15	Paris – Beaune	18.80	27.60
	Paris – Mâcon	24.50	36.10
	Paris – Lyon	29.60	43.60
E15	Orange – Montpellier	6.80	10.30
	Montpellier – Le Perthus (Spanish frontier)	14.60	22.80
E15/E17	Calais – Reims	18.60	28.00
	Reims – Troyes	9.60	14.10
E15/E17	Reims – Lyon	35.40	52.00
E15/E80	Lyon – Aix-en-Provence	21.00	33.00
E17	Dijon – Beaune	2.90	4.20
E17	Langres – Dijon	5.50	8.00
E17/E21/E62	Reims – Tunnel du Mont Blanc	49.60	75.80
E19	Valenciennes – Paris	12.40	18.30
E19/E17	Valenciennes – Reims	11.00	16.50
E21	Dijon – Dole	2.60	3.80
	Dole – Bourg-en-Bresse	8.70	12.80
E21	Nancy – Langres	6.30	9.20
E25	Metz – Strasbourg	11.20	17.30
E25	Genève – Tunnel du Mont Blanc	5.20	9.10
E44	Le Havre – St Saens (E402)	6.60	10.00
E44	Neufchâtel (E402) – Amiens	5.00	7.60
E44/E17	Amiens – Reims	11.30	17.00
E46/E5	Caen – Paris	12.70	19.20
E50	Paris – Reims	9.20	14.00
	Paris – Metz	21.60	32.70
E50	Paris – Rennes	25.40	39.70
E50/E25	Paris – Strasbourg	32.80	50.00
E50/E501	Paris – Angers	23.60	36.20
E54/E15	Paris – Lyon (via Troyes	29.10	43.00
E60	Angers – Nantes	7.60	11.40
E60	Angers – Tours	7.50	10.70
E60	Beaune – Besançon	6.50	9.50
	Besançon – Belfort	6.60	9.60
	Belfort – Mulhouse (German frontier)	2.60	3.80
E62	Mâcon – Genève	14.70	23.30
E70	Bordeaux – Brive	8.50	13.20
E70	Brive – Clermont-Ferrand	14.50	22.30
E70	Clermont-Ferrand – Lyon	9.50	14.90
E70	Lyon – Chambéry	9.80	15.50
E70	Chambéry – Albertville	4.70	7.40
E70/E711	Lyon – Grenoble	9.20	14.80
E72	Bordeaux – Toulouse	15.60	25.40
E80	Aix-en-Provence – Cannes	12.40	18.80
	Cannes – Nice	3.90	5.90
	Nice – Menton (Italian frontier)	1.90	2.90
E80	Bayonne – Toulouse	15.00	23.30
E80	Montpellier – Arles	4.70	7.30
E80/A54/A7	Montpellier – Aix-en-Prov	8.50	13.10
E80/E15	Toulouse – Montpellier	18.90	29.10
	Toulouse – Le Perthus (Spanish frontier)	17.50	27.10
E402	Rouen (E46/A13) – Le Mans	16.00	26.20
	Le Mans – Tours	7.50	11.50
E402/401	Calais – Paris	17.50	26.30
E604	Tours – Bourges	6.80	10.90
E611/E62	Lyon – Genève	13.70	21.60
E712	Aix-en-Provence – La Saulce (Sisteron)	10.70	16.20
E712	Chambéry – Genève	4.80	7.50
	Grenoble – Chambéry	5.30	7.70
E712	Grenoble – Sisteron	2.90	4.50
E712/E25	Chambéry – Chamonix	11.30	18.00
E713	Valence – Grenoble	7.90	12.40
A14	Orgeval (E5/A13) – Paris (La Défense)	6.90	13.80
A52/A50	Aix-en-Provence – Toulon	6.80	10.30
A57	Toulon – Le Cannet des Maures (E80)	3.70	5.60
A87	Angers – Les Sables d'Olonne	5.20	13.00
A131/E5	Le Havre – Paris	7.60	11.80

Bridges and Tunnels

Pont de Normandie	5.00	5.80
Pont de Tancarville	2.30	2.90
Tunnel du Puymorens	5.60	11.30
Tunnel Prado Carenage (**cars only**)	2.50	
Tunnel du Frejus	31.90	42.10
Tunnel du Mont Blanc	32.30	42.70
Le Viaduc de Millau	7.00	10.60

Driving in Germany (Central Europe)

The regulations below should be read in conjunction with the General motoring information on pages 18–21.

Drinking and driving

If the level of alcohol in the bloodstream is 0.049 per cent or more penalties include fines and the licence holder can be banned from driving in Germany. The blood alcohol level is nil per cent for drivers under 21 and those who have held a licence for less than 2 years; if even a small amount of alcohol is detected in the blood the fine is €125.

Driving licence

The minimum age at which a UK licence holder may drive a temporarily imported car and/or motorcycle is 18.

Fines

On-the-spot fines or a deposit can be imposed. Motorists can be fined for offences such as exceeding speed limits, using abusive language, making derogatory signs and running out of petrol on a motorway. Wheel clamps are not used in Germany but vehicles causing obstruction can be towed away.

Fuel

Unleaded petrol (91, 95 and 98 octane), diesel and LPG is available. Leaded petrol is no longer available, but you can buy a lead substitute additive. It is permitted to carry petrol in a can in Germany, but it is forbidden aboard ferries and Eurotunnel. Credit cards are accepted at most filling stations; check with your card issuer for usage in Germany before travel.

Lights

It is recommended to use dipped headlights at all times. It is compulsory during daylight hours if fog, snow or rain restrict visibility. Driving with sidelights (parking lights) alone is not allowed. Vehicles must have their lights on in tunnels.

Motorcycles

The use of dipped headlights during the day is compulsory. The wearing of a crash helmet is compulsory for both driver and passenger of a moped and motorcycle. Drivers of trikes and quads capable of exceeding 20km/h (12mph) must wear a helmet unless they use a seat belt.

Motor insurance

Third-party insurance is compulsory.

Passengers/children in cars

A child less than 1.5m (4ft 11in) travelling in any type of vehicle must be seated in a child seat or child restraint. Where a child restraint/seat is not available, a child, three years and over, must travel in the rear seat of the vehicle using a seat belt or other safety device attached to the seat. A child under three years old may not be transported in a vehicle without a suitable child restraint/seat. It is the responsibility of the driver to ensure that all children are safely restrained.

Seat belts

It is compulsory for front/rear seat occupants to wear seat belts, if fitted.

Speed limits

The standard legal limits, which may be varied by signs, for **private vehicles without trailers** are: in built-up areas 50km/h (31mph), outside built-up areas 100km/h (62mph) and on dual carriageways and motorways a recommended maximum of 130km/h (80mph). The minimum speed on motorways is 60km/h (37mph). Different speed limits apply in bad weather conditions. Lower limits apply for **private vehicles with a caravan or trailer** (up to 3.5 tonnes): Outside built-up areas the maximum limit is 80km/h (49mph) and on motorways (100km/h) 62mph. A 100km/h sticker must be fixed to the back of the caravan/trailer. The maximum speed limits for vehicles with snow chains is 50km/h (31mph).

Additional information

- It is not compulsory for visiting UK motorists to carry a warning triangle, but they are strongly advised to do so, as its use is compulsory.
- It is recommended that vehicles weighing more than 3.5 tonnes carry a yellow portable flashing light.
- It is recommended that visitors equip their vehicle with a first-aid kit and set of replacement bulbs.
- Slow-moving vehicles must stop at suitable places and let others pass.
- It is prohibited to overtake or pass a school bus that has stopped in a built-up area to let passengers on or off, a fine will be imposed for non-compliance.
- Spiked tyres and the use of radar detectors are prohibited.
- All motorists are obliged to adapt their vehicles to winter weather conditions. This includes but is not limited to winter tyres and anti-freeze fluid for the washer system. Extreme weather may additionally require snow chains. The law does not specify which type of tyre is 'appropriate'. The general opinion is that any type of tyre except summer tyres is appropriate, including all-year tyres. Winter tyres must bear the mark M&S or display the snowflake on the side wall. Motorists whose car is equipped with summer tyres while there is snow and ice may not take the car on the road. Motorists in violation face fines of €20. If they actually obstruct traffic, the fine is €40.

GERMANY, AUSTRIA & SWITZERLAND

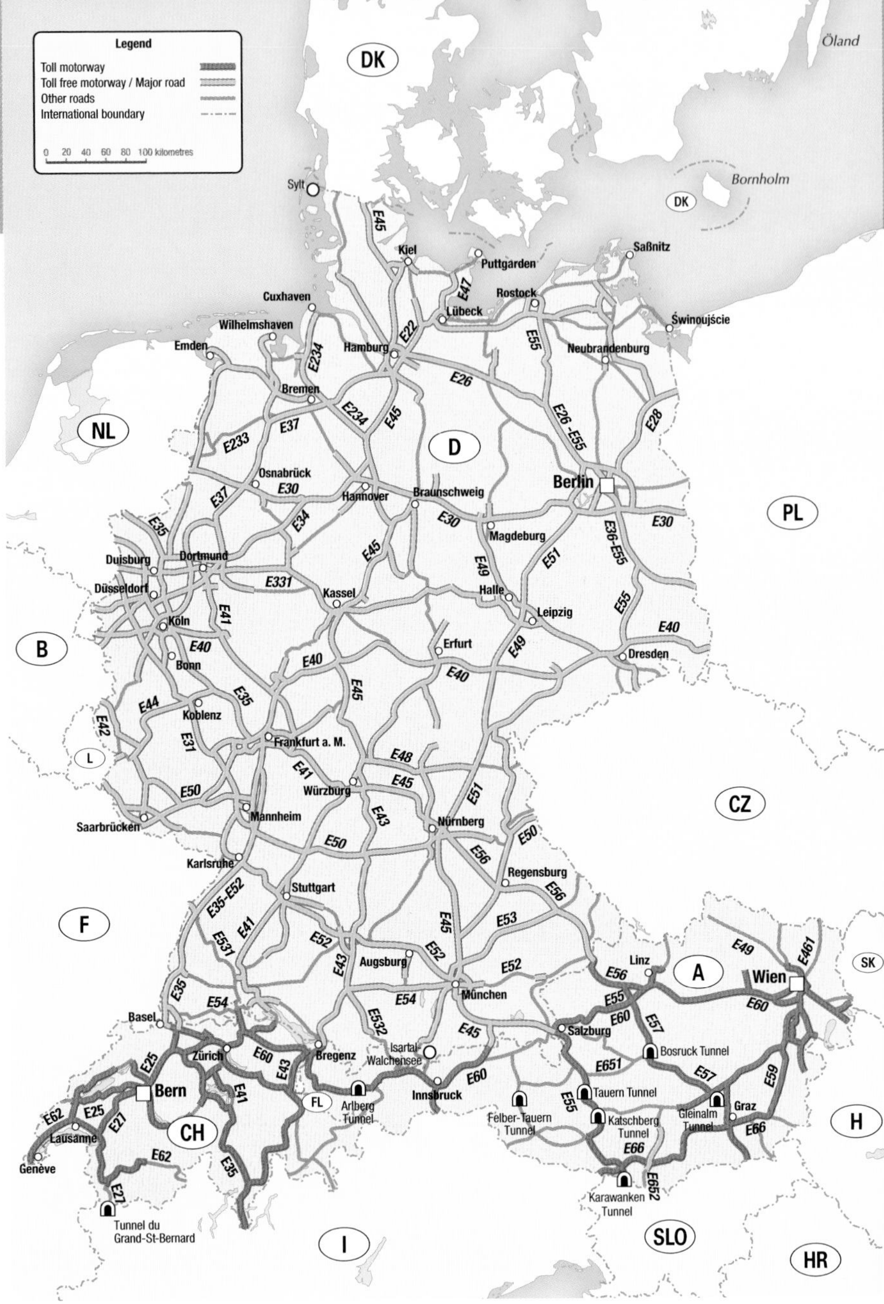

Travel facts: Germany

German National Tourist Office
PO Box 2695
London W1A 3TN
Tel: 020 9317 0908
www.germany-tourism.co.uk

Banking hours
Opening hours can vary greatly although they tend to open at 8.30 or 9am and close at 4pm (6pm Thursday). Banks are closed at weekends although many banks have a foyer with ATMs which can be accessed 24 hours a day.

Credit/debit cards
Credit cards are not accepted in many shops, restaurants and hotels in Germany, particularly in smaller outlets.

Currency
The currency in Germany is the Euro (€). Euro coins are issued in denominations of 1, 2, 5, 10, 20 and 50 cents and €1 and €2. Banknotes are issued in denominations of €5, €10, €20, €50, €100, €200 and €500.

Electricity
The power supply in Germany is 220 volts. Sockets accept two-round-pin (or increasingly three-round-pin) plugs, so an adaptor is needed for most non-Continental appliances. A transformer is needed for appliances operating on 110–120 volts.

Health care
Free or reduced-cost medical treatment is available in Germany to European visitors on production of a valid European Health Insurance Card (EHIC). See page 11. Comprehensive travel insurance is still advised and is essential for all other visitors.

Pharmacies
Pharmacies (*Apotheken*) can be found in every town and most villages throughout Germany. German pharmacists are highly trained and can offer excellent advice and over-the-counter medicines.

Post offices
Post offices are generally open Monday to Friday 8am to 6pm, Saturday 8am until noon. Post boxes are bright yellow.

Safe water
It is safe to drink tap water in Germany. Bottled mineral water (*Mineralwasser*) is also widely available.

Telephones
Local and long-distance calls can be made from post offices and public telephone booths. Telephone cards (available at post offices in denominations of €5 and €10) are required for most telephone booths. The country code for Germany is 49. To call home from Germany dial the international code (00) followed by the country code. To call the UK from Germany dial 00 44.

Time
Germany is on Central European Time, one hour ahead of Greenwich Mean Time (GMT + 1). From late March, when clocks are put forward one hour, until late October, Daylight Savings Time (GMT + 2) operates.

Emergency telephone numbers
Police **110**
Fire **112**
Ambulance **112**

Driving in Great Britain (Western Europe)

The regulations below should be read in conjunction with the General motoring information on pages 18–21.

Drystone walls divide fields in the Yorkshire Dales

Drinking and driving

The maximum permitted level of alcohol in the blood is 0.08 per cent. The police can ask a driver suspected of having committed an offence to undergo a breath test. A penalty of up to £5,000 and/or 6 months' imprisonment and 12 months withdrawal of driving licence, if the first time, can be imposed. The police may also carry out tests to detect a driver who may be under the influence of narcotics.

Driving licence

A visitor may use his national driving licence only if he has reached the minimum age to drive a vehicle in the UK: a motorcycle with or without sidecar, up to 25 kW and a power to weight ratio not exceeding 0.16 kW/kg – 17 years. A motorcycle with or without a sidecar above 25kW – 21 years.
A temporarily imported car 17 years.
A provisional (learner's) driving licence issued abroad is not valid for use in the UK.

Fines

Police officers can issue fixed penalty tickets for a range of offences, e.g. speeding, defective tyres, failure to wear a seat belt, etc. These tickets are issued at the discretion of the police. Offenders have 28 days in which to pay or to request a court hearing. If no action is taken on a ticket, the penalty is increased by 50 per cent or a summons issued for a court hearing. In practice, foreign visitors are not normally given tickets but are, where possible, taken straight before a court. In addition, traffic wardens as well as the police have power to issue tickets. Vehicles illegally parked are liable to a fine and may also be wheel-clamped or removed.

Fuel

Unleaded 95-octane petrol is sold as Premium Unleaded and unleaded 97-octane petrol as Super Unleaded. Ultra low sulphur diesel (ULSD) is sold at all filling stations;

City Diesel, a diesel with reduced sulphur is also available at some filling stations. There are more than 1,200 filling stations which sell Liquefied Petroleum Gas (LPG). Leaded 4-star petrol and Lead Replacement Petrol (LRP) are no longer available. Drivers of older cars designed to use leaded petrol are advised to use lead-replacement additives available widely in filling stations and accessory stores. Prices vary according to the region, fuel brand and type of outlet; supermarket prices may be lower priced.

Lights

Motorists must use sidelights between sunset and sunrise and headlights at night (between half an hour after sunset and half an hour before sunrise) on all roads without street lighting and on roads where the street lights are more than 185 metres apart or are not lit. Motorists must use headlights or front and rear fog lights when visibility is seriously reduced, generally to less than 100 metres, use dipped headlights at night in built-up areas unless the road is well lit, use headlights at night on lit motorways and roads with a speed limit in excess of 30mph (48km/h).

Motorcycles

It is compulsory for riders of motorcycles, scooters and mopeds to wear a safety helmet of an approved design. This also applies to passengers, except those in sidecars. The helmet must be manufactured to a standard similar to the British Standard. Use of headlights during the day is recommended.

Motor Insurance

It is prohibited to drive an imported vehicle in the UK without adequate motor insurance. If the importer does not hold an insurance certificate valid for the UK, arrangements should be made prior to travel. Minimum third party insurance, including trailers.

Motorway/bridge tolls

See motorway map on page 74. Tolls are payable when using certain motorway sections and some bridges and tunnels, see chart on page 75. Not all booths accept credit/debit cards. For information on the M6 Toll visit **www.m6toll.co.uk**

Passengers/children in cars

Children under three years must use a child restraint appropriate for their weight and height in any vehicle (including vans and other goods vehicles). The only exception is that a child under three may travel unrestrained in the rear of a taxi if the right child restraint is not available. Rear-facing car seats must not be used in a seat protected by a frontal air bag unless the air bag has been deactivated manually or automatically. In vehicles, where seat belts are fitted, children 3 years to 12 years and under 135cm in height (4ft 5in) must use the appropriate child restraint. These children

may also travel in the rear and use an adult belt in a taxi, if the right child restraint is not available; for a short distance in an unexpected necessity, or where two occupied child seats in the rear prevent the third being fitted. Drivers are responsible for making sure children under 14 years comply with these laws. Fines for non-compliance vary between £30 and £500

Seat belts

Seat belts must be worn in front and rear of vehicles, if fitted.

Speed limits

The standard legal limits, which may be varied by signs, for **private vehicles without trailers** are: In built-up areas up to 30mph (48km/h) unless otherwise indicated, outside built-up areas 60mph (96km/h), motorways and dual carriage ways up to 70mph (112km/h). Motor caravans with an unladen weight exceeding 3.5 tonnes or motor vehicles adapted to carry more than 8 passengers are banned from the outside lane of a motorway with 3 or more lanes. The limits for **cars towing a caravan or trailer** are: In built-up areas 30mph (48km/h), single carriageways 50mph (80km/h) and on dual carriageways and motorways 60mph (96km/h).

Additional information

- The rule of the road is drive on the left, overtake on the right.
- While it is not compulsory, it is recommended that you carry a warning triangle, first-aid kit and fire extinguisher.
- Motorists must not use a warning triangle on a motorway.
- It is an offence to use a hand-held phone or similar device when driving.
- It is prohibited to use the horn when the vehicle is stationary, except at times of danger due to another vehicle in movement, or as an anti-theft device. The use of the horn is prohibited in built-up areas from 11.30pm to 7am.
- A toll (congestion charge) is payable when driving or parking in central London on weekdays (Monday to Friday excluding public holidays) between 7am and 6.30pm. The entrances to the zone are indicated by the letter 'C' in white on a red background. Visit **www.cclondon.com** for further information. Tolls are also payable when using certain motorway sections, bridges and tunnels.
- Visiting motorists driving left-hand drive vehicles should ensure that their headlights are adjusted for driving on the left, otherwise they risk being stopped by the police and subsequently fined up to £1,000.

Travel facts: Great Britain

Britain and London Visitor Centre
1 Regent Street
London SW1Y 4XT

No telephone enquiries
www.visitbritain.com

Banking hours
Banks are generally open from Monday to Friday 9.30am to 4.30pm. Some banks open Saturday morning. Opening hours are can differ considerably from branch to branch. Some banks in Scotland close for an hour at lunchtime. Many banks have 24-hour banking lobbies where you can access a range of services via machines.

Credit/debit cards
All credit/debit cards that bear the Visa, MasterCard or American Express logo are widely accepted in Britain. Retailers can charge more for goods and services bought by credit card, but they must display a notice if any price increase applies.

Currency
Britain's currency is the pound sterling (£), issued in banknotes of £5, £10, £20 and £50. There are 100 pennies or pence (p) to each pound and coins come in denominations of 1p, 2p, 5p, 10p, 20p, 50p, £1 and £2. Scottish £1 notes are still in circulation in Scotland. The Channel Islands and the Isle of Man have some different coins and notes from the mainland but the monetary system is the same.

Electricity
The power supply in Britain is 240 volts. Sockets only accept three-square-pin plugs, so an adaptor is needed for Continental appliances. A transformer is needed for appliances operating on 110–120 volts.

Health care
Free or reduced-cost medical treatment is available in Great Britain to European visitors on production of a valid European Health Insurance Card (EHIC). See page 11. Comprehensive travel insurance is still advised and is essential for all other visitors.

Pharmacies
Prescription and non-prescription drugs and medicines are available from chemists/ pharmacies. Pharmacists can advise on medication for common ailments. Pharmacies operate a rota so there will always be one that is open 24 hours a day. Notices in pharmacy windows give details.

Post offices
Post offices are generally open Monday to Friday 9am to 5.30pm, Saturday 9am to noon.

Safe water
Tap water is safe to drink. Bottled mineral water is widely available.

Telephones
Coin operated public telephones take 10p, 20p, 50p and £1 coins, but card-operated ones are often more convenient. Phone cards are available from many shops. The country code for Britain is 44. To call home from Britain dial the international code (00) followed by the country code. To call Germany from Britain dial 00 49.

Time
Britain is on Greenwich Mean Time (GMT) in winter, but from late March to late October British Summer Time BST (GMT + 1) operates.

Emergency telephone numbers
Police **999** or **112**
Fire **999** or **112**
Ambulance **999** or **112**

GREAT BRITAIN

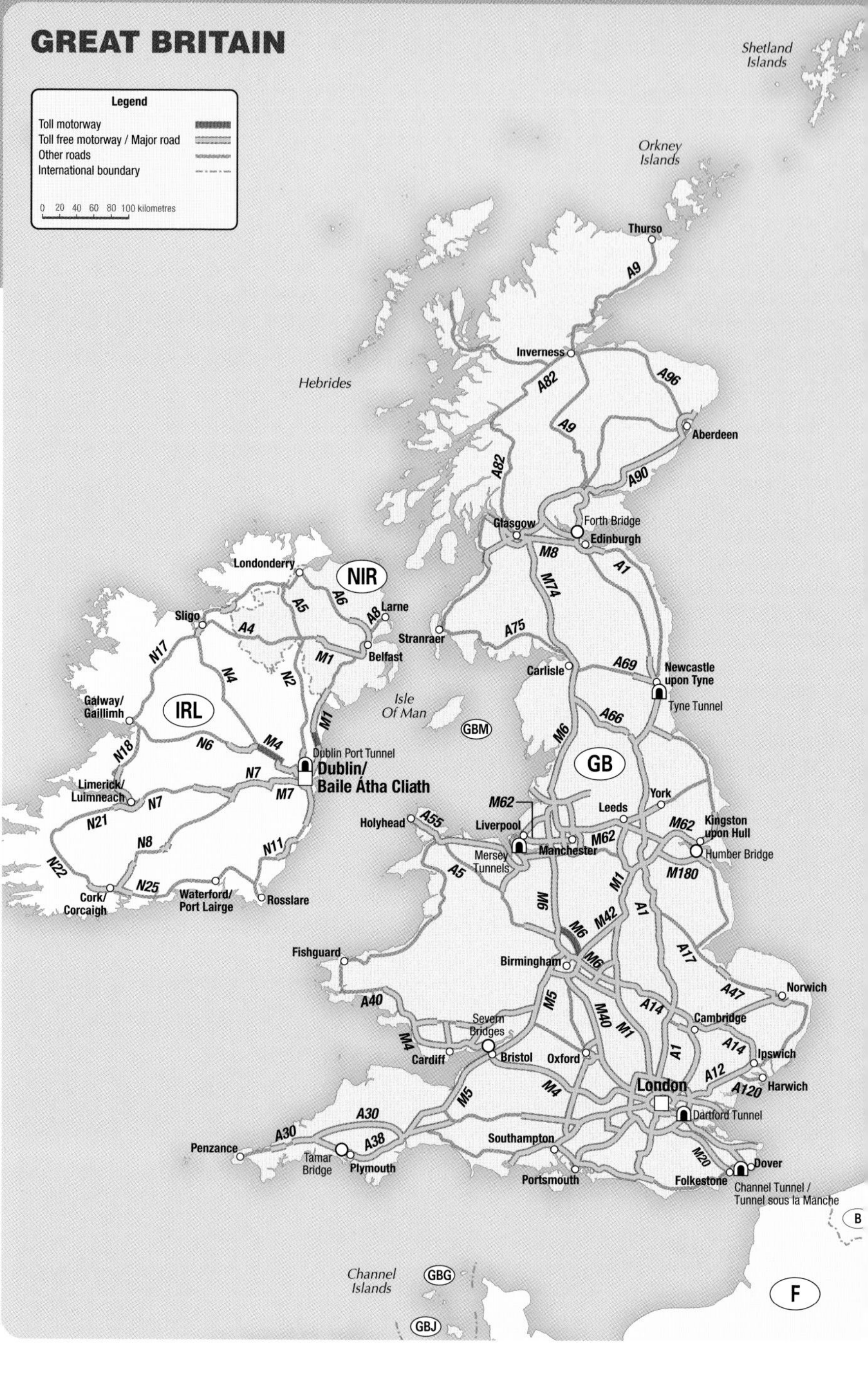
Legend
Toll motorway
Toll free motorway / Major road
Other roads
International boundary
0 20 40 60 80 100 kilometres
Shetland Islands
Orkney Islands
Thurso
A9
Inverness
A82
A96
Hebrides
A9
Aberdeen
A82
A90
Glasgow
Forth Bridge
Edinburgh
M8
A1
M74
Londonderry
NIR
A5
A6
A8
Larne
Sligo
A4
Stranraer
A75
Belfast
M1
N17
N4
N2
Carlisle
A69
Newcastle upon Tyne
Tyne Tunnel
Galway/ Gaillimh
IRL
M1
Isle Of Man
GBM
A66
N18
N6
M4
Dublin Port Tunnel
Dublin/ Baile Átha Cliath
M6
GB
N7
Limerick/ Luimneach
N7
M7
M62
York
Leeds
Holyhead
A55
Liverpool
M62
Kingston upon Hull
N21
N8
Mersey Tunnels
Manchester
Humber Bridge
N11
A5
M180
N22
N25
Cork/ Corcaigh
Waterford/ Port Lairge
Rosslare
M6
M1
A1
M42
M6
Fishguard
Birmingham
M6
A17
Norwich
A47
A40
M5
A14
Cambridge
Severn Bridges
M40
M1
M4
Cardiff
Bristol
Oxford
A1
A14
Ipswich
A12
London
A120
Harwich
M5
M4
A30
Dartford Tunnel
A30
A38
Southampton
Penzance
Tamar Bridge
Plymouth
M20
Dover
Portsmouth
Folkestone
Channel Tunnel / Tunnel sous la Manche
B
Channel Islands
GBG
F
GBJ

Toll charges in £ sterling

General	**Car**	**Car towing caravan/ trailer**
Central London	8.00	8.00
Central London congestion charge zone. Charge applies between 7am and 6pm weekdays and allows unlimited trips into or out of the zone in one day. For more information see page 72.		
Road		
M6 Toll Road		
(Night charge 11pm–6am)	3.00	6.00
(Day charge 6am–11pm)	4.00	7.00
Bridges and Tunnels		
Aldwark Toll Bridge between Little Ouseburn and Aldwark/ Linton on Ouse	0.40	1.00
Batheaston Bridge off **A4** near Bath	0.50	1.00
Cartford Bridge 5 miles (3km) east of Poulton-le-Fylde	0.40	0.80
Cleddau Bridge on **A477**	0.75	1.50
Clifton Suspension Bridge on **B3129**. Not suitable for caravans over 4 tonnes	0.30	0.60
Dartford River Crossing on **A282/ M25**	1.00	2.00

Bridges and tunnels	**Car**	**Car towing caravan/ trailer**
Dunham Bridge on **A57**	0.30	0.40
Humber Bridge on **A15**	2.70	4.90
Itchen Bridge on **A3025** (off-peak 0.50)	0.60	0.60
Mersey Tunnel (Kingsway) between Wallasey and Liverpool	1.30	2.60
Mersey Tunnel (Queensway) between Birkenhead and Liverpool	1.30	2.60
Middlesbrough transporter on **A178**	1.00	2.00
Penrhyndeudraeth Bridge (Briwet Bridge) (between **A496 and A487**)	0.40	0.70
Second Severn Crossing on **M4** (westbound only)	5.10	5.10
Severn Bridge on **M48** (westbound only)	5.10	5.10
Swinford Bridge on **B4044**	0.05	0.10
Tamar Bridge on **A38** (eastbound only)	1.00	2.00
Tyne Tunnel on **A19**	1.10	1.10
Warburton Bridge on **B5159**	0.12	0.12
Whitchurch Bridge on **B471**	0.20	0.20
Whitney-on-Wye Bridge on **B4350**	0.50	0.50

Brunel's spectacular Clifton Suspension Bridge spans the Avon Gorge

Driving in Greece (Southern Europe)

The regulations below should be read in conjunction with the General motoring information on pages 18–21.

The narrow paved alleyways of Greece

Drinking and driving

It is a criminal offence to drive if the level of alcohol in the bloodstream is 0.05 per cent or more. A lower unit of 0.02 per cent applies to drivers who have held a licence for less than two years, and to motorcyclists.

Driving licence

The minimum age at which a UK licence holder may drive a temporarily imported car and/or motorcycle (over 50cc) is 17.

Fines

Police can impose fines but not collect them on the spot. The fine must be paid at a Public Treasury office within 10 days. You can be fined for the unnecessary use of a car horn. Vehicles may be towed away if parked illegally, or if violating traffic regulations.

Fuel

Unleaded petrol (95 and 100 octane) and diesel (*petreleo*) is availableis. Leaded petrol is not available. Lead replacement petrol is sold as Super 2002 (98 octane). It is forbidden to carry petrol in a can in a vehicle. LPG may not be used in private cars, only in taxis. Credit cards are accepted at some filling stations. Check with your card issuer for use in Greece before travel.

Lights

Dipped headlights should be used in poor daytime visibility. The use of undipped headlights in towns is strictly prohibited.

Motorcycles

The use of dipped headlights during the day is compulsory. The wearing of crash helmets is also compulsory.

Motor insurance
Third-party insurance is compulsory.

Passengers/children in cars
It is prohibited for children over three years of age and under 1.5 metres (4ft 9in) to travel in the front seat of a vehicle. Children under five years of age must use the child restraint appropriate for their weight in all cars, vans and goods vehicles, except when travelling in the rear of taxis. They cannot be carried in the vehicle otherwise. Approved child restraints are those conforming with standard ECE R44/03 (or later). Children measuring 1.35 metres (4ft 4in) or over can use a seat belt. Placing a rear-facing child restraint in the front passenger seat is allowed only if the passenger airbag is deactivated.

Seat belts
It is compulsory for front-seat occupants to wear seat belts.

Speed limits
The standard legal limits, which may be varied by signs, for **private vehicles without trailers** are: in built-up areas 50km/h (31mph) for cars, 40km/h (24mph) for motorcycles; outside built-up areas 90km/h (55mph) or 110km/h (68mph) for cars, 70km/h (43mph) for motorcycles; motorways 120km/h (74mph) for cars and motorcycles over 125cc, 70km/h (43mph) for motorcycles under 125cc. Lower limits apply to **private cars towing a caravan or trailer:** Outside built-up areas and on motorways 80km/h (49mph).

Additional information
- A fire extinguisher, first-aid kit and warning triangle are compulsory.
- The police are empowered to confiscate the number plates of illegally parked vehicles throughout Greece. Generally this only applies to Greek-registered vehicles, but the drivers of foreign registered vehicles should be aware of parking illegally.

Travel facts and toll charges: Greece

Greek National Tourism Organisation
4 Conduit Street
London W1S 2DJ
Tel: 020 7495 9300 (enquiries and information)
www.visitgreece.gr

Banking hours
Banks are open Monday to Friday 8am to 2pm (Friday 1.30pm). They may stay open longer hours during peak season in resort areas.

Credit/debit cards
Cash is still the preferred method of payment in Greece. Only the larger and more expensive hotels, restaurants and shops will accept payment by credit card.

Currency
The currency in Greece is the Euro (€). Euro coins are issued in denominations of 1, 2, 5, 10, 20 and 50 cents and €1 and €2. Banknotes are issued in denominations of €5, €10, €20, €50, €100, €200 and €500.

Electricity
The power supply in Greece is 220 volts AC, 50Hz. Sockets accept two-round-pin plugs, so an adaptor is needed for most non-Continental appliances. A transformer is needed for appliances operating on 110–120 volts.

Health care
Free or reduced-cost medical treatment is available in Greece to European visitors on production of a valid European Health Insurance Card (EHIC). See page 11. Comprehensive travel insurance is still advised and is essential for all other visitors.

Pharmacies
Pharmacies (*farmakeío*), indicated by a green cross, give advice and prescriptions for common ailments. Codeine is banned in Greece and you can be fined for carrying it.

Post offices
Post offices, identified by a yellow OTE sign, are generally open Monday to Friday 8am to 2pm. Stamps (*ghramatósima*) are slos sold at kiosks or shops selling cards. Post boxes are yellow; use the slot marked *Exoterico* for overseas mail.

Safe water
Tap water is chlorinated and is regarded as safe to drink. Bottled mineral water it is cheap to buy and is widely available.

Telephones
Calls from phone booths can be made using a phonecard available from kiosks, OTE offices and some shops. They are sold in units of 100, 500 and 1,000). You can also make calls from street kiosks which have metered phones and pay at the end of the call, although connections tend to be poor. The country code for Greece is 30. To call home from Greece dial the international code (00) followed by the country code. To call Britain from Greece dial 00 44.

Time
Greece is on Eastern European Time. It is two hours ahead of Greenwich Mean Time (GMT + 2) and from late March to late October it is three hours ahead of Greenwich Mean Time (GMT + 3).

Emergency telephone numbers
Police, Fire and Amulance **100**
Athens only – Tourist Police **171**

Toll charges in Euros

Road		**Car**	**Car towing caravan/ trailer**
1/E75	Lamia – Inofita	1.20	1.80
1/E75	Katerini – Larisa	1.40	2.30
1/E75	Larisa – Lamia	1.40	2.30
1/E75	Thessaloniki – Katerini	1.40	2.30
1/E75	Lamia – Afidnes	1.40	2.30
1/E75	Afidnes – Athina	1.40	2.30
7/E65	Korinthos – Tripoli	2.70	3.50
8A/E65 – E55	Korinthos – Patra	1.80	3.00
8A/E94	Athina – Korinthos	1.40	2.30

Driving in Hungary (Central Europe)

The regulations below should be read in conjunction with the General motoring information on pages 18–21.

Drinking and driving

Nil per cent of alcohol is allowed in the driver's blood. Amounts of less than 0.08 per cent incur a fine, more than 0.08 per cent incur legal proceedings.

Driving licence

The minimum age at which a UK driving licence holder may drive a temporarily imported car and/or motorcycle is 17. All valid UK driving licences should be accepted in Hungary. This includes the older all-green paper style UK licences (in Northern Ireland older paper style with photographic counterpart) although the EC appreciates that these may be more difficult to understand and that drivers may wish to voluntarily update them before travelling abroad, if time permits. Alternatively, older licences may be accompanied by an International Driving Permit (IDP).

Fines

On-the-spot fines are only payable in the local currency, the Hungarian Forint (HUF). Credit cards are not accepted. On-the-spot fines can be paid by post within 30 days. The police must give a receipt for cash payments. Wheel clamps are in use.

Fuel

Unleaded petrol (95 and 98 octane), diesel (*Dizel* or *Gazolaj*) and LPG are available. Leaded petrol is not available. It is forbidden to import petrol in a can. Credit cards are accepted at some filling stations, check with your card issuer for usage in Hungary. Cash is the most usual form of payment.

Lights

The use of dipped headlights is compulsory at all times outside built-up areas. At night the use of full beam, in built-up areas, is prohibited.

Motorcycles

The use of dipped headlights is compulsory at all times. The wearing of crash helmets is compulsory for both driver and passenger.

Motor insurance

Third-party insurance is compulsory. Should a visitor cause an accident involving a Hungarian citizen they must report it to the Association of Hungarian Insurance Companies.

Passengers/children in cars

A child under 3 years of age may only travel in a vehicle if using a suitable child-restraint system appropriate for their weight, they are permitted to travel in the front of the vehicle using this restraint if it is rear facing and there is no airbag or it has been deactivated. Children under 1.5m (4ft 9in) and over 3 years of age must use a suitable child-restraint system and be seated in the rear of the vehicle.

Seat belts

It is compulsory for front/rear-seat occupants to wear seat belts, where fitted.

Speed limits

The standard legal limits, which may be varied by signs, for **private vehicles without trailers** are: In built-up areas 50km/h (31mph), outside built-up areas 90km/h (55mph) or 110km/h (68mph) on semi-motorways and 130km/h (80mph) on motorways. Lower limits apply to a **vehicle towing a caravan:** Outside built-up areas 70km/h (43mph), on semi-motorways 70km/h (43mph) and on motorways 80km/h (49mph). Vehicles with snow chains must not exceed 50km/h (31mph). In city centres, roads with an 30km/h (18mph) speed limit are increasingly common.

Additional information

- A first-aid kit and warning triangle are compulsory.
- Spare bulb kit recommended as its carriage is compulsory for Hungarian registered vehicles.
- It is recommended that the driver of a conspicuously damaged vehicle entering Hungary obtains a police report confirming the damage at the time of entry, otherwise lengthy delays may be encountered at the frontier when leaving Hungary. This report should be obtained from the police of the country where the car was damaged.
- Motorway tax is payable for use of: M1 (Budapest-Hegyeshalom), M3 (Budapest-Gorbehaza), M5 (Budapest-Kiskunfelegyhaza), the M6 (Erd-Dunaujvaros) and M7 (Budapest-Lake Balaton). A windscreen sticker must be displayed as evidence of payment. The sticker may be purchased only in Hungarian Forints from MAK office, large petrol stations near motorways and the offices of motorway companies and at some offices of automobile clubs in Austria and Slovakia – available for 4 days (vehicles up to 3.5 tonnes only), 10 days, one month or one year. Fines are imposed for non-display. See toll charges, opposite.
- Motorist should be wary of contrived incidents, particularly on the Vienna – Budapest motorway, designed to stop motorists and expose them to robbery.
- Spiked tyres are prohibited.
- The use of snow chains or their presence in a car can be made compulsory on some roads when weather conditions require.
- The use of the horn is prohibited in built-up areas, except in case of danger.

Travel facts and toll charges: Hungary

Hungarian Tourist Office
46 Eaton Place
London SW1X 8AL
Tel: 0800 360 00000
www.gotohungary.co.uk
www.hungary.com

Banking hours
Banks are generally open Monday to Friday 8am to 4pm, and until noon on Saturday.

Credit/debit cards
The acceptance of credit cards is limited; they are becoming increasingly popular but they are not accepted everywhere. Most ATMs in Hungary accept Visa, MasterCard (including Cirrus and Maestro), American Express and Diners Club.

Currency
Hungary's currency is the Forint (Ft or HUF). The denominations of Forint banknotes are Ft200, 500, 1,000, 2,000, 5,000, 10,000 and 20,000. There are coins of 1, 2, 5, 10, 20, 50 and 100 forints.

Electricity
Hungary has 220–230V power supply. Electrical sockets take two round pin-plugs.

Health care
Free or reduced-cost medical treatment is available in Hungary to European visitors on production of a valid European Health Insurance Card (EHIC). See page 11. Comprehensive travel insurance is still advised and is essential for all other visitors.

Pharmacies
A pharmacy (*gyógyszetár* or *patica*) sells both prescription and non-prescription medicines (bring your own medication if you need a specific product). Information about the nearest 24-hour facility is posted at all pharmacies.

Post offices
Buy stamps (*bélyeg*) at a post office (*posta*), news-stand or tobacconist (*dohanyaruds*) or from a hotel. Post boxes are wall mounted and red with a calling-horn emblem.

Safe water
Although tap water is safe, you may find it causes mild upsets. Bottled mineral water and soda water are widely available and advised.

Telephones
You can use cash and prepaid phone cards to make a call in Hungary. For direct dialing national and international calls use Ft20, Ft50 and Ft100 coins. International calls can be made from red phone booths. Phone cards on 50 and 100 units can be bought from newsstands, tobacconists, petrol stations, post offices and hotels. The country code for Hungary is 36. To call home from Hungary dial the international code (00) followed by the country code. To call the UK from Hungary dial 00 44.

Time
Hungary is on Central European Time, one hour ahead of GMT (GMT + 1). Daylight Savings Time comes into effect from the end of March to the end of October CET + 1 (GMT + 2).

Emergency telephone numbers
Police **107** Fire **105** Ambulance **104**

Toll charges in Forints
For details of where to buy the motorway tax see page 80.

General	**Car**	**Car towing caravan/ trailer**
4-day vignette (May to September) **M1/M3/M5/M7**	1530.00	1530.00
4-day vignette (September to May) **M1/M3/M5/M7**	1170.00	1170.00
10-day vignette **M1/M3/M5/M7**	2550.00	2550.00
1 month **M1/M3/M5/M7**	4200.00	4200.00
1 year **M1/M3/M5/M7**	37200.00	37200.00

Driving in Ireland (Republic of) (Western Europe)

The regulations below should be read in conjunction with the General motoring information on pages 18–21.

Picturesque Kylemore Abbey stands in wooded grounds on the edge of a lake in Connemara

For regulations covering Northern Ireland see Great Britain, pages 70–75.

Drinking and driving

If the level of alcohol in the bloodstream is more than 0.08 per cent or more, severe penalties including a fine and/or imprisonment plus disqualification can be imposed.

Driving licence

The minimum age at which a UK licence holder may drive a temporarily imported car or motorcycle (exceeding 150cc) is 17.

Fines

There are on-the-spot fines for parking and speeding offences. Wheel clamps are in use. In some areas parked cars can be towed away if causing an obstruction and a significant fee is charged for release.

Fuel
Unleaded petrol (95 octane) and diesel are sold. Leaded petrol is not available. The use of lead replacement petrol and LPG is extremely limited in Ireland. Petrol in a can is permitted but forbidden on board ferries. Credit cards are accepted at most filling stations; check with your card issuer for usage in Ireland before travel.

Lights
Dipped headlights should be used in poor daytime visibility.

Motorcycles
The use of dipped headlights during the day is recommended. The wearing of crash helmets is compulsory for both driver and passenger.

Motor insurance
Third-party insurance is compulsory.

Passengers/children in cars
A child under 12 cannot travel as front seat passenger unless using suitable restraint system. Children under 12 years of age and less than 1.5m (4ft 9in) high must use a suitable child seat e.g. a booster cushion.

Seat belts
It is compulsory for front/rear-seat occupants to wear seat belts, if fitted.

Speed limits
The standard legal limits, which may be varied by signs, for **private vehicles without trailers** are: In built-up areas are: 50km/h (31mph), outside built-up areas 60–100km/h (37–62mph) according to road signs and 120km/h (75mph) on motorways. Lower limits apply to **vehicles with trailers:** Outside built-up areas and on motorways 80km/h (40mph)

Special features
- The rule of the road is drive on the left; overtake on the right.
- A warning triangle is compulsory for vehicles with an unladen weight exceeding 1,524kg (1.5 tons).
- Horns must not be used between 11:30pm and 7am.
- Distances are given in kilometres.
- Some level crossings have manual gates which motorists must open and close.
- Radar detectors are forbidden.

Travel facts and toll charges: Ireland

Irish Tourist Board
Nations House, 103 Wigmore Street
London W1U 1QS
Tel: 020 7518 0800; 0800 039 7000 (brochures)
www.tourismireland.com
www.visitireland.com

Banking hours
Banks are generally open Monday to Friday 10am to 4pm. Some banks in small towns close 12.30 to 1.30pm. Banks open until 5pm one day a week (Thursday in Dublin).

Credit/debit cards
Credit and debit cards are accepted in major hotels, restaurants and large stores. Check first in small or rural establishments.

Currency
The monetary units in the Republic of Ireland is the Euro (€); in Northern Ireland it is the pound sterling (£), see page 73. These are not interchangeable. Euro banknotes come in denominations of €500, €200, €100, €50, €20, €10 and €5; coins in denominations of €2 and €1 and 50, 20, 10, 5, 2 and 1 cents.

Electricity
The power supply in the Republic of Ireland is: 230 volts. Electrical sockets take either plugs with two round pins or three square pins.

Health care
Free or reduced-cost medical treatment is available in the Republic of Ireland to European visitors on production of a valid European Health Insurance Card (EHIC). See page 11. Comprehensive travel insurance is still advised and is essential for all other visitors.

Pharmacies
Prescription and non-prescription drugs and medicines are available from pharmacies.

Post offices
Opening hours are generally Monday to Friday 9am to 5.50pm, Saturday 1pm.

Safe water
Tap water in Ireland is safe to drink. Bottled mineral water is widely available.

Telephones
Public telephone boxes, blue and cream in the Republic, are being replaced by glass and metal booths. To make a call, lift the handset, insert the correct coins (10, 20 or 50 cents) or phonecard and dial. The country code for Ireland is 353.
To call home from the Republic dial the international code (00) followed by the country code. To call the UK from the Republic dial 00 44.

Time
Ireland observes Greenwich Mean Time (GMT), but from late March, when clocks are put forward one hour, until late October, summer time (GMT + 1) operates.

Emergency telephone numbers
Police, Fire, Ambulance and Coastal Rescue
999 or **112**

Toll charges in Euros

Roads	**Car**	**Car towing caravan/ trailer**
M1 Toll Drogheda Bypass	1.70	1.70
M4 Toll Kinnegad – Enfield – Kilcock	2.60	2.60
M8 Toll Rathcormac – Fermoy	1.60	1.60
Bridges and Tunnels		
East Link Toll Bridge East of Dublin	1.45	1.45
M50 Dublin Port Tunnel (northbound, afternoon peak rate)	12.00	12.00
M50 Dublin Port Tunnel (southbound, morning peak rate)	12.00	12.00
West Link Toll Bridge on M50 West of Dublin (peak time)	3.00	3.00

Driving in Italy and San Marino (Southern Europe)

The regulations below should be read in conjunction with the General motoring information on pages 18–21.

Drinking and driving

If the level of alcohol in the bloodstream is 0.051 per cent or more, severe penalties, which include fines, confiscation of vehicle and imprisonment can be imposed.

Driving licence

The minimum age at which a UK licence holder may drive a temporarily imported car and/or motorcycle (over 125cc or with passenger) is 18. All valid UK driving licences should be accepted in Italy. This includes the older all-green style UK licences (in Northern Ireland older paper style with photographic counterpart) although the EC appreciates that these may be more difficult to understand and that drivers may wish to voluntarily update them before travelling abroad, if time permits. Alternatively, older licences may be accompanied by an International Driving Permit (IDP).

Fines

On-the-spot fines can be imposed. Fines for speeding offences are particularly heavy. The police can impose the fine and collect one quarter of the maximum fine; they must give a receipt for the amount of the fine paid. Illegally parked vehicles can be clamped or towed away and a fine imposed.

Fuel

Unleaded petrol (95 octane and 98 octane), diesel (*gasolio*) and LPG are available. Leaded petrol is not available, but you can buy a lead substitute additive. Carrying petrol in a can is permitted. Credit cards are accepted at most filling stations. Check with your card issuer for usage in Italy and San Marino before travel.

The magnificent view over the rooftops of Florence from the city's Duomo

Lights

The use of dipped headlights during the day is compulsory outside built-up areas and during snow and rain or poor visibility.

Driving in Italy and San Marino continued

A farmhouse sits on the crest of a hill in green Tuscan countryside near San Gimignano

Rear fog lights may only be used when visibility is less than 50 metres or in case of strong rain or intense snow. Lights must be switched on in tunnels.

Motorcycles

The use of dipped headlights during the day is compulsory on all roads. The wearing of crash helmets is compulsory for both driver and passenger. The vehicle can be seized for non-compliance. It is prohibited to carry a child less than 4 years on a moped or motorcycle. The registration certificate must state that the moped/motorcycle is designed to carry a passenger. Motorcycles under 150cc are not allowed on motorways.

Motor Insurance

Third-party insurance is compulsory.

Motorways

See map, page 89. To join a motorway follow the green signposts (vehicles which cannot exceed 40kmh/25mph and motorcycles under 150cc are prohibited). On the majority of the toll motorways a ticket is issued on entry (do not enter in the yellow TELEPASS lanes) and toll is paid on leaving the motorway. The entry ticket gives information about the toll charges, including the toll category of the vehicle. At the exit use either the white or blue lanes, return your ticket and pay. Blue lanes are self service and take credit cards or Viacard. White lanes are self service and take cash, credit cards or Viacard. White lanes with operators take cash, credit cards and prepaid Viacard. Toll booths will not exchange traveller's cheques, If paying with cash ensure you have sufficient Euros to meet the high toll charges. Credit cards are accepted at the majority of toll booths. Visit **www.autostrade.it** for further information.

It is usually possible to obtain services for a car and/or occupants every 30–50km (18–31 miles). Emergency telephones are sited every 2km (1.24 miles) on most motorways.

Passengers/children in cars

Children under 1.5m (4ft 9in) have to use a suitable restraint system or an adaptor for a seat belt. Where no restraint system is available children aged 3 or under are not permitted to travel. Children over 3 years of age should travel on the rear seats, they are permitted to travel in the front seats if they are taller than 1.5m (4ft 9in). A child must not be seated in a restraint system with their back to the road if the vehicle is fitted with an airbag, unless it is deactivated.

Seat belts

It is compulsory for front/rear-seat occupants to wear seat belts, if fitted.

Speed limits

The standard legal limits, which may be varied by signs, for **private vehicles without trailers** are: In built-up areas 50km/h (31mph), outside built-up areas 90km/h (55mph) on ordinary roads, 110km/h (68mph) on dual carriageways and 130km/h (80mph) on motorways. Note: in wet weather lower speed limits of 90km/h (55mph) apply on dual carriageways and 110km/h (68mph) on motorways. Restrictions apply if vehicles are using spiked tyres. Lower limits apply to **cars towing a caravan or trailer**: Outside built-up areas 70km/h (43mph) and on motorways 80km/h (49mph).

Additional information

- A warning triangle is compulsory for all vehicles with more than two wheels.
- It is recommended that visitors equip their vehicles with a set of replacement bulbs.
- Any vehicle with an overhanging load (e.g. carrying bicycle at rear) must display reflective square panel, a fine may be imposed if the sign is not displayed.
- The wearing of reflective jacket/waistcoat compulsory if driver and/or passenger(s) exits vehicle which is immobilised on the carriageway at night or in poor visibility.
- Tolls are levied on the majority of motorways. See page 88.
- In built-up areas the use of the horn is prohibited except in cases of immediate danger.
- In the area of Val d'Aosta, vehicles must be equipped with winter tyres or snow chains from 15 October until 15 April.
- The transportation or use of radar detectors is prohibited, violation of this regulation will result in a fine between €708 and €2,834 and confiscation of the device.

Toll charges in Euros

Road		Car	Car towing caravan/ trailer
E25 (A26)			
	Génova – Alessandria	3.90	4.90
	Genova – Iselle (Swiss frontier)	11.30	14.20
E25 (A5)	Santhià – Aosta	13.00	19.30
E33 (A15)			
	Parma – La Spezia	10.30	14.10
E35 (A1)	Milano – Bologna	10.90	13.70
	Bologna – Firenze	5.90	7.30
	Firenze – Roma	13.20	16.60
E35 (A8/A9)			
	Milano – Chiasso (Swiss frontier)	3.70	4.70
E35/E45 (A1)			
	Milano – Nápoli	40.80	51.50
E45 (A1)	Roma – Nápoli	10.50	13.30
E45 (A3)	Nápoli – Salerno	1.50	3.20
E45/A14 Dir			
	Bologna – Ravenna	3.70	4.70
E45 (A18)			
	Messina – Catánia	3.00	5.50
E45 (A22)			
	Brenner Pass – Trento	8.40	10.50
	Trento – Verona	5.10	6.40
	Verona – Modena	4.90	6.20
E45/E55 (A14)			
	Bologna – Ancona	10.30	13.00
E45/E55 (A14)			
	Bologna – Táranto	38.40	48.50
E55 (A14)			
	Ancona – Pescara	7.90	9.90
	Pescara – Bari	16.10	20.30
E55 (A14)			
	Pescara – Táranto	19.50	24.60
E55 (A23)			
	Udine – Tarvisio (Austria)	5.50	6.80
E62 (A7)	Milano – Tortona	3.30	4.30
	Milano – Génova	6.90	8.80
E62 (A8)	Milano – Varese	3.20	4.00
E64 (A4)	Torino – Milano	6.90	8.70
	Milano – Bréscia	6.20	7.8
E64/E70 (A4)			
	Milano – Venézia	14.50	18.50
E70 (A4)	Bréscia – Verona	2.60	3.30
	Verona – Pádova	3.40	4.30
	Pádova – Venézia	1.70	2.10
E70 (A4)	Venézia – Trieste	5.50	6.90
E70 (A21)			
	Torino – Alessandria	4.80	6.20
	Alessandria – Piacenza	5.10	6.30
	Torino – Piacenza	10.20	13.00
	Piacenza – Brescia	3.60	4.50
E70 (A32)			
	Torino – Tunnel del Fréjus (France)	9.00	16.10
E76 (A11)			
	Firenze – Pisa	5.40	7.00
E80 (A10)			
	Génova – Savona	2.20	2.70
	Savona – Ventimiglia – Border	11.10	20.70
E80 (A12)			
	Génova – La Spezia	8.50	11.30
	La Spezia – Livorno	10.20	14.00
	Génova – Viareggio (E76)	10.50	14.10
	Génova – Livorno	16.40	22.20
	Livorno – Roma	3.40	4.20
E80 (A24)			
	Roma – Téramo	10.70	13.40
E80 (A25)			
	Roma – Pescara	12.80	16.00
E90 (A20)			
	Messina – Palermo	6.40	8.50
E612/E25 (A5)			
	Torino – Aosta	14.40	21.30
E717 (A6)			
	Torino – Savona	9.70	13.50
E842 (A16)			
	Napoli – Bari	15.10	19.00
E843 (A14)			
	Bari – Táranto	3.50	4.40
A13	Bologna – Pádova	5.10	6.40
	Bologna – Ferrara	1.70	2.20
	Ferrara – Padova	4.00	5.10
A22	Brenner Pass (Austria) – Modena	18.40	23.10
A27	Venezia – Belluno	4.90	6.20
A30	Caserta – Salerno	5.10	6.40
A31	Vicenza – Trento	1.80	2.30

Bridges and Tunnels

E25	Tunnel Monte Bianco	32.30	42.70
E70	Tunnel dél Fréjus	31.90	42.10
	Tunnel Munt La Schera	10.00	20.00
	Sankt Bernhard Tunnel	22.40	34.80

ITALY
Legend
Toll motorway
Toll free motorway / Major road
Other roads
International boundary
0 20 40 60 80 100 kilometres
CH
FL
A
SLO
HR
BIH
MC
F
V
RSM
I
Tunnel du
Iselle
Bolzano/
Bozen
Belluno
Trento
Udine
Trieste
Santhià
Milano
Bréscia
Verona
Vicenza
Padova
Venézia
Torino
Alessandria
Tortona
Piacenza
Parma
Modena
Ferrara
Savona
Genova
Bologna
Ravenna
La Spézia
Firenze
Pisa
Livorno
Siena
Ancona
Perugia
Téramo
Pescara
Corse
Roma
Manfredonia
Foggia
Caserta
Bari
Napoli
Salerno
Potenza
Brindisi
Taranto
Lecce
Porto Torres
Olbia
Sardegna
Cagliari
Catanzaro
Sicilia
Trapani
Palermo
Messina
Reggio di Calabria
Catania
Agrigento
Gela
E66
E45
A8
E62
E55
E70
E64
E612
E25
E74
E717
E35
E33
E80
E76
E78
E842
E843
E847
E90
E844
E846
E848
E933
E932
E391

Travel facts: Italy and San Marino

Italian State Tourist Board
1 Princes Street
London W1B 2AY
Tel: 020 7408 1254
www.italiantouristboard.co.uk

Banking hours
Banks are generally open Monday to Friday 8.30am to 1.30pm and 3 to 4.30pm. Some banks open Saturday morning until 1.30pm. Traveller's cheques can be exchanged at most hotels and shops and at the foreign exchange offices in main railway stations and at the airports.

Credit/debit cards
All major credit cards are widely accepted in Italy. Check with your provider.

Currency
The currency in Italy is the Euro (€). Euro coins are issued in denominations of 1, 2, 5, 10, 20 and 50 cents and €1 and €2. Banknotes are issued in denominations of €5, €10, €20, €50, €100, €200 and €500.

Electricity
The power supply is 220 volts (125 volts in parts of Italy). Type of socket: Round two- or three-hole sockets taking plugs of two round pins, or sometimes three pins in a vertical line. British visitors should bring an adaptor.

Health care
Free or reduced-cost medical treatment is available in Italy to European visitors on production of a valid European Health Insurance Card (EHIC). See page 11. Comprehensive travel insurance is still advised and is essential for all other visitors.

Pharmacies
A pharmacy (*farmacia*), recognised by a green cross sign, will have highly trained staff able to offer medical advice on minor ailments and provide a wide range of prescribed and non-prescribed medicines and drugs.

Post offices
Buy stamps (*francobolli*) at a post office (*ufficio postale*) or at a tobacconist (*tabaccaio*). Post boxes (red or blue) often have two slots, one for local mail (*per la città*), the other for out-of-town destinations (*tutte le alter destinazioni*).

Safe water
In some rural areas it is not advisable to drink the tap water ('*acqua non potabile*' means 'the water is unsafe to drink'). However, across most of the rest of the country the water is perfectly safe, although most Italians prefer to drink bottled mineral water.

Telephones
Almost every bar in Italy has a telephone, and there are many in public places. Most of them operate with phone cards (*schede telefoniche*) for €2.5, €5 or €16, which can be bought from tobacconists, bars, post offices, news-stands and other public places. Some take coins of 10, 20 or 50 cents, €1 or €2, and some take credit cards. The country code for Italy is 39. To call home from Italy dial the international code (00) followed by the country code. To call the UK from Italy dial 00 44.

Time
Italy is on Central European Time, one hour ahead of Greenwich Mean Time (GMT +1). From late March, when clocks are put forward one hour, until late October, Daylight Savings Time (GMT + 2) operates.

Emergency telephone numbers
General emergencies **112**
Police **112**
Fire **115**
Ambulance **118**

Driving in Latvia (Eastern Europe)

The regulations below should be read in conjunction with the General motoring information on pages 18–21.

The historic buildings of Riga's Old Town viewed from across the Daugava River

Drinking and driving

The maximum permitted level of alcohol in the bloodstream for drivers with more than 2 years experience is 0.05 per cent. For drivers with less than 2 years experience the maximum permitted level of alcohol in the bloodstream is 0.02 per cent. Penalties are severe if the levels are exceeded.

Driving licence

The minimum age at which a UK licence holder may drive a temporarily imported car and/or motorcycle (over 125cc) is 18.

Fines

The police cannot collect fines on the spot. Police control speeds closely and give fines for even the smallest of speeding offences.

Fuel

Unleaded petrol (95 octane), diesel and LPG are available. There is no leaded petrol, but

Driving in Latvia continued

petrol with lead substitute is available. Carrying petrol in a can is permitted (duty payable). Visa and MasterCard are accepted at most filling stations; check with your card issuer for usage in Latvia before travel. Cash payments are only accepted in the local currency.

Lights

The use of dipped headlights during the day is compulsory.

Motorcycles

The use of dipped headlights during the day is compulsory. The wearing of crash helmets is compulsory for both driver and passenger.

Motor insurance

Third-party insurance is compulsory.

Passengers/children in cars

A child less than 1.5m (4ft 9in) in height must use a child-restraint restraint system appropriate to height and weight or the lap strap of an adult seat belt.

Seat belts

It is compulsory for front/rear seat occupants to wear seat belts, if fitted.

Speed limits

The standard legal limits, which may be varied by signs, for **private vehicles without trailers** are: in built-up areas 50km/h (31mph), outside built-up areas 90km/h (55mph), dual carriageways 100km/h (62mph). In some residential areas the speed limit is 20km/h (12mph).

Additional information

- A first-aid kit, fire extinguisher and warning triangle are compulsory. Winter tyres are compulsory from 1 December until 1 March.
- Spiked tyres are prohibited from 1 May until 1 October.
- It is recommended that visitors carry an assortment of spares for their vehicle, such as a fan belt, replacement bulbs and spark plugs.
- Latvia has very little signposting and very few road markings.

Travel facts: Latvia

Latvia Tourism Bureaux
72 Queensborough Terrace
London W2 3SH
Tel: 020 7229 8271
www.latviatourism.lv

Banking hours
Banks and their retail branches are usually open Monday to Friday 9am to 5 or 6pm; branches at supermarkets close at 8 or 9pm on weekdays. Some banks open 9am to 1pm on Saturday.

Credit/debit cards
Many transactions in Hungary are still dealt with in cash. The most commonly used credit cards accepted in Latvian hotels, larger shops, restaurants, cafés and supermarkets are Eurocard, MasterCard, Visa, JCB, Diners Club, American Express and Eurocheque. ATMs can be found in cities and towns.

Currency
Latvian national currency is the Lat (LVL), 1 Lats consists of 100 santims. Bank notes are in denominations of LVL500, 100, 50, 20, 10 and 5. Coins are in denominations of LVL2 and 1, and 50, 20, 10, 5, 2 and 1 santims.

Electricity
The electrical supply in Latvia is 220V, 50Hz. Sockets take two-round-pin plugs.

Health care
Free or reduced-cost medical treatment is available in Latvia to European visitors on production of a valid European Health Insurance Card (EHIC). See page 11. Comprehensive travel insurance is still advised and is essential for all other visitors.

Pharmacies
There is an extensive network of pharmacies throughout Latvia, some are at hospitals and health centres, shopping malls, stations etc. Opening hours vary; 24-hour pharmacies are denoted with the letter 'A'.

Post offices
Opening hours at post offices (*Pasts*) are Monday to Friday 8am to 5 or 6pm and 8am to 4pm on Saturday. Opening hours for sub-post offices in small villages vary.

Safe water
Drinking water in major towns is generally safe, though you may prefer to buy bottled mineral water.

Telephones
Public phone boxes can be found on the streets and in train and bus stations, shopping malls etc, and contain information about how to make calls within Latvia, international country codes and local telephone books. Public pay phones accept phone cards, credit cards or coins. Phone cards are available from kiosks, shops, post offices and petrol stations where the *Lattelekom* sign is displayed. The country code for Latvia is 371. To call home from Latvia dial the international code (00) followed by the country code. To call the UK from Latvia dial 00 44.

Time
Latvia is on Eastern European Time. It's two hours ahead of Greenwich Mean Time (GMT + 2), but from late March, when clocks are put forward one hour, to late October, summer time (GMT + 3) operates.

Emergency telephone numbers
Police: **02**
Fire: **01**
Ambulance: **03**
Common telephone number for all types of emergency calls: **112**

Driving Lithuania (Eastern Europe)

The regulations below should be read in conjunction with the General motoring information on pages 18–21.

Sailing the waters of Lake Galve offers a different perspective of Trakai's Gothic castle and museum

Drinking and driving

If the level of alcohol in the bloodstream is 0.04 per cent or more severe penalties include a fine and/or withdrawal of your driving licence for up to 1.5 years.

Driving licence

The minimum age at which a UK licence holder may drive a temporarily imported car and/or motorcycle is 18. **Note:** UK licences that do not incorporate a photograph must be accompanied by photographic proof of identity e.g. a passport.

Fines

On-the-spot fines can be imposed (some fines may be paid at a local bank depending on the amount/traffic violation). Wheel clamps are in use.

Fuel

Leaded petrol is sold at Statoil petrol stations. Unleaded petrol (92, 95 and 98 octane), diesel and LPG are available. Petrol in a can is permitted (duty payable). Credit cards are accepted at filling stations, check with your card issuer for usage in Lithuania before travel.

Lights

The use of dipped headlights during the day is compulsory, there is a fine for non-compliance.

Motorcycles

The use of dipped headlights during the day is compulsory, a fine can be imposed for non-compliance. The wearing of crash helmets is compulsory for both driver and passenger. A child under 12 cannot travel as a passenger.

Motor insurance

Third-party insurance is compulsory, but fully comprehensive insurance is recommended.

Passengers/children in cars

A child under 12 cannot travel as a front seat passenger unless using a child restraint appropriate to age and size.

Seat belts

It is compulsory for front seat occupants to wear seat belts, if fitted.

Speed limits

The standard legal limits, which may be varied by signs, for **private vehicles without trailers** are: in built-up areas 50km/h (31mph), outside built-up areas 90km/h (55mph) and on dual carriageways 110km/h (68mph). **Note:** In summer time a limit of 130km/h (80mph) applies on the dual carriageways between (i) Vilnius and Panevezys and (ii) Kaunas and Klaipeda. The police control speeds closely and impose fines for even the smallest of speeding offences.

Additional information

- A first-aid kit, fire extinguisher and a warning triangle are compulsory.
- It is recommended that visitors carry an assortment of spares for their vehicle for example, a fan belt, replacement bulbs and spark plugs.

A pavement café in Kaunas Old Town sqaure

- Winter tyres are compulsory between 1 November and 1 April, spiked tyres may also be used during this period.
- It is compulsory to call the police to the scene of an accident.
- Lithuania has almost no signposting.
- For safety reasons a reflective jacket is recommended.

Travel facts: Lithuania

Embassy of the Republic of Lithuania
84 Gloucester Place
London
W1U 6AU
Tel: 020 7486 6401
http://lithuania.embassy-uk.co.uk

The embassy can provide information for visitors to the Republic of Lithuania.

Banking hours
Banks are generally open Monday to Friday 9am to 5pm, some banks also open Saturday 9am to 1pm. Currency can be exchanged at banks and bureaux de change. There are ATMs in most cities.

Credit/debit cards
Most major credit and debit cards are accepted in the main hotels, restaurants, shops and in some petrol stations. Check with your credit and debit card company for usage in Lithuania before you travel.

Currency
The official currency of the country is the Lithuania Litas (Lt) which is divided into 100 centas. Banknotes come in denominations of Lt500, 200, 100, 50, 20, 10, 5, 2 and 1. Coins are in denominations of Lt5, 2 and 1, and the worthless 50, 20, 10, 5, 2 and 1 centas. The Litas is pegged to the Euro. Cash payments will be accepted only in the Litas, however many shopping centres and other service outlets take credit cards.

Electricity
The electricity supply is 220 volts AC, 50Hz. European two-pin plugs are in use.

Health care
Free or reduced-cost medical treatment is available in Lithuania to European visitors on production of a valid European Health Insurance Card (EHIC). See page 11. Comprehensive travel insurance is still advised and is essential for all other visitors.

Pharmacies
Pharmacies in major cities will generally have regular prescription drugs readily available; there is usually at least one that is open 24 hours a day.

Post offices
In major towns, post offices (*pastas*) are open Monday to Friday 8am to 6pm, Saturday 8am to 3pm. Post boxes are yellow.

Safe water
It is advisable to drink bottled or filtered water.

Telephones
There are two kinds of payphone: rectangular telephones which take magnetic strip cards and rounded telephones which take chip cards. Phonecards are sold at kiosks and post offices. There are plans to introduce one type of phonecard, compatible for use with both phones. The country code for Lithuania is 370. To call home from Lithuania dial the international code (00) followed by the country code. To call the UK from Lithuania dial 00 44.

Time
Lithuania is on Eastern European Time. It's two hours ahead of Greenwich Mean Time (GMT + 2), but from late March, when clocks are put forward one hour, to late October, summer time (GMT + 3) operates.

Emergency telephone numbers
For all emergency calls: **112**

Driving in Luxembourg (Western Europe)

The regulations below should be read in conjunction with the General motoring information on pages 18–21.

Drinking and driving

If the level of alcohol in the bloodstream is 0.05 per cent or more severe penalties include fines and/or prison. The blood alcohol level for young driver is 0.019 per cent.

Driving licence

The minimum age at which a UK licence holder may drive a temporarily imported car and/or motorcycle 18.

Fines

On-the-spot fines can be imposed. Unauthorised and dangerous parking can result in the car being impounded or removed.

Fuel

Unleaded petrol (95 and 98 octane) is available, along with diesel and LPG. It is forbidden to carry petrol in a can. Credit cards are accepted at filling stations, but check with your card issuer for usage in Luxembourg before you travel.

Lights

Sidelights are required when parking where there is no public lighting. When visibility is below 100 metres (110 yards) due to fog, snow, heavy rain etc, dipped headlights must be used. It is compulsory to flash headlights at night when overtaking outside built-up areas. In tunnels indicated by a sign, drivers must use their passing lights. The use of dipped headlights during the day is recommended.

Mondorf-Les-Bains, to the south of Luxembourg City, is a popular spa town

Motorcycles

The use of dipped headlights during the day is compulsory. The wearing of crash helmets is also compulsory for both driver and passenger. A child under 12 is not permitted to ride as a passenger.

Driving in Luxembourg continued

The River Alzette in Luxembourg City

Motor insurance

Third-party insurance is compulsory.

Passengers/children in cars

A child under the age of 11 or 1.5 metres (4ft 9in) in height cannot travel as a front seat passenger unless using a suitable restraint system appropriate to their weight and height. In the rear children under three must be seated in suitable restraint system and children over three must wear a normal seat belt in the absence of a child seat, however they are permitted to wear only the lap part of the belt if under 1.5 metres (4ft 9in).

Seat belts

It is compulsory for front/rear seat occupants to wear seat belts, if fitted.

Speed limits

The standard legal limits, which may be varied by signs, for **private vehicles without trailers** are: In built-up areas 50km/h (31mph), outside built-up areas 90km/h (55mph) and motorways 130km/h (80mph). In rain or snow 110 km/h (68mph), 70km/h (43mph) speed limit for vehicles with spiked tyres. Lower limits apply **vehicles towing a trailer**: In built-up areas 75km/h (46mph) on motorways 90km/h (55mph).

Additional information

- Any vehicle immobilised on the motorway must use a warning signal, either by a warning triangle or a displaying a flashing light at the rear.
- The use of spiked tyres is permitted from 1 December to 31 March.
- In built-up areas the use of the horn is prohibited except in case of immediate danger.

Travel facts: Luxembourg

Luxembourg Tourist Office
122 Regent Street
London W1B 5SA
Tel: 020 7434 2800
www.luxembourg.co.uk

Banking hours
Banks generally open from Monday to Friday 9am to 12 noon and 2pm to 4pm. Some banks open over lunch, and some stay open until 6pm. Some ATMs (e.g. near the Grand Ducal Palace) are open 24 hours.

Credit/debit cards
The use of credit/debit cards is becoming ever more common, but many retailers require a minimum sales amount before accepting them. American Express, Diners Club, MasterCard, Visa and others are all accepted, as well as Eurocheque cards.

Currency
The currency in Luxembourg is the Euro (€). Euro coins are issued in denominations of 1, 2, 5, 10, 20 and 50 cents and €1 and €2. Banknotes are issued in denominations of €5, €10, €20, €50, €100, €200 and €500.

Electricity
The power supply in Luxembourg is 220 volts AC, 50Hz. Sockets accept two-round-pin plugs, so an adaptor is needed for most non-Continental appliances.

Health care
Free or reduced-cost medical treatment is available in Luxembourg to European visitors on production of a valid European Health Insurance Card (EHIC). See page 11. Comprehensive travel insurance is still advised and is essential for all other visitors.

Pharmacies
Prescription medicines and advice can be obtained from a pharmacy (*pharmacie*) identified by a green cross. Information about the nearest 24-hour facility is posted at all pharmacies.

Post offices
Post offices are open Monday to Friday 8am to 12 noon, and 1:30 to 5pm. The Luxembourg-Ville main office (opposite the railway station) is open Monday to Friday 6am to 7pm, Saturday 6am to 12 noon. Smaller offices may open for only a few hours.

Rule of the road
Drive on the right and overtake on the left.

Safe water
Tap water is considered safe to drink and bottled mineral water (*eau minérale*) is widely available.

Telephones
Public telephone booths (*cabine télephonique*) normally have pictorial instructions with French and German text. Most take coins or buy a pre-paid phone card (*télecarte*) from a post office or rail stations. International phone booths have a yellow sign showing a telephone dial with a receiver in the centre. The country code for Luxembourg is 352. To call home from Luxembourg dial the international code (00) followed by the country code. To call the UK from Luxembourg dial 00 44.

Time
Luxembourg is on Central European Time, one hour ahead of Greenwich Mean Time (GMT + 1). From late March, when clocks are put forward one hour, until late October, Daylight Savings Time (GMT + 2) operates.

Emergency telephone numbers
General emergencies **112**
Police **112** or **113**
Fire **112**
Ambulance **112**

Driving in Macedonia (Former Yugoslav Republic of Macedonia) (South East Europe)

The regulations below should be read in conjunction with the General motoring information on pages 18–21.

Drinking and driving

If the level of alcohol in the bloodstream is 0.05 per cent or more, severe penalties, including a fine, imprisonment and/or suspension of driving licence, can be imposed.

Driving licence

The minimum age at which a UK licence holder may drive a temporarily imported car and/or motorcycle (exceeding 125cc) is 18.

Fines

On-the-spot fines can be imposed by police officers. An official receipt should be obtained. Police can impound a vehicle that is wrongly parked and can detain a vehicle with worn tyres.

Fuel

Leaded – super petrol (96 octane) and unleaded petrol (91, 95 and 98 octane) are available. Carrying petrol in a can is permitted. Diesel, Euro diesel and LPG are available. Credit cards are accepted at some filling stations, check with your card issuer for usage in Macedonia before travel. Usually payment can only be made in the local currency.

Lights

The use of dipped headlights during the day is compulsory. Police can impose an on-the-spot fine for non-compliance.

A minaret rises above the red-tiled roofs and cobbled streets in Skopje

Motorcycles

The use of dipped headlights during the day is compulsory. The wearing of crash helmets is also compulsory for both driver and passenger.

Motor insurance

A Green Card is accepted; third party insurance is compulsory.

Passengers/children in cars
A child under 12 is not permitted to travel in the front seats of a vehicle.

Seat belts
It is compulsory for front/rear-seat occupants to wear seat belts, if fitted.

Speed limits
The standard legal limits, which may be varied by signs, for **private vehicles with or without trailers** are: In built-up areas 50km/h) (31mph), outside built-up areas 80km/h (49mph) but 100km/h (62mph) on dual carriageways and 120km/h (74mph) on motorways.

A boy and his dog tend a flock of sheep in rural Macedonia

Additional information

- It is compulsory for visitors to equip their vehicle with a set of replacement bulbs. A first-aid kit and a warning triangle compulsory, two triangles are required if towing a trailer. A reflective jacket is compulsory for drivers, in case of an accident.
- A person visibly under the influence of alcohol is not permitted to travel in a vehicle as a front seat passenger.
- The authorities at the frontier must certify any visible damage to a vehicle entering Macedonia and a certificate obtained; this must be produced when leaving. A certificate must also be obtained if the damage occurs while in Macedonia.
- From 15 November to 15 March all motor vehicles must be equipped to travel in snow conditions. Snow chains must be carried to use with all-year tyres or winter tyres must be fitted on all wheels.
- Spiked tyres are prohibited.

Travel facts: Republic of Macedonia

Embassy of the Republic of Macedonia
Suite 2.1/2.2 Buckingham Court
75/83 Buckingham Gate
London SW1E 6PE
Tel: 020 7976 0535
www.exploringmacedonia.com

Banking hours
Banks are generally open Monday to Friday 8am to 7pm, Saturday 8am to noon or 1pm. Banks at airports, railway and bus stations are open longer hours. Money should be exchanged in official exchange offices (banks, post offices, hotels, tourist agencies) according to current exchange rates. When leaving Macedonia visitors can exchange MKDs back into foreign currency (at official places) only after presenting the evidence of exchange for Denars when entering the country.

Credit/debit cards
Some major credit cards (Diners, American Express, Visa and MasterCard/EuroCard) and Euro-cheques can be used for payment wherever a notice is displayed, as a rule in hotels, shops, and restaurants, but acceptance throughout the country is limited. Check with your credit card provider. Credit card fraud is widespread in Macedonia so you should take care when making a purchase using this method. ATMs are widely available in Skopje, less so in other main towns, although the number is increasing making the withdrawal of local currency much easier. Cash is the most common form of payment.

Currency
The Macedonian currency is the Macedonian Denar (MKD) which is divided into 100 deni. Banknotes come in denominations of Den5,000, 1,000, 500, 100, 50 and 10. Coins are in denominations of Den5, 2 and 1, and 50 deni. All major currencies may be exchanged, but Euros are easiest to exchange.
Note: You must declare all foreign currency on arrival.

Electricity
The electrical current is 220 volts AC, 50Hz.

Health care
Comprehensive travel insurance is essential for all visitors.

Pharmacies
You'll find a pharmacy in all bigger towns, service is good and prices moderate. Prescribed medicines must be paid for.

Post offices
Post offices are generally open Monday to Friday 8am to 8pm or 9am to 5pm.

Safe water
Mains water is normally chlorinated and, while relatively safe, may cause mild stomach upsets. Bottled mineral water is available and is advised for the first few weeks of the stay.

Telephones
The country code for Macedonia is 389. To call home from Macedonia dial the international code (00) followed by the country code. To call the UK from Macedonia dial 00 44.

Time
Macedonia is on Central European Time, one hour ahead of GMT (GMT + 1). Daylight Savings Time comes into effect from the end of March to the end of October (GMT + 2).

Emergency telephone numbers
Police **92**
Fire **93**
Ambulance **94**
Road assistance **987**

Driving in Montenegro (South East Europe)

The regulations below should be read in conjunction with the General motoring information on pages 18–21.

Drinking and driving

If the level of alcohol in the bloodstream is 0.05 per cent or more or if a medical examination shows that normal bodily functions are impaired, severe penalties can include a fine, imprisonment and/or suspension of driving licence.

Driving licence

The minimum age at which a UK licence holder may drive a temporarily imported car and/or motorcycle (exceeding 125cc) is 18. We recommend that you obtain an International Driving Permit to accompany your UK driving licence.

Fines

Officials can issue an on-the-spot fine notice, but cannot collect the payment. Fines vary according to the gravity of the offence. Penalties are higher if the motorist endangers other people or causes an accident.

Fuel

Unleaded petrol (95 and 98 octane) and Diesel (*Dizel*) are available. You can carry a small amount of petrol in a can. Credit cards are generally accepted; check with your card issuer for usage in Montenegro before travel.

Lights

Dipped headlights are compulsory at all times.

A bridge spans a gorge in the highlands of Montenegro

Motorcycles

The use of dipped headlights is compulsory at all times. The wearing of crash helmets is compulsory for both driver and passenger.

Motor insurance

A Green Card is recognised; third-party insurance is compulsory.

Driving in Montenegro continued

A decorated arch in Kotor's medieval Old Town

Passengers/children in cars

A person visibly under the influence of alcohol or child under 12 is not permitted to travel in a vehicle as a front-seat passenger.

Seat belts

It is compulsory for front/rear-seat occupants to wear seat belts, if fitted.

Speed limits

The standard legal limits, which may be varied by signs, for **private vehicles without trailers** are: In built-up areas 50km/h (31mph), outside built-up areas 80km/h (49mph) and 100km/h (62mph) on fast roads.

Additional information

- It is compulsory for visitors to equip their vehicle with a set of replacement bulbs. A first-aid kit is compulsory (excluding mopeds) and a warning triangle is compulsory (excluding motorcycles), two triangles are required if towing a trailer.
- The authorities at the frontier must certify any visible damage to a vehicle entering Montenegro and a certificate obtained; this must be produced when leaving otherwise you may experience serious difficulties when leaving.
- It is compulsory for accidents resulting in serious injury or material damage to be reported to the police.
- Spiked tyres are prohibited. In winter snow chains may be necessary on some roads.
- Vehicles entering a roundabout have right of way.
- Horns must not be used in built-up areas or at night except in cases of imminent danger.
- School buses must not be overtaken or passed when they stop for children to board or alight.

Travel facts: Montenegro

Montenegro does not at present have an embassy or tourist office in London.

www.visit-montenegro.org
www.montenegro.org.uk

Banking hours
Banks are generally open Monday to Friday 8am to 7pm, Saturday 8am to 1pm.

Credit/debit cards
The most widely accepted cards are Visa, Master, Maestro and Diners. American Express cards are not accepted in Montenegro. ATMs increasingly accept international bank cards.

Currency
The currency in Montenegro is the Euro (€). Euro coins are issued in denominations of 1, 2, 5, 10, 20 and 50 cents and €1 and €2. Banknotes are issued in denominations of €5, €10, €20, €50, €100, €200 and €500.

Electricity
The power supply is 20 volts AC, 50Hz. Round two-pin plugs are used.

Health care
Comprehensive travel insurance is essential for all visitors.

Pharmacies
Medicines and basic medical supplies are largely available from private pharmacies. Prescribed medicines must be paid for.

Post offices
Postal services within Montenegro are reasonably good.

Safe water
During the holiday season water shortages can affect quality and the locals will often stop taking ice in drinks. To avoid stomach upsets, drink bottled mineral water and avoid ice in drinks.

Telephones
Public telephones take pre-paid cards which can be bought in post offices, operators' outlets or tobacco shops/newsagents. The country code for Montenegro is 382. To call home from Montenegro dial the international code (00) followed by the country code. To call the UK from Montenegro dial 00 44.

Time
Montenegro is on Central European Time, one hour ahead of Greenwich Mean Time (GMT + 1). From late March, when clocks are put forward one hour, until late October, Daylight Savings Time (GMT + 2) operates.

Emergency telephone numbers
Police **92**
Fire Department **93**
Ambulance **94**

Driving in The Netherlands (Western Europe)

The regulations below should be read in conjunction with the General motoring information on pages 18–21.

Elegant gabled houses fronted by leafy trees line Amsterdam's canals

Drinking and driving

If the level of alcohol in the bloodstream is over 0.05 per cent, severe penalties include a fine, withdrawal of driving licence and imprisonment. The lower limit of 0.02 per cent applies to new drivers for the first five years and moped riders up to the age of 24.

Driving licence

The minimum age at which a UK licence holder may drive a temporarily imported car and/or motorcycle is 18.

Fines

On-the-spot fines can be imposed. In the case of illegal parking the police can impose on-the-spot fines or tow the vehicle away.

Fuel

Unleaded petrol (95 and 98 octane), diesel and LPG are available. There is no leaded petrol (lead substitute petrol is available as 'super' 98 octane). Petrol in a can is permitted but forbidden aboard ferries and Eurotunnel. Credit cards are accepted at most filling stations; check with your card issuer for use before travel.

Lights

The use of dipped headlights during the day is recommended. At night it is prohibited to drive with only sidelights.

Motorcycles

The use of dipped headlights during the day is recommended. The wearing of crash helmets is compulsory on all motorcycles which are capable of exceeding 25km/h (15mph).

Motor insurance

Third-party insurance is compulsory.

Passengers/children in cars

Children up to the age of 18 and less than 1.35m (4ft 4in) in height cannot travel as a front or rear seat passenger unless using a suitable restraint system adapted to their weight and height. Suitable child restraint systems must meet the safety approval of ECE 44/03 or 44/04. If the vehicle is not fitted with rear seat belts children under 3 are not permitted to travel in the vehicle.

Children under 3 are permitted to travel in the front seats if using a rear-facing child seat with the airbag deactivated (if fitted). If the vehicle's front seats are not fitted with seat belts, only passengers measuring 1.35m (4ft 4in)or more may travel in the front seat.

Seat belts

It is compulsory for front/rear-seat occupants to wear seat belts, if fitted.

Speed limits

The standard legal limits, which may be varied by signs, for **private vehicles without trailers** are: In built-up areas 50km/h (31mph), outside built-up areas 80km/h (49mph) or 100km/h (62mph) and motorways 120km/h (74mph). There is no minimum speed on motorways. Lower limits apply to **vehicles towing a trailer:** Outside built-up areas, on main roads and motorways 80km/h (40mph).

Additional information

- A warning triangle or hazard warning lights must be used in case of accident or breakdown (it is recommended that a warning triangle is always carried).
- Buses have the right of way when leaving bus stops in built-up areas.
- Trams have right of way except when crossing a priority road.
- Beware of large numbers of cyclists and skaters.
- Spiked tyres are prohibited.
- Vehicles can be confiscated in cases of heavy excess of speed and drink driving.
- The use of a radar detector is prohibited, if you are caught using such a device by the police the radar detector will be confiscated and you will be fined €250.
- Horns should not be used at night and in moderation during the day.

Road signs (a selection of standard and non-standard)

Residential zone

Parking for permit holders only

Disc parking zone

Park and ride

Maximum speed limit

Built-up areas

Travel facts: The Netherlands

Netherlands Board of Tourism
PO Box 30783
London WC2B 6DH
Tel: 020 7539 7958
www.holland.com/uk

Banking hours
Banks are generally open Tuesday to Friday from 9am to 4pm. On Monday banks open at 1pm. Banks are closed Saturday and Sunday.

Credit/debit cards
The major credit cards are widely accepted, but if in doubt, ask in advance. ATMs for cash advances can be found outside banks in all the major towns.

Currency
The currency in the Netherlands is the Euro (€). Euro coins are issued in denominations of 1, 2, 5, 10, 20 and 50 cents and €1 and €2. Banknotes are issued in denominations of €5, €10, €20, €50, €100, €200 and €500.

Electricity
The electrical current in Holland is 230 volts. Hotels may have a 110-volt or 120-volt outlet for shavers, but travellers are advised to bring a converter and an adapter for two-round-pin plugs.

Health care
Free or reduced-cost medical treatment is available in the Netherlands to European visitors on production of a valid European Health Insurance Card (EHIC). See page 11. Comprehensive travel insurance is still advised and is essential for all other visitors.

Pharmacies
Prescription and non-prescription drugs and other medical products are sold in pharmacies (*apotheeken*), recognised by a green cross sign. Despite their name, drug stores (*drogerijen*) do not sell medicines, but toiletries and cosmetics. Pharmacies are Monday to Friday from 8 or 9am to 5:30 or 6pm.

Post offices
Most PTT post offices (*postkaantoren*) are generally open Monday to Friday 9am to 5pm. Larger ones are also open on Saturdays between 9am and 12 noon or 12:30pm.

Safe water
Tap water is safe to drink. Bottled mineral water, often called by the generic name '*spa*', after a popular Belgian label, is readily available.

Telephones
Orange-and-grey coloured phone booths are located at most Netherlands railway stations. These booths accept coins, credit cards and telephone cards. *Telfort* telephone cards are available from the GWK – Holland Welcome Service, Wizzl Shops at many railway stations and all ticket offices at the Netherlands Railway stations. To make a telephone call from a green telephone booth (located outside railway stations) you need a different telephone card. These are available from, among other places, the GWK – Holland Welcome Service offices, post offices and major department stores. The country code for the Netherlands is 31. To call home from the Netherlands dial the international code (00) followed by the country code. To call the UK from the Netherlands dial 00 44.

Time
The Netherlands is on Central European Time (GMT + 1). Dutch Summer Time (GMT+2) operates from late March, when clocks are put forward 1 hour, until late October.

Emergency telephone numbers
Police **112**
Fire **112**
Ambulance **112**

Toll charges in Euros

Bridges and tunnels	Car	Car towing caravan/ trailer
Westerschelde Tunnel	4.50	6.70

Driving in Norway (Northern Europe)

The regulations below should be read in conjunction with the General motoring information on pages 18–21.

The mountainous Telemark region at the heart of southern Norway

Drinking and driving

If the level of alcohol in the bloodstream exceeds 0.020 per cent severe penalties can incur heavy fines and/or prison, and the surrender of your driving licence.

Driving licence

The minimum age at which a UK licence holder may drive a temporarily imported car is 18, for a motorcycle up to 11kw the minimum age is 16, 11-25kw 18 and over 25kw 20.

Fines

On-the-spot fines for infringement of traffic regulations can be imposed. Vehicles illegally parked may be towed away.

Fuel

Unleaded petrol (95 and 98 octane) and diesel is available, there is limited LPG available. Petrol in a can is permitted but not aboard ferries. Credit cards are accepted at

Driving in Norway continued

Sparkling waters at Inndyr in the north of Norway

filling stations, check with your card issuer for usage in Norway before travel.

Lights
The use of dipped headlights during the day is compulsory.

Motorcycles
The use of dipped headlights during the day compulsory. The wearing of crash helmets is compulsory for both driver and passenger.

Motor insurance
Third-party insurance is compulsory.

Passengers/children in cars
A child under 4 cannot travel as a front or rear seat passenger unless seated in a child restraint. Children over 4 must use a child-restraint system or a seat belt.

Seat belts
It is compulsory for front/rear-seat passengers to wear seat belts, if fitted.

Speed limits
The standard legal limits, which may be varied by signs, for **private vehicles without trailers** are: In built-up areas 50km/h (31mph), outside built-up areas 80km/h (49mph) and up to 90km/h, 100km (55mph or 62mph) on motorways. Lower limits apply to **motor vehicles towing a trailer** equipped with a braking device: Outside built-up areas, on main roads and motorways 80km/h (49mph). Without a braking device and weighing more than 300kg the limit is 60km/h (37mph).

Additional information
- A warning triangle is compulsory for all vehicles with more than two wheels. We recommended that visitors equip their vehicle with a first-aid kit, fire extinguisher and a set of replacement bulbs.
- In addition to some road, bridge and tunnel tolls, city tolls are payable by

motorists entering Bergen, Oslo, Stavanger and Trondheim, see panel opposite.

- Spiked tyres may be used between 1 November and the first Sunday after Easter, cars with spiked tyres will be charged a fee by the municipalities of Oslo, Bergen and Trondheim, the stickers are available to purchase daily, monthly or yearly. In the three Northern counties of Nordland, Troms and Finnmark, spiked tyres are permitted from 15 October to 1 May.
- Snow chains may be used on all types of tyres, in the event that there is snow or ice covering the roads winter tyres or any tyres and snow chains must be used.
- A vehicle towing a caravan must be equipped with special rear-view mirrors.
- Trams always have right of way.
- The use of radar detectors is forbidden.
- The wearing of a reflective jacket/ waistcoat is compulsory requirement for residents, while this legislation does not apply to foreign registered vehicles we strongly recommend that a reflective jacket be carried and worn if the driver and/or passenger(s) need to exit a vehicle which is immobilised on the carriageway of all motorways and main or busy roads. We recommend the jacket be carried in the passenger compartment of the vehicle (not the boot). Visitors renting a car in Norway will have to make sure the hired vehicle is supplied with a jacket.

Toll charges in Norwegian Kroner

Road		**Car**	**Car towing caravan/ trailer**
E6	Trondheim – Stjordal	25.00	50.00
E18/E134	Oslo – Drammen	20.00	40.00
E18	Larvik – Porsgrunn	20.00	40.00
E18	Kristiansaund City	10.00	20.00

A charge is made for travelling on the following ring roads (charges apply Mon–Fri 6am–6pm)

Oslo	20.00	40.00
Bergen	15.00	30.00
Trondheim	15.00	30.00
Stavanger	13.00	26.00

Bridges and Tunnels

Askim on **E18**	20.00	40.00
Aust-Agder on **E18**	20.00	40.00
Folgefonntunnelen	60.00	120.00
Hvalertunnelen	50.00	100.00
Moss on **E6**	15.00	30.00
Nappstraumen Tunnel on **E10**	65.00	130.00
Nordkapp **E39**	68.00	140.00
North Hordaland Tunnel **E39**	45.00	140.00
Oslofjord Tunnel	55.00	120.00
Oysand-Thamshamn **E39**	15.00	30.00
Rennfast on **E39**	90.00	280.00
Sunnfjordtunnelen	45.00	135.00
Svinesundsforbindelsen on **E6**	18.00	89.00
Trekantsambanet on **E39**	85.00	270.00
Vestfold on **E18**	30.00	60.00
Ostfold on **E18/E6**	14.00	28.00

Travel facts: Norway

Innovation Norway
Charles House
5 Regent Street
London SW1Y 4LR
Tel: 020 7389 8800
www.visitnorway.com

Banking hours
Banks are generally open from 9am to 3.30pm. They generally close half an hour earlier from mid-May to mid-August, but stay open until 5pm on Thursday all year. They are closed weekends.

Credit/debit cards
The use of credits cards is widespread in Norway, and they are accepted almost everywhere. Eurocard/MasterCard, Visa, American Express and Diners Club are the most common. Not all petrol stations accept credit cards, so make sure you have enough cash when buying fuel. Check with your card provider about acceptability and available services.

Currency
Norway's currency is the Krone (NOK or Kr), which is divided into 100 øre. The denominatoins of Krone banknotes are Kr50, Kr100, Kr200, Kr500 and Kr1,000. There are coins of 50 øre and Kr1, Kr5, Kr10 and Kr20.

Electricity
Norway has a 220-volt power supply. Electrical sockets take plugs with two round pins.

Health care
Free or reduced-cost medical treatment is available in Norway to European visitors on production of a valid European Health Insurance Card (EHIC). See page 11. Comprehensive travel insurance is still advised and is essential for all other visitors.

Pharmacies
A pharmacy (*apotek*) sells prescription medicines; many pharmacists speak English. Information about the nearest late-night or 24-hour facility is posted at all pharmacies.

Post offices
Post offices are generally open Monday to Friday 8am to 5pm; hours for rural post offices may vary. Buy stamps (*frimerker*) at a post office (*posten*), a news-stand/tobacconist, such as Narvesen or MIX or from a hotel. Post boxes boxes are red.

Safe water
Tap water is safe to drink throughout Norway. Bottled mineral water (*mineralvann*) is widely available.

Telephones
You can use cash or a telephone card (*telekort*) to make a calling Norway. Most phone booths have direct dialing for international calls. Use Kr1, Kr5, Kr10 and Kr20 coins (minimum charge Kr2). Greencard phones accept phone cards Kr40, Kr90 and Kr140), available from Narvesen and MIX kiosks. Some card phones accept credit cards. The country code for Norway is 47. To call home from Norway dial the international code (00) followed by the country code. To call the UK from Norway dial 00 44.

Time
Norway is on Central European Time, one hour ahead of Greenwich Mean Time (GMT + 1). From late March, when clocks are put forward one hour, until late October, Daylight Savings Time (GMT + 2) operates.

Emergency telephone numbers
Police **112**
Fire **110**
Ambulance **113**

Driving in Poland (Central Europe)

The regulations below should be read in conjunction with the General motoring information on pages 18–21.

Drinking and driving

The maximum level of alcohol permitted in the bloodstream is 0.02 per cent. If between 0.021% and 0.05% per cent a heavy fine can be imposed and your driver's licence suspended. If over 0.05% a fine is determined by a tribunal along with a prison sentence and suspension of licence.

Driving licence

The minimum age at which a UK licence holder may drive a temporarily imported car and/or motorcycle (over 125cc) is 18. All valid UK driving licences should be accepted in Poland.

Fines

On-the-spot fines can be imposed. An official receipt should be obtained. The police are authorised to request foreign motorists pay their fines in cash. Wheel clamps are in use. Illegally parked cars causing an obstruction may be towed away and impounded.

Fuel

Unleaded petrol (95 and 98 octane), diesel and LPG are available. Leaded petrol (95 octane petrol with lead replacement additive) is available. You can carry 10 litres of petrol in a can but not aboard ferries and Eurotunnel. Credit cards are accepted at most filling stations; check with your card issuer for usage in Poland before travel.

Lights

Dipped headlights or daytime running lights are compulsory for all vehicles at all times. A fine can be imposed for non-compliance.

Motorcycles

Dipped headlights or daytime running lights are compulsory for all vehicles at all times. The wearing of crash helmets is compulsory for both driver and passenger.

Motor insurance

Third-party insurance is compulsory.

Passengers/children in cars

A child under 12 and 1.5 m (4ft 9in) in height cannot travel as front or rear seat passenger unless using suitable child restraint system adapted to their size. If a car is equipped with front seat airbags it is prohibited to place a child in a rear-facing seat.

Seat belts

It is compulsory for front/rear-seat occupants to wear seat belts, if fitted.

Driving in Poland continued

Krakow's imposing Royal Castle and cathedral are situated on the banks of the River Vistula

Speed limits

The standard legal limits, which may be varied by signs, for **private vehicles without trailers** are: In built-up areas 60km/h (37mph) from 11pm to 5am and 50km/h (31mph) from 5am to 11pm, outside built-up areas 90km/h (55mph), on express roads (2 x 1 lane) 100km/h (62mph) or (2 x 2 lanes) 110km/h (68mph) and 130km/h (80mph) on motorways. The minimum speed on motorways is 40km/h (24mph). Some residential zones are 20km/h (13mph).

Additional information

- A warning triangle is compulsory for all vehicles with more than two wheels.
- It is recommended that visitors equip their vehicle with a first-aid kit and a set of replacement bulbs. It is recommended that a fire extinguisher is carried as this is compulsory for Polish registered vehicles.
- The use of spiked tyres is prohibited. Snow chains may be used only on roads covered with snow.
- It is prohibited to carry or/and use a radar detector.
- The use of the horn is not authorised in built-up areas except to avoid an accident.

Travel facts and toll charges: Poland

Polish National Tourist Office
Level 3, Westec House
West Gate
London W5 1YY
Tel: 08700 675 010 (brochure line)
www.visitpoland.org

Banking hours
Banks are generally open Monday to Friday 9am to 4pm and Saturday 9am to 1pm. Hours are limited in smaller towns.

Credit/debit cards
Major credit cards are widely accepted in Poland, most hotels, restaurants, shops and petrol stations accept payments with credit cards. Stickers on the doors and windows of businesses usually indicate which credit cards will be accepted.

Currency
The Polish currency is Zloty (Zl) = 100 Groszy. Banknotes come in denominations of Zl10, Zl20, Zl50, Zl100 and Zl200 and coins of Zl1, Zl2 and Zl5 and 1, 2, 5 and 10 Groszy.

Electricity
The power supply is 220 volts AC, 50Hz. Sockets take two-round-pin continental-style plugs. Visitors from the UK require an adaptor.

Health care
Free or reduced-cost medical treatment is available in Poland to European visitors on production of a valid European Health Insurance Card (EHIC). See page 11. Comprehensive travel insurance is still advised and is essential for all other visitors.

Pharmacies
Prescriptions are necessary for most medications. In every bigger Polish city there is at least one pharmacy on night duty

Post offices
Post offices are usually open from 8am to 8pm. In large cities at least one post office stays open 24 hours.

Safe water
Tap water is normally chlorinated, and may cause mild abdominal upsets. Bottled mineral water is available.

Telephones
Phone cards can be purchased from post offices and newsagents. The country code for Poland is 48. To call home from Poland dial the international code (00) followed by the country code. To call the UK from Poland dial 00 44.

Time
Poland is on Central European Time, one hour ahead of Greenwich Mean Time (GMT + 1). From late March, when clocks are put forward one hour, until late October, Daylight Savings Time (GMT + 2) operates.

Emergency telephone numbers
Police **997**
Fire Brigade **998**
Ambulance **999**

Toll charges in Zlotys

Road		**Car**	**Car towing caravan/ trailer**
A4	Katowice – Kraków	11.00	15.00
A2	Wrzesnia – Konin	11.00	18.00
A2	Krzesiny – Wrzesnia	11.00	18.00
A2	Komorniki – Nowy Tomysl	11.00	18.00

Driving in Poland

Driving in Portugal (South West Europe)

The regulations below should be read in conjunction with the General motoring information on pages 18–21.

Amarante, in the Duoro region, has grown up along the banks of the River Tamega

Drinking and driving

If the level of alcohol in the bloodstream is between 0.05 per cent and 0.08 per cent, a fine and withdrawal of driving licence for a minimum of one month to a maximum of one year can be imposed; if more than 0.08 per cent, there is a fine and withdrawal of driving licence for a minimum of two months up to a maximum of two years.

Driving licence

The minimum age at which UK licence holder may drive a temporarily imported car and/or motorcycle (over 50cc) is 17; however visitors under the age of 18 years may encounter problems even though they hold a valid UK licence. All valid UK driving licences should be accepted in Portugal. This includes the older all-green style UK licences (in Northern Ireland older paper style with photographic counterpart) although the EC appreciates that these may be more difficult to understand and that drivers may wish to voluntarily update them before travelling abroad if time permits. Alternatively, older licences may be accompanied by an International Driving Permit (IDP).

Fines

On-the-spot fines can be imposed. An official receipt showing the maximum amount of the fine should be obtained. **Note:** Foreign motorists refusing to pay an on-the-spot fine will be asked for a deposit to cover the maximum fine for the offence committed. If a motorist refuses to do this, the police can take the driving licence, registration document or failing that they can confiscate the vehicle. Wheel clamping and towing are in operation for illegally parked vehicles.

Fuel
Unleaded petrol (95 and 98 octane), diesel and LPG are available. There is no leaded petrol (lead replacement petrol is available as 98 octane). Petrol in a can is permitted. Credit cards are accepted at most filling stations; check with your card issuer for use in Portugal before travel. **Note:** a tax of €0.50 is added to credit card transactions.

Lights
Dipped headlights must be used in poor daytime visibility and in tunnels.

Motorcycles
The use of dipped headlights during the day is compulsory. The wearing of crash helmets is compulsory. A child under seven is not permitted to ride as a passenger.

Motor insurance
Third-party insurance is compulsory.

Motorways
See Spain/Portugal motorway map on page 136.

Passengers/children in cars
Children under 12 and less than 1.5m (4ft 9in) in height cannot travel as front seat passengers. They must travel in the rear in a special restraint system adapted to their size, unless the vehicle has only two seats, or is not fitted with seat belts.
Children under 3 can be seated in the front

The Torre de Belém, Lisbon's most emblematic building, guards the entrance to the harbour

passenger seat if using a suitable child restraint however, the airbag must be demolbilsed off if using a rear-facing child restraint system.

Seat belts
It is compulsory for front/rear-seat occupants to wear seat belts, if fitted.

Speed limits
The standard legal limits, which may be varied by signs, for **private vehicles without trailers** are: In built-up areas 50km/h (31mph), outside built-up areas 90km/h (55mph) or 100km/h (62mph) and on motorways 120km/h (74mph). The minimum speed on motorways is 50km/h (31mph). Motorists who have held a driving licence for

Driving in Portugal continued

less than one year must not exceed 90km/h (55mph) or any lower speed limit. Lower limits apply to **cars towing a trailer or caravan:** Outside built-up areas 70–80km/h (43–49mph) and on motorways 100km/h (62mph).

Additional information

- A warning triangle is recommended as the use of hazard warning lights or a warning triangle is compulsory in an accident/breakdown situation.
- It is prohibited to carry and/or use a radar detector.
- Spiked tyres and winter tyres are prohibited. Snow chains may be used, where the weather conditions require.
- It is illegal to carry bicycles on the back of a passenger car.
- The wearing of reflective jacket/waistcoat is recommended if the driver and/or passenger(s) exits a vehicle which is immobilised on the carriageway on all motorways and main or busy roads. We recommend that the jacket is carried in the passenger compartment of the vehicle (not the boot). This is a compulsory requirement for residents.
- In built-up areas the use of the horn is prohibited during the hours of darkness except in the case of immediate danger.

Toll charges in Euros

Road		**Car**	**Car towing caravan/ trailer**
E1 (A1)	Lisboa – Porto	18.65	18.65
E1 (A2)	Lisboa – VLA (Algarve)	17.05	17.05
E1 (A3)	Porto – Valença do Minho (Spain/Vigo)	7.50	7.50
E82 (A4)	Porto – Amarante	3.50	3.50
A5	Lisboa – Cascais	1.15	1.15
E90 (A6)	E1/E90 (Marateca) – Badajoz (Spanish border)	9.70	9.70
A7	Vila do Conde – A24	7.85	7.85
A8	Lisboa – Leiria	8.00	8.00
A11	Braga – Guimaraes – A4	4.75	4.75
A12	Setúbal – Ponte Vasco de Gama	1.75	1.75
A15	Obidos – Santarem (E1)	3.25	3.25
A21	Malveria (A8) – Mafra (north of Lisboa)	0.55	0.55
A10	A9 – Arruda dos Vinhos – E1	0.80	0.80
A13	Santo Estevao – Marateca (E1/E90)	6.30	6.30
A14	Figueira da Foz – Coimbra Norte	1.80	1.80

Bridges and Tunnels

Lisbon Tagus Bridge (Ponte 25 de Abril) on **A2** (tolls are payable in one direction only, when travelling north into Lisbon)	1.25	1.25
Vasco da Gama Bridge (Ponte Vasco da Gama) on **A12** (tolls are payable in one direction only when travelling north)	2.20	2.20

Note: It is a legal requirement in Portugal that everyone carries photographic proof of identity at all times.

Travel facts: Portugal

Portuguese National Tourist Office,
Portuguese Embassy
11 Belgrave Square
London SW1X
Tel: 0845 355 1212
www.visitportugal.com

Banking hours
Banks are open Monday to Friday from 8.30am to 3pm. Portugal has a national network of ATMs identified by the symbol MB (*Multibanco*), from which you can withdraw cash 24 hours a day.

Credit/debit cards
In Portugal, the most commonly used credit cards are Visa, American Express, Diners Club, Europay/MasterCard, JCB and Maestro.

Currency
The currency in Portugal is the Euro (€). Euro coins are issued in denominations of 1, 2, 5, 10, 20 and 50 cents and €1 and €2. Banknotes are issued in denominations of €5, €10, €20, €50, €100, €200 and €500. €500. **Note:** €200 and €500 notes are not issued in Portugal, but those issued elsewhere are valid.

Electricity
The native power supply is 220 volts AC, 50Hz. Sockets take two-round-pin continental-style plugs. Visitors from the UK require an adaptor.

Health care
Free or reduced-cost medical treatment is available in Portugal to European visitors on production of a valid European Health Insurance Card (EHIC). See page 11. Comprehensive travel insurance is still advised and is essential for all other visitors.

Pharmacies
Prescription and non-prescription drugs and medicines are available from pharmacies (*fármacias*), distinguished by a large green cross. Pharmacists can prescribe remedies for a wide range of ailments.

Post offices
There is at least one post office (*correio*) in every town and reasonably large village. They sell stamps as do many places with correios signs. In small towns they close for lunch, otherwise hours are Monday to Friday 8.30am to 6pm.

Safe water
Tap water is generally safe but not too pleasant. Anywhere, but especially outside the main cities, towns and resorts, it is advisable to drink bottled water (*água mineral*), either still (*sem gás*) or carbonated (*com gás*).

Telephones
Most public telephones now accept coins and credit cards or phone cards. Phone cards are available from post offices, kiosks and shops displaying the PT (*Portugal Telecom*) logo and can be used for international calls. International calls are cheaper between 9pm and 9am and at weekends. The country code for Portugal is 351. To call home from Portugal dial the international code (00) followed by the country code. To call the UK from Portugal dial 00 44.

Time
Portugal is on Greenwich Mean Time (GMT), the same as the UK, and one hour behind most of continental Europe. During the summer, from the last Sunday in March to the last Sunday in October, the time in Portugal is GMT plus one hour (GMT + 1).

Emergency telephone numbers
Police **112**
Fire **112**
Ambulance **112**
Forest safety **117**

Driving in Romania (South East Europe)

The regulations below should be read in conjunction with the General motoring information on pages 18–21.

A horse and cart is still an accepted form of transport in rural villages

Drinking and driving

Drinking and driving is strictly forbidden. Nil percentage of alcohol is allowed in drivers' blood. Your driving licence can be suspended for a maximum of 90 days or a prison sentence imposed for offenders.

Driving licence

The minimum age at which a UK licence holder may drive a temporarily imported car and/or motorcycle (for up to 90 days) is 18. Driving licences issued in the UK that do not incorporate a photograph must be accompanied by an International Driving Permit (IDP).

Fines

Police can impose fines but not collect them on the spot. A vehicle which is illegally parked may be clamped and removed.

Fuel

Lead replacement petrol (95 and 99 octane), unleaded petrol, diesel and LPG are available. Petrol in a can is permitted (must be empty when leaving Romania). Tax is payable on petrol and diesel in the vehicle tank when leaving Romania. Credit cards are accepted at many stations; check with your card issuer for usage in Romania before travel. Payment is usually made in local currency.

Lights

It is forbidden to drive at night if the vehicle lighting is faulty. Additional headlamps are prohibited. Dipped headlights must be used outside built-up areas during the day.

Motorcycles

The use of dipped headlights during the day is compulsory. The wearing of crash helmets

is compulsory for the driver and passenger of machines of 50cc and above.

Motor insurance

A Green Card/third-party insurance is compulsory. Drivers of vehicles registered abroad who are not in possession of a valid Green Card must take out short term insurance at the frontier.

Passengers/children in cars

A child under 12 cannot travel as a front-seat passenger.

Seat belts

It is compulsory for front/rear-seat occupants to wear seat belts, if fitted.

Speed limits

The standard legal limits, which may be varied by signs, for **private vehicles without trailers** are: In built-up areas 50km/h (31mph), outside built-up areas 90km/h (55mph) and 120km/h (74mph) on motorways. There is no minimum speed on motorways.

Additional information

- A fire extinguisher, first-aid kit and a warning triangle are compulsory.
- It is against the law to drive a dirty car.
- If a temporarily imported vehicle is damaged before arrival in Romania, the importer must ask a Romanian customs or police officer to write a report on the damage so that he can export the vehicle without problems. If any damage occurs inside the country a report must be obtained at the scene of the accident. Damaged vehicles may only be taken out of the country on production of this evidence.
- The use of the horn is prohibited between 10pm and 6am in built-up areas. '*Claxonarea interzisa*' – use of horn prohibited.
- Spiked tyres are prohibited.
- The use of snow chains is recommended for winter journeys to the mountains and may be compulsory in case of heavy snow.
- A road tax is levied on all motor vehicles (residents and visitors). Road tax 'stickers' (*rovinieta)* are available from border crossing points, petrol stations and post offices in Romania. The cost depends on emissions category and period of use in Romania. Foreign drivers failing to purchase a *rovinieta* during their stay may incur a fine between €90 and €2,000 when leaving the country. Proof of insurance and the cars registration document is required when purchasing the *rovinieta.*

Travel facts: Romania

Romanian National Tourist Office
22 New Cavendish Street
London W1G 8TT
Tel: 020 7224 3692
www.romaniarourism.com
www.romaniatravel.com

Banking hours
Banks are generally open Monday to Friday 9am to 1pm.

Credit/debit cards
Romania is largely a cash-only economy. American Express, Diners Club, MasterCard and Visa are accepted by an increasing number of hotels and some restaurants and shops, but you are advised to use cash due to the risk of credit card fraud. There are an increasing number of ATMs (*bancomat*) throughout the major cities. Do not expect to find ATMs in remote areas or villages.

Currency
The monetary unit of Romania is the new Lei (RON), divided into 100 bani. Notes are in denominations of Lei500, 100, 50, 10, 5 and 1. Coins are in denominations of Bani 50, 10, 5 and 1. It is recommended that visitors bring Euros, as these can be easily exchanged by shops, restaurants and hotels. Dollars and Sterling are not always easy to exchange for the local currency especially outside of Bucharest. Money should be changed in recognised exchange shops, banks and hotels. It is illegal to change money on the black market.

Electricity
The electrical supply is 220 volts AC, 50Hz. Plugs are of the two-pin type.

Health care
Comprehensive travel insurance is essential for all visitors.

Pharmacies
Pharmacies (*farmacie*) in Bucharest are well stocked and pharmacists may be able to suggest a medication for certain complaints. Some pharmacies in the city are open 24 hours a day.

Post offices
Post offices are generally open Monday to Friday 7.30am to 8pm, Saturday 8am to 2pm. Airmail to Western Europe takes one week.

Safe water
Mains water is normally chlorinated, and whilst relatively safe, may cause abdominal upsets. You are advised to drink bottled mineral water which is widely available.

Telephones
Public telephones are widely available and can be used for direct international calls; most require a phone card. Hotels often impose a high service charge for long-distance calls. The country code for Romania is 40. To call home from Romania dial the international code (00) followed by the country code. To call the UK from Romania dial 00 44.

Time
Romania is on Eastern European Time which is two hours ahead of Greenwich Mean Time (GMT + 2), but from the last Sunday in March to the last Sunday in October, when clocks are put forward one hour, summer time (GMT + 3) operates.

Emergency telephone numbers
Police **112**
Fire **112**
Ambulance **112**

Driving In Serbia (South East Europe)

The regulations below should be read in conjunction with the General motoring information on pages 18–21.

Drinking and driving
If the level of alcohol in the bloodstream is 0.05 per cent or more or if a medical examination shows that normal bodily functions are impaired, severe penalties can include a fine, imprisonment and/or suspension of driving licence.

Driving licence
The minimum age at which a UK licence holder may drive a temporarily imported car and/or motorcycle (exceeding 125cc) is 18. We recommend that you obtain an International Driving Permit (IDP) to accompany your UK driving licence.

Fines
On-the-spot fines can be imposed. An official receipt should be obtained. Fines vary according to the gravity of the offence. Penalties are higher if the motorist endangers other people or causes an accident.

Fuel
Leaded (95 and 98 octane), unleaded petrol (95 octane), diesel (*dizel*) and LPG are available. Petrol in a can is permitted (duty payable). Credit cards are generally accepted; check with your card issuer for usage in Serbia before travel.

Lights
Dipped headlights should be used in poor daytime visibility.

The parliament building in Belgrade

Motorcycles
Use of dipped headlights during the day is compulsory outside built-up areas. The wearing of crash helmets is compulsory for both driver and passenger.

Motor insurance
A Green Card is recognised, third-party insurance is compulsory.

Driving In Serbia continued

Outside Belgrade's National Museum

Passengers/children in cars

A person visibly under the influence of alcohol or child under 12 is not permitted to travel in a vehicle as a front-seat passenger.

Seat belts

It is compulsory for front/rear-seat occupants to wear seat belts, if fitted.

Speed limits

The standard legal limits, which may be varied by signs, for **private vehicles without trailers** are: In built-up areas 60km/h (37mph), outside built-up areas 80km/h (49mph) but 100km/h (62mph) on dual carriageways and 120km/h (74mph) on motorways.

Additional information

- It is compulsory for visitors to equip their vehicle with a set of replacement bulbs. A first-aid kit and a warning triangle are compulsory, two triangles are required if towing a trailer.
- Tolls are payable on most sections of motorway. See page 125.
- The authorities at the frontier must certify any visible damage to a vehicle entering Serbia and a certificate obtained; this must be produced when leaving otherwise you may experience serious difficulties on leaving the country.
- Spiked tyres are prohibited.
- If winter conditions require, snow tyres marked M&S on the side wall must be fitted on the driving wheels. We recommend that snow chains are carried as their use may become compulsory if the international snow chains sign is displayed.
- Vehicles entering a roundabout have right of way.
- Horns must not be used in built-up areas or at night except in cases of imminent danger.
- School buses must not be overtaken when they stop for children to board or alight.

Travel facts and toll charges: Serbia

Embassy of the Republic of Serbia
28 Belgrave Square
London SW1X 8QB
Tel: 020 7235 9049
www.serbianembassy.org.uk
www.serbia-tourism.org

Banking hours
Banks are generally open Monday to Saturday 6am to 7pm. Some banks open on Sunday.

Credit/debit cards
Major credit cards such as Visa, MasterCard and Diners Club are accepted in most shops, hotels and restaurants in Serbia. Very few ATMs accept international bank cards. There are several money-exchange machines in Belgrade (including one at the airport), which accept Pounds Sterling, US Dollars and Euros, giving back Dinars. Scottish and Northern Irish Pound Sterling bank notes are not accepted.

Currency
The official currency in Serbia is the Dinar which is divided into 100 paras. Bank notes are in denominations of CSD5,000, 1,000, 200, 100, 50, 20 and 10 and coins in denominations of CSD20, 10, 5, 2 and 1 and 50 paras. Money should be exchanged through official exchange offices only.

Electricity
The electric current in Serbia 220 volts AC, 50Hz. Two-round-pin plugs are used.

Health care
Comprehensive travel insurance is essential for all visitors.

Pharmacies
Pharmacies are open Monday to Friday from 8am to 8pm and on Saturdays from 8am to 1pm. Each city has a pharmacy that is open on Sundays and throughout the night.

Post offices
Most post offices are open Monday to Friday from 8am to 7pm and on Saturday from 8am to 3pm. On Sunday there is usually a designated post office that maintains services.

Safe water
Mains water is normally chlorinated and, while relatively safe, may cause mild abdominal upsets. Bottled water is available.

Telephones
The country code for Serbia is 381. To call home from Serbia dial the international code (00) followed by the country code. To call the UK from Serbia dial 00 44.

Time
Serbia observes Central European Time (CET) which is one hour ahead of Greenwich Meantime (GMT + 1), until late March to late October, when clocks are put forward one hour (GMT + 2).

Emergency telephone numbers
Police **92**
Fire **93**
Medical emergency **94**

Contact the Serbian Embassy for details of specific entry/exit requirements.

Toll charge in Dinars

Road		**Car**	**Car towing caravan/ trailer**
E75	Beograd – Novi Sad	430.00	690.00
E75	Novi Sad – Feketic	430.00	690.00
E75	Beograd – Nis	1130.00	1650.00
E75	Nis – Leskovac	260.00	430.00
E70	Beograd – Sid	520.00	780.00

Driving in Slovakia (Central Europe)

The regulations below should be read in conjunction with the General motoring information on pages 18–21.

Drinking and driving
Drinking and driving is strictly forbidden. Nil percentage of alcohol allowed in the driver's blood. Penalties include a fine, withdrawal of licence and imprisonment.

Driving licence
The minimum age at which a UK licence holder may drive a temporarily imported car is 18, for a motorcycle (exceeding 50cc) it is 17. An IDP is required for car hire.

Fines
On-the-spot fines (up to SKK5,000) can be imposed, an official receipt should be obtained. Wheel clamps are in use and vehicles may be towed away.

Fuel
Unleaded petrol (95 and 98 octane), diesel (*Nafta*) and LPG are available. There is no leaded petrol. Petrol in a can is permitted. LPG can only be used for road vehicles on the condition that a safety certificate covers the equipment for its combustion. Credit cards are accepted at filling stations, check with your card issuer for usage in Slovakia before travel.

Lights
The use of dipped headlights during the day is compulsory from 15 October to 15 March. Any vehicle warning lights, other than those supplied with the vehicle as original equipment, must be made inoperative.

Motorcycles
The use of dipped headlights during the day is compulsory. The wearing of a crash helmet is compulsory when riding a machine over 50cc. It is forbidden for motorcyclists to smoke while riding their machine.

Motor insurance
Third-party insurance is compulsory.

Passengers/children in cars
No person under 1.5m (4ft 9in) in height or a child under 12 may travel in a vehicle as a front seat passenger. The use of child seats is compulsory for children under 12 years of age or 1.5m (4ft 9in) tall.

Seat belts
It is compulsory for all occupants to wear seat belts, if fitted.

Speed limits
The standard legal limits, which may be varied by signs, for **private vehicles without trailers**, are: In built-up areas 60km/h (37mph), outside built-up areas including dual carriageways for vehicles not exceeding 3,500kg 90km/h (55mph) and motorways 130km/h (80mph). The minimum speed on motorways is 50km/h (31mph). Drivers must not exceed a speed of 30km/h (18mph) 30 metres before a level crossing, and while crossing over it.

Additional information

- A first-aid kit, warning triangle, spare tyre (and tool kit for tyre change) and a tow rope are compulsory. Visitors must also equip their vehicles with a set of replacement bulbs and fuses.
- Motorway tax is payable for use of certain highways and motorways. A windscreen sticker must be displayed on all vehicles, except motorcycles, as evidence of payment. Stickers may be purchased at border crossings and from selected filling stations and post offices for periods of one year, one month or one week. Fines are imposed for non-display.
- The authorities at the frontier must certify any visible damage to a vehicle entering Slovakia. If any damage occurs inside the country a police report must be obtained at the scene of the accident. Damaged vehicles may only be taken out of the country on production of this evidence.
- Spiked tyres are prohibited, snow chains may be used but only where there is enough snow to protect the road surface. Winter tyres recommended during winter months.
- All foreign visitors are required to show proof of medical insurance cover on entry.
- A reflective jacket is compulsory for 2- and 4-wheeled vehicles on all roads outside built-up areas, day and night. The person getting out of the vehicle as a result of a breakdown, puncture or accident must wear a reflective jacket. A fine of up to SKK5,000 will be imposed for non compliance. Reflective jackets must comply with EU standard EN 471.
- Horns may only be used to warn of danger or to signify intention to overtake.

Bratislava's town hall is topped by an ornate clock tower

Travel facts and toll charges: Slovakia

Slovakian Tourist Board
Slovak Tourist Centre
16 Frognal Parade
Finchley Road
London NW3 5HG
Tel: 020 7794 3263 or **0800 026 79432**
www.slovakiatourism.sk

Banking hours
Banks are generally open Monday to Friday 8am to 6pm.

Credit/debit cards
Major credit cards (American Express, Diners Club, MasterCard and Visa) and debit cards (Maestro and Visa Electron) are widely accepted in Slovakia

Currency
The currency of Slovakia is the Slovak Koruna or Slovak Crown (SKK; symbol Sk). One Slovak Koruna is divided into 100 hellers (*hal*).
Banknotes are issued in denominations of Sk5,000, Sk1,000, Sk500, Sk200, Sk100, Sk50 and Sk20 and coins in denominations of Sk10, Sk5, Sk2, Sk1 and 50 hal.

Electricity
The power supply in Slovakia is 230 volts/50 Hz. Sockets take two-round-pin plugs.

Health care
Free or reduced-cost medical treatment is available in Slovakia to European visitors on production of a valid European Health Insurance Card (EHIC). See page 11. Comprehensive travel insurance is essential for all visitors. All visitors must show proof of medical insurance cover on entry.

Pharmacies
Pharmacies (*apothéka*) are the only places to sell over-the-counter medicines. They also dispense many drugs (*leky*) normally available on prescription in other Western countries.

Post offices
Post offices are usually open between 8am and 5pm Monday to Friday. Stamps (*známky*) are available from newsagents and kiosks as well as post offices, though often only for domestic mail.

Safe water
The tap water is normally be safe to drink in Slovakia. If you are in any doubt about this, bottled mineral water is widely available.

Telephones
Public phones (*telefón*) in Slovakia are pretty reliable, with instructions in English. Phone cards (*telefonní karty*) can be bought at post offices and most tobacconists and kiosks.
If you have any problems, dial 149 and ask for an English-speaking operator. The country code for Slovakia is 421. To call home from Slovakia dial the international code (00) followed by the country code. To call the UK from Slovakia dial 00 44.

Time
Slovakia is on Central European time (GMT + 1), Daylight Savings Time comes into effect on the last Sunday in March and end on the last Sunday in October (GMT + 2).

Emergency telephone numbers
Police **112**
Fire **112**
Ambulance **112**

Toll charges in Slovakian Koruna

Road	Car	Car towing caravan/ trailer
15 days	150.00	750.00
1 year	750.00	5000.00

Driving in Slovenia (Central Europe)

The regulations below should be read in conjunction with the General motoring information on pages 18–21.

Drinking and driving
If the level of alcohol in the bloodstream is 0.05 per cent or more, severe penalties including a fine or suspension of driving licence can be imposed. The driver can still be fined for levels under 0.05 per cent if unable to drive safely. These rules also apply to narcotics.

Driving licence
The minimum age at which a UK licence holder may drive a temporarily imported car and/or motorcycle exceeding 125cc is 18. An Internatioinal Driving Permit is compulsory for holders of driving licences not incorporating a photograph and is also recommended for photo card licence holders.

Fines
On-the-spot fines must be paid in local currency. Refusal to pay could result in your passport being held. Illegally parked vehicles will be towed away or clamped.

Fuel
Unleaded petrol (95 and 98 octane), diesel and LPG are available. There is no leaded petrol (a lead substitute additive is available). Petrol in a can is permitted. Credit cards are accepted at filling stations, but check with your card issuer for usage in Slovenia before travel.

Lights
The use of dipped headlights during the day is compulsory.

Motorcycles
The use of dipped headlights during the day is compulsory. The wearing of crash helmets is also compulsory for both driver and passenger. A child under 12 is not permitted as passenger.

Motor insurance
Third-party insurance is compulsory.

Passengers/children in cars
Children under 12 and shorter than 1.5m (4ft 9in) must use suitable restraint system for their age and size and are only permitted to travel in the rear seats. Children over 12 may wear normal seat belts.

Seat belts
It is compulsory for front/rear-seat occupants to wear seat belts, if fitted.

Speed limits
The standard legal limits, which may be varied by signs, for **private vehicles without trailers** are: In built-up areas 50km/h (31mph), outside built-up areas 90km/h (55mph) but 100km/h (62mph) on 'fast roads' (dual carriageways) and 130km/h (80mph) on motorways. There are areas

Driving in Slovenia continued

Medieval Predjama Castle, near Postojna, is built into the side of a cliff

with a restricted speed limit of 30km/h (18mph). Lower limits apply to **private cars with a trailer or caravan:** outside built-up areas, on fast roads and motorways 80km/h (49mph).

Additional information

- A warning triangle is compulsory, two triangles are required if towing trailer.
- A warning triangle and/or hazard warning lights must be used in an accident/ breakdown situation.
- At night, if hazard lights fail, in addition to a warning triangle a yellow flashing light or position lights must mark the vehicle.
- A fire extinguisher, first-aid kit and a set of replacement bulbs are recommended.
- Foreign drivers involved in an accident must call the police and obtain a written report. On leaving the country, damaged vehicles must be accompanied by this report, as Customs will ask to see it, to allow exit.
- It is prohibited to overtake a bus transporting children when passengers are getting on/off.
- The use of the horn is prohibited in built-up areas or at night, except in cases of danger/injury/illness.
- From 15 November to 15 March, and beyond these dates during winter weather conditions (e.g. during snowfall, black ice, etc), private cars and vehicles up to 3.5 tonnes must have winter equipment as follows: winter tyres on all four wheels or summer tyres on all four wheels and snow chains in car boot. In both cases, the minimum tyre tread depth must be 3mm. This regulation also applies to vehicles with foreign registration plates but only during winter weather conditions (e.g. during snowfall, black ice, etc).
- Spiked tyres are prohibited.

Travel facts and toll charges: Slovenia

Slovenian Embassy
10 Little College Street,
London SW1P 3SJ
Tel: 020 7222 5400
www.slovenia.embassy-uk.co.uk

Banking hours
Banks are open Monday to Friday 9am to 12 noon and 2 to 5pm, some banks open on Saturday from 9am to 12 noon. Money can also be exchanged in exchange offices, at hotel reception desks, tourist agencies, petrol stations and larger supermarkets.

Credit/debit cards
Major cards accepted for payment are MasterCard, Maestro, Visa, Visa Electron, American Express and Diners. ATMs are located across the country.

Currency
The Euro (€) is the official currency of Slovenia. Coins are issued in denominations of 1, 2, 5, 10, 20 and 50 cents and €1 and €2. Notes are issued in denominations of €5, €10, €20, €50, €100, €200 and €500.

Electricity
The power supply is 220 volts AC, 50Hz. Sockets take round plugs with two round pins.

Health care
Free or reduced-cost medical treatment is available in Slovenia to European visitors on production of a valid European Health Insurance Card (EHIC). See page 11. Comprehensive travel insurance is still advised and is essential for all other visitors.

Post offices
Post offices are generally open Monday to Friday 8am to 6pm, Saturday 8am to 12 noon. The post office at Cigaletova 5, Ljubljana is open 24 hours. Stamps can be bought at bookstalls.

Safe water
Mains water is considered safe to drink. However, bottled mineral water is available and is advised for the first few weeks of the stay.

Telephones
Calls can be made with phone cards which are sold at post offices, newspaper kiosks and tobacco shops. The country code for Slovenia is 386. To call home from Slovenia dial the international code (00) followed by the country code. To call the UK from Slovenia dial 00 44.

Time
Slovenia is on Central European time (GMT +1), Daylight Savings Time comes into effect on the last Sunday in March and end on the last Sunday in October (GMT + 2).

Emergency telephone numbers
Police **113**
Fire **112**
Ambulance **112**

Toll charges in Euros

Road		Car	Car towing caravan/ trailer
A1	Ljubljana – Postojna	5.10	7.60
A1	Ljubljana – Videz	24.50	32.95
A1	Maribor – Ljubljana	9.05	13.55
A2	Ljubljana – Podtabor	1.60	2.35
A2	Ljuibljana – Pluska	1.70	2.60
A3	Ljubljana – Sezana	20.10	26.25
H4	Podnanos – Nova Gorica	1.50	2.25
A2	Tunel Karavanke	6.50	10.50
A2	Kronovo – Obre (Croatia frontier)	3.50	5.30

Driving in Spain (South West Europe)

The regulations below should be read in conjunction with the General motoring information on pages 18–21.

The 16th-century windmills at Castilla La Mancha in central Spain

Drinking and driving

If the level of alcohol in the bloodstream is 0.05 per cent or more, severe penalties can include a fine and withdrawal of the visitor's driving licence. The level for drivers with less than 2 years experience is 0.03 per cent.

Driving licence

The minimum age at which a UK licence holder may drive a temporarily imported car and/or motorcycle (over 75cc) is 18. All valid UK driving licences should be accepted in Spain. This includes the older all-green style UK licences (in Northern Ireland older paper style with photographic counterpart) although the EC appreciates that these may be more difficult to understand and that drivers may wish to voluntarily update them before travelling abroad, if time permits. Application form D1 (in Northern Ireland DL1) is available from most post offices. Alternatively, older licences may be accompanied by an IDP.

Fines

On-the-spot fines can be imposed. An official receipt should be obtained. Illegally parked vehicles can be towed away. Wheel clamps are also in use.

Fuel

Unleaded petrol (95 and 98 octane) is available. There is no leaded petrol. Petrol in a can is permitted. Diesel (Gasoleo 'A' or Gas-oil) is available. **Note:** Gasoleo 'B' is heating oil only. LPG is available under the name of Autogas, but there are only a few sales outlets at present. For locations visit www.repsolypf.com to view map. Credit cards are accepted at most filling stations; check with your card issuer for usage in Spain before travel.

Lights

The use of full headlights in built-up areas is prohibited; use sidelights or dipped headlights depending on how well lit the roads are. Dipped headlights must be used in tunnels.

Motorcycles

The use of dipped headlights during the day is compulsory. The wearing of crash helmets is also compulsory for riders of motorcycles 125cc and over, this includes trikes and quads unless equipped with seat belts.

Motor Insurance

Third-party insurance is compulsory.

Motorways

On Spanish motorways tolls can be paid in cash (Euros), credit card or electronic toll collection (ETC). Visit www.aseta.es for details of ETC and other information. Manual lanes, with toll collectors, accept cash and most major credit cards. Other lanes (VIAS AUTOMATICAS) are exclusively for motorists paying by credit card. See motorway map and toll charges on pages 136–137.

Passengers/Children in cars

Children up to the age of 12 and measuring less than 1.35m (4ft 5in) travelling in the front seat of a car must be seated in a child restraint system adapted to their size and weight. Children measuring more than 1.35m (4ft 5in) may use an adult seat belt. Children under 1.35m (4ft 5in) travelling on the rear seat must also be placed in a child restraint system adapted to their height and weight, except when travelling in a taxi in an urban area.

Seat belts

It is compulsory for front/rear-seat occupants to wear seat belts, if fitted.

Speed limits

The standard legal limits, which may be varied by signs, for **private vehicles without trailers** are: In built-up areas 50km/h (31mph), outside built-up areas 90km/h (55mph), on 2nd category roads

100km/h (62mph), on 1st category roads and 120km/h (74mph) on motorways. On motorways and dual carriage ways in built-up areas 80km/h (49mph). The minimum speed on motorways is 60km/h (37mph). The limit in some residential zones is 20km/h (13mph). Lower limits apply to **cars towing a caravan or trailer:** Outside built-up areas 70km/h (43mph), on dual carriageways 80km/h (49mph), on motorways 90km/h (55mph).

Additional information

- It is compulsory for visitors to equip their vehicles with a set of replacement bulbs, the tools to fit them and a warning triangle (one warning triangle is compulsory for foreign registered vehicles; two are recommended as, in an accident/breakdown situation, local officials may impose a fine if only one is produced).
- A Bail Bond is no longer a legal requirement and many insurance companies have stopped issuing them.
- A driver who wears glasses should carry a spare pair with them.
- Apparatus with a screen which can distract a driver (such as a television, video, DVD equipment) are prohibited. This excludes GPS systems.
- The use of radar detectors is prohibited.
- In urban areas it is prohibited to sound the horn at any time, except in an emergency. Lights may be flashed in place of using the horn.
- The use of snow chains are recommended in snow conditions.
- It is not mandatory to carry a reflective jacket in the vehicle and Spanish police cannot fine a foreign motorist who does not carry one however, the wearing of reflective jacket/waistcoat is compulsory if driver and/or passenger(s) exits vehicle which is immobilised on the carriageway of all motorways and main or busy roads. Car hire companies are not under legal obligation to supply them to persons hiring vehicles, so often don't.
- In winter, spikes on spiked tyres must not exceed 2mm in length and must only be used on roads covered with snow or ice.

Road signs (a selection of standard and non-standard)

Use dipped headlights | Motorway | Dual carriageway | Turning permitted | Limited parking zone | Viewpoint | Water

Travel facts: Spain

Spanish Tourist Office
22–23 Manchester Square
London W1M 5AP
Tel: 020 7486 8077
www.tourspain.co.uk

Banking hours
Banks are generally open Monday to Friday 8.30am to 1pm. Some banks open Saturday (October to May only) 8.30am to 1pm.

Credit/debit cards
Credit cards are widely accepted in shops, restaurants and hotels. Visa, MasterCard and Diners Club cards with four-digit PINs can be used in most ATM cash dispensers.

Currency
The Euro (€) is the official currency of Spain. Coins are issued in denominations of 1, 2, 5, 10, 20 and 50 cents and €1 and €2. Notes are issued in denominations of €5, €10, €20, €50, €100, €200 and €500.

Electricity
The power supply is 220/230 volts (in some bathrooms and older buildings it is 110/120 volts). Round two-hole sockets take two-round-pin plugs. British visitors will need an adaptor.

Health care
Free or reduced-cost medical treatment is available in Spain to European visitors on production of a valid European Health Insurance Card (EHIC). See page 11. Comprehensive travel insurance is still advised and is essential for all other visitors.

Pharmacies
Prescription and non-prescription drugs and medicines are available from pharmacies (*farmacias*) distinguished by a large green cross. They are able to dispense over the counter many drugs which would be available only on prescription in other countries.

Post offices
Post offices (*correos*) are generally open 9am to 2pm (1pm Saturday). In main centres they may open extended hours. Stamps (*sellos*) can also be bought at tobacconists (*estancos*). Post boxes are yellow.

Safe water
Tap water is chlorinated and generally safe to drink; however, unfamiliar water may cause mild abdominal upsets. Bottled mineral water (*agua mineral*) is cheap and widely available. It is sold still (*sin gas*) and carbonated (*con gas*).

Telephones
All telephone numbers throughout Spain now consist of nine digits (incorporating the former area code, preceded by 9), and no matter where you call from, you must always dial all nine digits. Many public telephones (*teléfono*) take phonecards (*credifone*), which are available from post offices and some shops for €6 or €12. The country code for Spain is 34. To call home from Spain dial the international code (00) followed by the country code. To call the UK from Spain dial 00 44.

Time
Spain is on Central European Time (GMT + 1), Daylight Savings Time comes into effect on the last Sunday in March and end on the last Sunday in October (GMT + 2).

Emergency telephone numbers
Police (national) **091**
Police (local) **092**
Fire **080**
Ambulance **061**

SPAIN & PORTUGAL

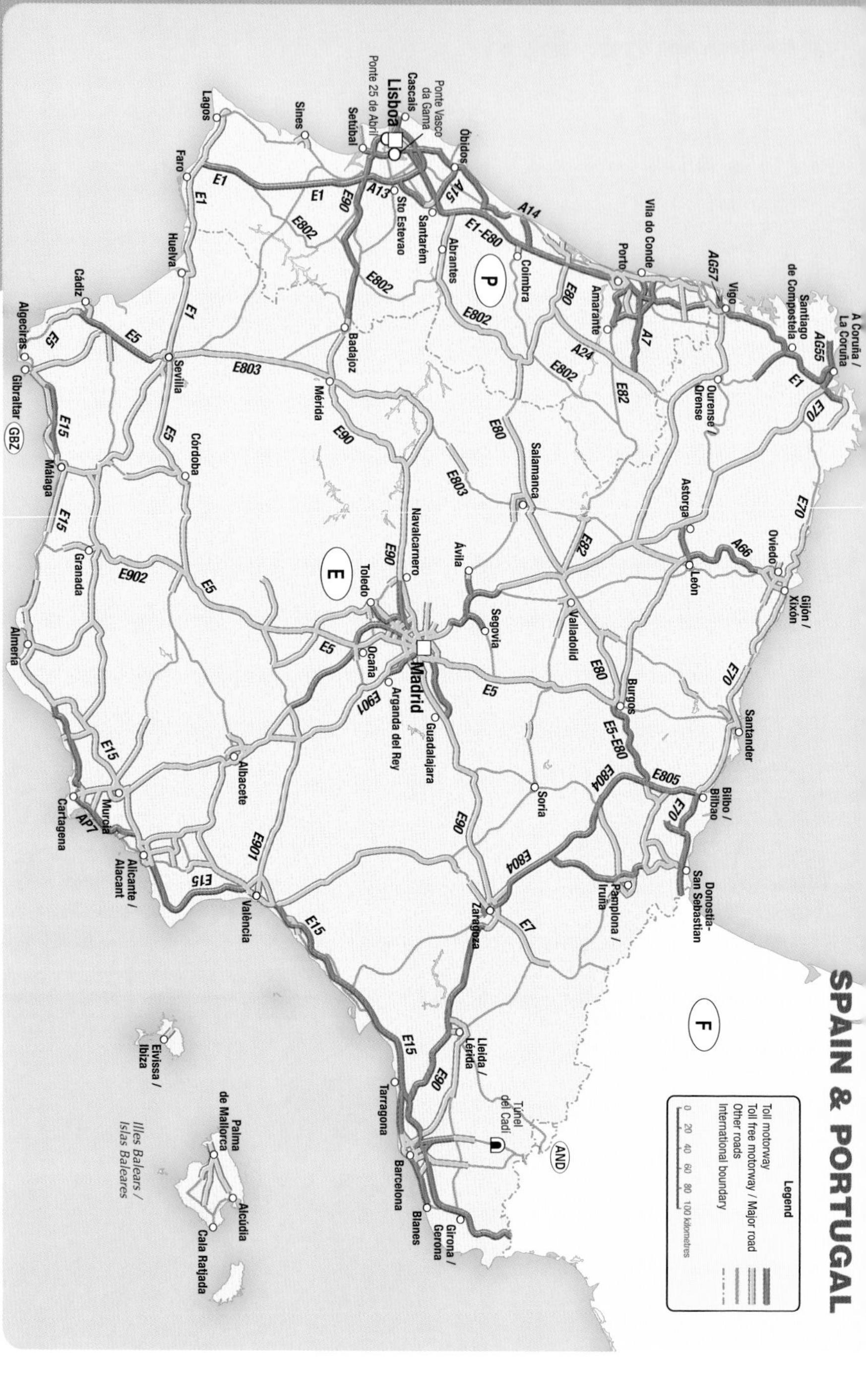

Toll charges in Euros

Road		Car	Car towing caravan/ trailer
E1 (A9)	Santiago de Compostela – Vigo	6.85	6.85
E1 (A9)	La Coruna – Santiago de Compostela	4.80	4.80
E5 (A4)	Cadiz – Dos Hermanas (Sevilla)	5.50	5.50
E5 (A4)	Madrid – Ocana	7.45	7.45
E5/E80 (A1)	Burgos – E804 (Miranda de Ebro)	8.75	8.75
E9	Barclelona – Túnel del Cadi	10.96	10.96
E15 (A7)	Barcelona – Tarragona	7.00	7.00
E15 (A7)	Tarragona – Valencia	19.60	19.60
E15 (A7)	La Jonquera (French frontier) – Barcelona	12.16	12.16
E15 (A7)	Malaga – Algeciras	12.30	12.30
E15 (A7)	Valencia – Alicante (Alacant)	12.95	12.95
E70 (A8)	Bilbao (Bilbo) – Irun (French frontier)	8.30	8.30
E90 (A2)	Zaragoza – Tarragona	21.45	21.45
E90 (R2)	Madrid – Guadalajara	5.95	5.95
E90 (R5)	Madrid – Navalcarnero	3.30	3.30
E804 (A68)	Zaragoza – Miranda de Ebro (E5/E80)	18.00	18.00
E805 (A68)	Miranda de Ebro (E5/E80) – Bilbao (Bilbo)	8.15	8.15

Road		Car	Car towing caravan/ trailer
E901 (R3)	Madrid – Arganda del Rey	3.15	3.15
M12	Madrid (Barajas) Airport – E5 (A1)	1.60	1.60
A6	Madrid – Valladolid – Adanero	8.30	8.30
A7	Cartagena – Alicante (Alacant)	2.95	2.95
A15	Pamplona (Irurtzun) – E804	9.35	9.35
A37	Alicante (Alacant) – Cartagena	5.50	5.50
A41	Madrid – Toledo	6.20	6.20
A51	Madrid – Avila	7.45	7.45
A55	La Coruna – Carballo	2.05	2.05
A57	Vigo – Baiona	1.35	1.35
A61	Madrid – Ségova	6.30	6.30
A66	Leon – Oviedo	9.90	9.90
A71	Leon – Astorga	3.60	3.60
AP53	Santiago – Ourense	4.80	4.80
C32 (A19)	Barcelona – Blanes	3.70	3.70
C32	Barcelona Airport – Tarragona	7.57	7.57

Bridges and tunnels

E9	Barcelona:		
	Túnel del Cadi	10.04	10.04
	Tunels de Vallvidrera	3.22	3.22

The spectacular Puente Nuevo (New Bridge), spans El Tajo gorge in the town of Ronda, Andalucia

Driving in Sweden (Northern Europe)

The regulations below should be read in conjunction with the General motoring information on pages 18–21.

Stockholm takes on a rosey hue at sunset

Drinking and driving

If the level of alcohol in the bloodstream is 0.02 per cent or more severe penalties including fines, withdrawal of licence and/or prison can be imposed.

Driving licence

The minimum age at which a UK licence holder may drive a temporarily imported car is 18, for a motorcycle it is 17.

Note: UK driving licences which do not incorporate a photograph, will not be recognised unless accompanied by photographic proof of identity e.g. a passport.

Fines

Police can impose but not collect fines on the spot. Illegally parked vehicles may be towed away, the release charge is up to SEK1,400.

Fuel

Unleaded (*Blyfri*) petrol (95, 96 and 98 octane) and diesel are available. Very limited LPG available. Petrol in a can is permitted (duty plus VAT payable). Credit cards are accepted at filling stations, check with your card issuer for usage in Sweden before travel.

Lights

The use of dipped headlights during the day is compulsory. Fines will be imposed for inadequate lighting.

Motorcycles

The use of dipped headlights during the day is compulsory. The wearing of crash helmets is also compulsory.

Motor insurance

Third-party insurance is compulsory.

Passengers/children in cars

It is compulsory for all children up to the age of seven or smaller than 135cm (4ft 5in) to be seated in a special child seat allowing them to use the normal seat belts in the car or use a suitable child restraint for their height/weight. This applies to front and rear seats.

Seat belts

It is compulsory for front/rear seat occupants to wear seat belts, if fitted.

Speed limits

The standard legal limits, which may be varied by signs, for **private vehicles without trailers** are: In built-up areas 50km/h (31mph), outside built-up areas on minor roads up to 90km/h (55mph) and those with a high-traffic density; on major roads and motorways up to 120km/h (74mph) according to signs. A lower limit of 30km/h (18mph) applies in many city centres and built-up areas. The limit for a **car towing a trailer** with effective brakes in 80km/h (49mph).

Additional information

- A warning triangle, first-aid kit and fire extinguisher are recommended.
- Beware game (moose, deer, elk, etc – a yellow warning triangle with a red border, see below, depicts animals most common on a particular stretch of road), as they constitute a very real danger on many roads.
- From 1 December to 31 March, when the roads are covered in snow and ice, it is strongly recommended that winter tyres are used, as these are compulsory for vehicles registered in Sweden.
- Spiked tyres (which must be fitted on all wheels) may be used 1st October to the 30th April.
- Snow chains may also be used if the weather or road conditions require.
- Congestion charges in Stockholm do not apply to foreign registered vehicles.
- The use of radar detectors is strictly forbidden.

Road signs (a selection of standard and non-standard)

Elks

Additional stop sign

Slow lane

End of lane

Travel facts and toll charges: Sweden

Swedish Travel and Tourism Council
11 Montagu Place
London W1H 2AL
Tel: 020 7870 5600
www.visitsweden.com

Banking hours
Banks are generally open Monday to Friday 10am to 3pm (in some cities until 6pm), Saturday 8am to noon or 1pm. Banks are also open on Thursday until 4 to 5.30pm.

Credit/debit cards
Major credit cards are widely accepted at banks, hotels, stores and restaurants. Most shops and restaurants require an identity card when paying with a credit card. You can get cash with your Visa, MasterCard, Maestro or Cirrus card at any '*Bankomat*' or '*Minuten*' ATM.

Currency
Sweden's currency is the Krona (SEK, SKr or Kr; plural Kronor), which is divided into 100 öre. Bank notes are issued in values of SEK20, 50, 100, 500 and 1,000; coins 50 öre, 1SEK, 5 and 10.

Electricity
Sweden has a 220 volts AC, 50Hz power supply. Electrical sockets take two-round-pin plugs.

Health care
Free or reduced-cost medical treatment is available in Sweden to European visitors on production of a valid European Health Insurance Card (EHIC). See page 11. Comprehensive travel insurance is still advised and is essential for all other visitors.

Pharmacies
Prescription and non-prescription medicines are available from a pharmacy (*apotek*). A 24-hour service is available in most cities.

Post offices
You'll find post offices in various shops, stores, kiosks and petrol stations. The opening hours differ according to the specific establishment. Buy stamps (*frimarken*) at a post office (*postkontoret*), supermarket, news-stand (*nyhetsbyra*), or kiosk displaying a blue-and-yellow post sign. Hours for rural post offices may vary. There are two different types of post boxes – the blue box is for local deliveries, the yellow box for national and international deliveries.

Safe water
Tap water is safe to drink, and bottled mineral water (*mineralvatten*) is widely available.

Telephones
You can use prepaid phone cards or credit cards to make a call from a public phone (*telefon*) in Sweden. A telephone card (*telefonkort*) can be bourght from news-stands, shops, hotels or magazine kiosks. Post offices do not have telephone facilities. Long-distance calls can be made from offices called Telebutik marked '*Tele*'. Operators speak English. The country code for Sweden is 46. To call home from Sweden dial the international code (00) followed by the country code. To call the UK from Sweden dial 00 44.

Time
Sweden is on Central European Time, which is one hour ahead of Greenwich Mean Time (GMT + 1). Daylight savings time (GMT + 2) is in effect from the last weekend in March to the last weekend in October.

Emergency telephone numbers
Police **112**
Fire **112**
Ambulance **112**

Toll charges in Swedish Krona

Bridges and tunnels	**Car**	**Car towing caravan/ trailer**
Oresund Bridge (one way)	300.00	600.00

Driving in Switzerland and Liechtenstein (Central Europe)

The regulations below should be read in conjunction with the General motoring information on pages 18–21.

Drinking and driving
If the level of alcohol in the bloodstream is 0.05 per cent or more, severe penalties include a fine or prison. The police may request any driver to undergo a breath test or drugs test. Visiting motorists may be forbidden from driving in Switzerland for a minimum of two months.

Driving licence
The minimum age at which a UK licence holder may drive a temporarily imported car is 18, for a motorcycle (50–125cc) it is 16, for a motorcycle (over 125cc) it is 18.

Fines
On-the-spot fines can be imposed. Vehicle clamps are not used in Switzerland but vehicles causing an obstruction can be removed. Fines/penalties are imposed for even minor traffic infringements.

Fuel
Unleaded petrol (95 and 98 octane) and diesel (*gasoil*) are available. There is no leaded petrol (a lead substitute additive is available). There is limited LPG availability (only eight outlets). Petrol in a can is permitted. Credit card acceptance is variable, especially at night due to automatic pumps not recognising UK chip and PIN cards; check with your card issuer for usage in Switzerland and Liechtenstein before travel. Some automatic pumps accept bank notes.

Lights
The use of dipped headlights during the day is recommended for all vehicles; it is compulsory when passing through tunnels even if they are well lit, a fine will be imposed for non-compliance.

Motorcycles
The wearing of crash helmets is compulsory. The use of dipped headlights during the day is recommended.

Motor insurance
Third-party insurance is compulsory.

Passengers/children in cars
Vehicles registered outside Switzerland, i.e. visiting Switzerland, must comply with the requirements of their country of registration with regard to child-restraint regulations.

Seat belts
It is compulsory for front/rear-seat occupants to wear seat belts, if fitted.

Speed limits
The standard legal limits, which may be varied by signs, for **private vehicles with or without trailers** are: In built-up areas 50km/h (31mph), outside built-up areas 80km/h (49mph), semi-motorways 100km/h (62mph) and 120km/h (74mph) on motorways. The minimum speed on motorways is 80km/h (49mph). **Note:** Towing cars on the motorway is only

permitted up to next exit at a maximum speed of 40km/h (24mph).

Additional information

- A warning triangle is compulsory, this must be kept within easy reach (not in the boot).
- Hitchhiking is prohibited on motorways and semi-motorways.
- The Swiss authorities levy an annual motorway tax and a vehicle sticker (costing CHF40 for vehicles up to 3.5 tonnes maximum total weight and known locally as a '*vignette*') must be displayed in the prescribed manner by each vehicle (including motorcycles, trailers and caravans) using Swiss motorways and semi-motorways. The fine for non-display of the *vignette(s)* is the cost of *vignette(s)* plus CHF100. Motorists may purchase the stickers in the UK (telephone the Swiss Centre on free-phone 00800 100 20030 for information) or in Switzerland from customs offices at the frontier or service stations and garages throughout the country.
- Vehicles over 3.5 tonnes maximum total weight are taxed on all roads; coaches and caravans pay a fixed tax for periods of one day, 10 days, one month or one year but lorries are taxed on weight and distance travelled.
- Radar detectors are prohibited even if not switched on.
- All vehicles with spiked tyres are prohibited on motorways and semi-motorways except for certain parts of the A13 and A2.
- Snow tyres are not compulsory, however vehicles which are not equipped to travel through snow and which impede traffic are liable to a fine.
- Snow chains are compulsory in areas where indicated by the appropriate road sign. They must be fitted on at least two drive wheels.
- Drivers who are involved in an accident who do not call the police must complete a European Accident Claim Form.
- During daylight hours outside built-up areas drivers must sound their horns before sharp bends where visibility is limited, after dark this warning must be given by flashing headlights.
- In Switzerland, pedestrians generally have right of way and expect vehicles to stop. Some pedestrians may just step into the road and will expect you to stop.

Travel facts and toll charges: Switzerland

Switzerland Tourism
30 Bedford Street
London WC2E 9ED
Tel: 020 7845 7680
www.MySwitzerland.com

Banking hours
Banks are generally open Monday to Friday from 8.30am to 4.30pm. Once a week they extend their hours. Please check locally. They are closed Saturday, Sunday and public holidays. Many banks have ATMs that accept overseas bank cards. Check with your local bank before leaving if your bank card is valid in Switzerland.

Credit/debit cards
The cards most used are Visa, MasterCard and American Express. Many Swiss banks have ATMs for cash advances with your credit card.

Currency
Switzerland's currency is the Swiss Franc (CHF) issued in CHF1,000, CHF200, CHF100, CHF50, CHF20 and CHF10 notes, and 5CHF, 2CHF and 1CHF coins. There are 100 centimes in a franc and 20, 10 and 5 centime coins. Many prices are indicated in Euros to aid comparing prices. Merchants may accept Euros but are not obliged to do so. Change will likely be in Swiss Francs.

Electricity
The power supply in Switzerland is 220 volts AC, 50Hz. Most power sockets take three round-pin-plugs. The standard continental plug with two round pins may be used without a problem.

Health care
Free or reduced-cost medical treatment is available in Switzerland to European visitors on production of a valid European Health Insurance Card (EHIC). See page 11. Comprehensive travel insurance is still advised and is essential for all other visitors.

Pharmacies
Many prescription and non-prescription medicines are available from pharmacists.

Post offices
Post offices are usually open Monday to Friday from 8am to 12 noon and 2 to 5pm. Branches located in shopping centers are usually open the same hours as the shopping centers, including the extended business times that are often offered once a week. On Saturday, post offices in large cities are open from 8.30am to 12 noon.

Safe water
The tap water is safe to drink. Bottled mineral water is readily available.

Telephones
Public payphones take the Swiss phone card, Taxcard, on sale for CHF5, CHF10 and CHF20 at post offices, newsagents, railway stations, etc. The country code for Swizerland is 41. To call home from Swizerland dial the international code (00) followed by the country code. To call the UK from Swizerland dial 00 44.

Time
Switzerland is on Central European Time which is one hour ahead of Greenwich Meantime (GMT + 1), until late March to late October, when clocks are put forward one hour (GMT + 2).

Emergency telephone numbers
Police **711** Fire **811**
Ambulance (not all areas) **144**

Toll charges in Swiss Francs
For details of where to buy the motorway tax (*vignette*) see page 142.

General	**Car**	**Car towing caravan/ trailer**
Annual vignette (includes use of Gotthard Tunnel and San Bernardino Tunnel)	40.00	40.00
Bridges and tunnels		
Munt La Schera Tunnel	10.00	20.00
Sankt Bernhard Tunnel	18.70	29.00

Driving in Turkey (South East Europe)

The regulations below should be read in conjunction with the General motoring information on pages 18–21.

The road winds through rock formations which make up Cappadocia's surreal landscape

Drinking and driving

If the level of alcohol in the bloodstream is 0.05 per cent or more, penalties imposed can be severe. For drivers of cars with caravans or trailers the alcohol level in the bloodstream is nil.

Driving licence

The minimum age at which a UK licence holder may drive a temporarily imported car and/or motorcycle is 18. A UK driving licence is valid for 90 days; licences that do not incorporate a photograph must be accompanied by an International Driving Permit (IDP).

Fines

On-the-spot fines can be imposed. Vehicles may be towed away if causing an obstruction.

Fuel

Leaded (96 octane), unleaded petrol (95 octane) and diesel are available. LPG is available in large centres. Petrol in a can is permitted (fireproof container). Credit cards are accepted at many filling stations, check with your card issuer for usage in Turkey before travel.

Lights

Dipped headlights should be used in poor daytime visibility, and also after sunset in built-up areas.

Motorcycles

The wearing of crash helmets is compulsory.

Motor insurance

Third-party insurance is compulsory. The Green Card is recognised (it must cover the whole of Turkey). Alternatively, insurance can be obtained at the border.

Passengers/children in cars

A child under 12 cannot travel as a front-seat passenger.

Seat belts

It is compulsory for front-seat occupants to wear seat belts, if fitted.

Speed limits

The standard legal limits, which may be varied by signs, for **private vehicles without trailers** are: In built-up areas 50km/h (31mph), outside built-up areas 90km/h (55mph) for cars, 70km/h (43mph) for motorcycles; motorways 120km/h (74mph) for cars and 80km/h (49mph) for motorcycles. The minimum speed on motorways is 40km/h (24mph). Speed limits are 10km/h (6mph) **less if the car has a trailer**.

Additional information

- A fire extinguisher, first-aid kit and two warning triangles are compulsory.
- The use of the horn is generally prohibited in towns from 10pm until sunrise.
- The use of spiked tyres is prohibited.
- It is recommended that winter tyres are used in snowy areas and snow chains are carried.
- In the event of an accident it is compulsory for the police to be called and a report obtained.

Travel facts and toll charges: Turkey

Turkish Tourist Office
Egyptian House
170 Piccadilly
London W1J 9EJ
Tel: 020 7629 7771
www.gototurkey.co.uk
www.tourismturkey.org

Banking hours
Banks are generally open Monday to Friday 8.30am to 12 noon and 1.30 to 5pm. Some banks open weekends in tourist areas.

Credit/debit cards
Credit cards are widely accepted in hotels, restaurants and shops. ATMs are located in convenient locations in cities, towns and resorts. There are also cash machines in the arrivals halls at most airports.

Currency
Turkey's currency is the New Turkish Lira (YTL) divided into 100 New Kurus (YKr). Banknotes are issued in denominations of 1, 5, 10, 20, 50 and 100YTL. Coins in 1, 5, 10, 25 and 50YKr and 1YTL. Many shops and restaurants in the coastal resorts and big cities accept payment in foreign currency. But if you are planning to travel to other parts of the country, it is advisable to take some Turkish Lira.

Electricity
The power supply in Turkey is 220 volts. Sockets take two-round-pin plugs but there are two sizes in use. Bring your own adaptor. Power cuts are frequent in rural areas but usually short lived.

Pharmacies
Prescription and non-prescription drugs and medicines are available from pharmacies (*eczane*). They are able to dispense many drugs that would normally be available only on prescription in many countries.

Post offices
Post offices (PTT) are easily recognisable by a black-on-yellow logo. In major resorts and larger towns the main PTT will stay open for phone calls until midnight. Post offices are generally open Monday to Friday from 8am to 7 or 8pm and Saturday mornings. Stamps are usually also available where postcards are sold.

Safe water
Tap water is generally safe to drink, though it can be heavily chlorinated and taste unpleasant. Bottled mineral water is inexpensive and is sold either sparkling (*maden suyu*) or still (*memba suyu*).

Telephones
There are pay-phones on many streets, and at PTT offices. Phone cards are sold at post offices and newsagents. Most phones also accept credit cards. The country code for Turkey is 90. To call home from Turkey dial the international code (00) followed by the country code. To call the UK from Turkey dial 00 44.

Time
Turkey is on Eastern European Time which is two hours ahead of Greenwich Mean Time (GMT + 2), but from the last Sunday in March to the last Sunday in October, when clocks are put forward one hour, summer time (GMT + 3) operates.

Emergency telephone numbers
Police **155** Traffic police **154** Fire **110**
Emergency (including ambulance) **112**

Toll charges in Turkish Lira

Road		Car	Car towing caravan/ trailer
E80	Edirne – Istanbul	2.30	3.50
E80/89	Istanbul – Ankara	3.70	5.10
E90	Pozanti – Tarus (Adana)	10.00	15.00
O31	Izmir – Aydin	7.00	9.00
O32	Izmir – Cesme	8.00	10.00
Bridges and tunnels			
Bosphorus and Fatih Sultan Mehmet Bridge		25.00	25.00

Part 3
Car tours

The Western Loire Valley

Starting in Nantes, this tour soon leaves all Breton influences behind as it heads for the valleys of the Loire and the Sarthe. You will find some of France's finest *son et lumière* presentations here, one of the world's most famous motor-racing circuits, and the Pays Nantais and Anjou are packed with vineyards.

5 days 512km (319 miles)

ITINERARY

NANTES • Clisson (27km/17 miles)
CLISSON • Cholet (36km/22.5 miles)
CHOLET • Doué-la-Fontaine (58km/36 miles)
DOUÉ-LA-FONTAINE • St-Hilaire (29km/18 miles)
ST-HILAIRE • Saumur (4km/2.5 miles)
SAUMUR • Baugé (44km/27 miles)
BAUGÉ • Le Lude (24km/15 miles)
LE LUDE • Le Mans Circuit (75km/47 miles)
LE MANS CIRCUIT • Le Mans (10km/6 miles)
LE MANS • Angers (106km/66 miles)
ANGERS • Nantes (99km/62 miles)

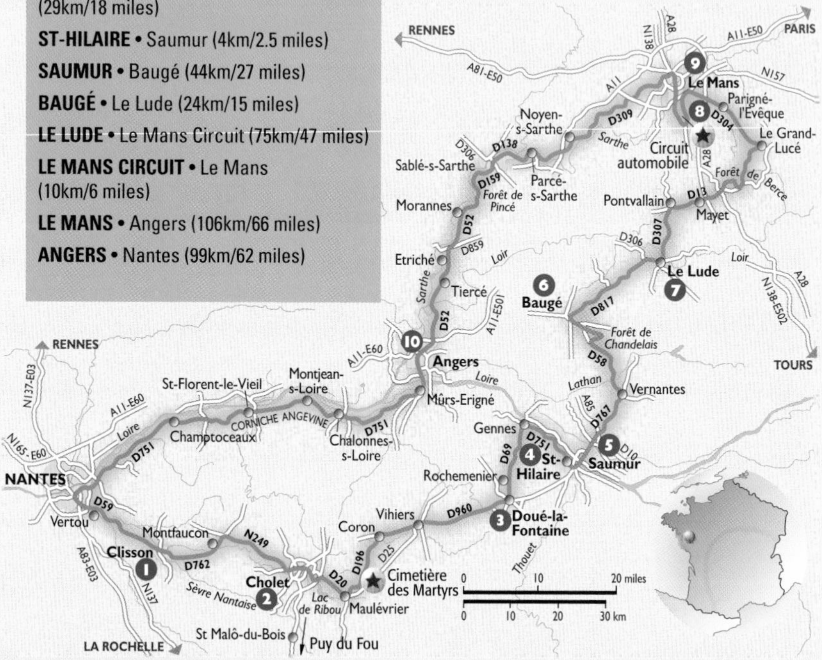

Leave Nantes for Clisson on the D59 through St-Fiacre. In Gorges go left of the D113 then take the D59 again into Clisson.

❶ Clisson, Loire Valley West
The Vendée Wars and the savage reprisals of the Revolutionary government army all but obliterated this little town. Then it was completely rebuilt, but not as it had been before. Present-day Clisson is mostly a tribute to Palladian Italy, with colonnades, loggias and bell-towers of a style seen nowhere else in western France.

Look for the stabilised but unfurnished ruin of the 13th- to 15th-century castle, the 15th-century market hall, the two medieval bridges contrasting with the soaring 19th-century road viaduct, and Italianate creations such as the Temple d'Amitié and the Church of Notre-Dame.

There are beautiful walks in the valleys of the Sèvre Nantaise and the Moine. Local

Clisson's impressive ruined 13th- to 15th-century castle sits atop a rocky outcrop

wines may be tasted. But Clisson itself is the great attraction, especially its Italianate skyline and leafy riverside view.

Leave Clisson on the N149. Turn left as for Beaupréau on the D762 then go along the N249 and follow signs to Cholet.

❷ Cholet, Loire Valley West
Only 20 buildings were left standing in the brutal aftermath of the Vendée Wars of 1793–96. A section of the Musée d'Art et de l'Histoire explains how the Vendée rising against the Revolutionary government's policies of mass conscription and the overthrow of all previous loyalties, was at first successful, then viciously crushed. Other exhibitions are at the Musée Paysan with its old-style dairy and country house interiors in the leisure park by the Ribou lake.

This is a famous textile town with a Musée du Textile illustrating the industry. Its trademark is the red-and-white handkerchief – the *mouchoir de Cholet* – whose design is rooted in another incident of the Vendée Wars. The town also has a shoe museum and at nearby Maulévrier there is a fine Oriental Garden which mirrors the Buddhist stages of human existence.

Leave Cholet on the D20 as for Poitiers. In Maulévrier turn left and right as for Vihiers, then left on the D196 through Chanteloup to Coron. Go right on the D960 to Doué-la-Fontaine.

❸ Doué-la-Fontaine, Loire Valley West
If you arrived in the middle of Doué without paying attention to its outskirts, you might shrug it off as an ordinary little town. It is far from that. The zoo, adapted from the cliffs, caverns and ditches of a disused limestone quarry, houses lions, tigers, lemurs, birds of prey, deer, emus, rarities such as snow panthers, and 15 separate monkey enclosures. Its Naturoscope has displays relating to the problems of threatened species and the destruction of their habitats.

The Musée des Commerces Anciens old-style shops and a rose-water distillery, in partly restored 18th-century stables.

Nobody is certain about the origins of Doué's arena, which is Roman in style but of a much later date. However, there is no doubt about the Moulin Cartier. Built in 1910, it was the last windmill raised in the region of Anjou (closed to visitors).

Leave Doué on the D69 to Gennes. Go right as for Saumur on the D751 through La Mimerolle and into St-Hilaire.

❹ **St-Hilaire,** Loire Valley West
Just before this village – a suburb of Saumur – the Musée du Champignon, in a cave system cut into the roadside cliffs, is more than simply an exhibition about mushrooms and how they are grown. The underground galleries were dug in medieval times, part of a network of more than 480km (300 miles) throughout the district, which produces 75 per cent of France's cultivated mushrooms.

Turn right in St-Hilaire for the École National d'Équitation. This is France's national riding academy, excellently housed and staffed. In the practice arena, in front of high wall mirrors, you may see members of the acadamy's Cadre Noire put their horses through the intricate, disciplined and stylish movements for which they are famous all over Europe. They also perform summer season shows.

Continue on the D751 into Saumur.

❺ **Saumur,** Loire Valley West
Straddling the Loire, this very appealing town is passionate about horses and the cavalry, wines, museums and exuberant outdoor displays. The Château de Saumur, overlooking the river, houses two separate collections. The Musée des Arts Décoratifs concentrates on the decorative arts – ceramics, enamelware, carvings in wood and alabaster. Another, Musée du Cheval, celebrates centuries of horsemanship.

The cavalry has two separate exhibitions, one recalling its mounted days, the other taking the story to more recent times with a comprehensive display of tanks and armoured cars.

The château at Saumur has been dubbed 'the castle of love'

Second only to Champagne, Saumur is famous for its sparkling wines. Several firms welcome visitors to their cellars. Notre-Dame de Nantilly, dating from the 12th century, houses a valuable collection of medieval and Renaissance tapestries.

And the old quarter of Saumur with its narrow streets and restored 17th-century houses adds to the attractions of a justifiably self-confident town.

Leave Saumur on the N147 as for Le Mans. At the roundabout take the second exit to Vernantes on the D767. In Vernantes, turn sharp left at the traffic lights as for Baugé, then right on the D58 as for Baugé through Mouliherne. In Le Guédéniau go right on the D186 as for Lasse. Turn left following 'Les Caves de Chanzelles' sign. At the roundabout in the forest take the fifth exit for Baugé. Rejoin the D58 and continue to Baugé.

❻ Baugé, Loire Valley West
Plenty of space has been left around Baugé's 15th-century castle, originally a hunting lodge of Good King René, Duke of Anjou. Holding displays of weapons, coins and ceramics, it stands beside public gardens dipping to an attractive riverside. The Convent of La Girouardière houses a venerated relic – a jewelled cross believed to contain a piece of the True Cross brought to France by a crusader knight. Its unusual design was adopted as the Cross of Lorraine. Look also for Baugé's charming 17th-century Hospice-St-Joseph (not open to the public).

Sometimes an unfamiliar language may be seen or spoken here, describing Baugé, for instance, as '*bela kaj malmova urbeto*': the Château de Grésillon, on your exit route from 'this fine old town', is an international Esperanto centre (not open to the public).

Leave Baugé on the D817, which becomes the D305, go right on the D306 to Le Lude.

❼ Le Lude, Loire Valley West
Pride of this little town is the richly furnished château, rebuilt in Renaissance style after an English garrison was driven out – with heavy damage to the fabric – in 1427. The town's situation is most attractive, above balustraded gardens rising from the River Loir, whose waters eventually feed the larger Loire. Cultural life in Le Lude includes a number of special events and festivals featuring horticulture, theatre, music and children's activities.

Leave Le Lude on the D307 to Pontvallain. Go right on the D13 through Mayet and across the N138 to Le Grand-Lucé. Turn left at the give way sign and left on the D304 as for Le Mans. Go under the bridge, then left following the 'Angers' sign, under another bridge and follow the 'Tours' signs along the N138. Go right at the roundabout on the D140 as for Arnage, then right on the D139 to the grandstands of the racing circuit.

❽ Le Mans Circuit, Loire Valley West
Prosaically, they may be the N138, D140 and D139, but these roads are also part of the great motor-racing circuit where the Le Mans 24-Hour Race is held every June.

The N138 is the Mulsanne Straight, along which Jaguars, Porsches and Mercedes howl at speeds of over 320km/h (200mph).

There is a smaller but linked Bugatti Circuit. The two tracks play host to five major car and motorcycle events, plus a 24-hour truck race! You can watch test sessions from the main grandstands, which are informally open to the public on non-competition days.

An excellent motor museum also recalls that this was where Wilbur Wright, over from the United States, made the first powered flight in Europe in 1908.

Continue on the D139 into Le Mans.

9 Le Mans, Loire Valley West
Many first-time visitors to Le Mans will notice a familiarity – if, that is, they saw the films *Cyrano de Bergerac* and the 1997 version of *The Man in the Iron Mask* which were shot here. It lies at the heart of a warren of cobbled medieval streets, lined with half-timbered buildings and attractive Renaissance mansions.

One of the loveliest of these houses the Musée de la Reine Bérengère, a celebration of Sarthe history. Queen Bérengère was Richard the Lionheart's widow, and she built the Cistercian abbey outside the town. Art lovers should make for the Musée de Tessé, with its superb collection of paintings. In July, a lively street festival takes over the town.

Leave Le Mans on the D309 as for Sablé. In Parcé cross the river then go first right at the crossroads, left to Solesmes then continue to Sablé-sur-Sarthe. Go straight across the D306 for Centre-Ville. At the roundabout take the last exit, then a side road right for Pincé. This is the D159. Bear right on the C15 for 'Pincé par la Forêt'. Rejoin the D159, then follow the D18 and D52 through Morannes. Continue through Etriché and Tiercé. Go straight on along the N160 then right on the N23 to Angers.

Fascinating exhibits in the Le Mans' automobile museum

10 Angers, Loire Valley West
Here in the heart of Anjou lies a university town of parks, gardens and colourful floral decorations, with a grand Plantagenet castle rising in towers of banded stonework. The Cathédrale Saint Maurice, is best approached by the Montée St-Maurice, a stairway climbing from the River Maine.

The longest tapestry in France, La Tenture de l'Apocolypse, completed in the late 14th century to show the Apocalypse, is on display in the castle. Angers is a tapestry town. Many others, ancient and modern, are on show in the castle itself and in individual museums and galleries.

Fine Renaissance buildings survive, both around the cathedral and elsewhere. River cruises follow the Maine, and for the adventurous there are hot-air balloon flights to waft you high above the castles, vineyards and villages of Anjou.

Alternatively, visit the stunningly converted 13th-century abbey, now home to the monumental sculptures of David d'Angers (1788–1856).

Leave Angers through Les-Ponts-de-Cé on the N160. In Mûrs-Érigné, turn right to go through Chalonnes-sur-Loire and Champtoceaux on the D751 and return on the N249 to Nantes.

The Enchanting Mosel Valley

Long before Rome was founded – legend says around 2050 BC – there was a settlement at Trier. The city blossomed under the Romans, but later was repeatedly attacked by invading Vandals. It is now a major tourist attraction.

2/3 days 432km (267 miles)

ITINERARY

TRIER • Bernkastel-Kues (60km/37.5 miles)

BERNKASTEL-KUES • Traben-Trarbach (26km/16 miles)

TRABEN-TRARBACH • Cochem (52km/32 miles)

COCHEM • Burg Eltz (20km/12 miles)

BURG ELTZ • Koblenz (35km/22 miles)

KOBLENZ • Boppard (22km/13.5 miles)

BOPPARD • St Goar (15km/9 miles)

ST GOAR • Bingen (34km/21 miles)

BINGEN • Bad Kreuznach (13km/8 miles)

BAD KREUZNACH • Trier (155km/96 miles)

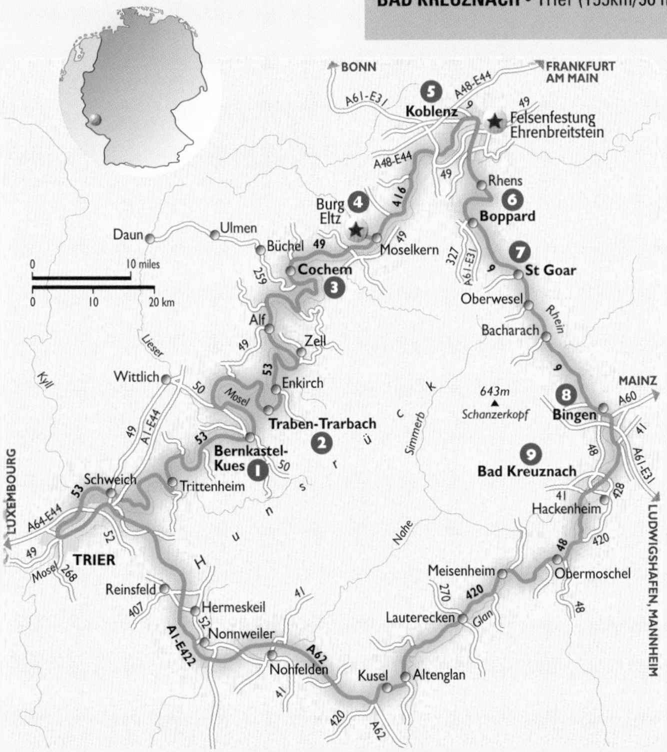

From Trier join the B53 northeast to Bernkastel-Kues, 60km (37.5 miles).

❶ Bernkastel-Kues, Rheinland-Pfalz
The square of this picturesque town is surrounded by timber-framed houses, with the fountain of St Michael in its centre, and the Rathaus (Town Hall) which was built in 1608. Fascinating but not quite so picturesque are the iron chains of the Pranger (stocks), the public punishment of the Middle Ages, preserved here. The parish

church of St Michael dates from the 14th century and contains interesting works by a local sculptor, H R Hoffmann. Bernkastel-Kues has a wine museum, and the excellent Bernkastler wine is well known.

South of Bernkastel stands the ruin of the Landshut, the second fortress to be built on the same site, in 1280.

Continue on the B53 for 26km (16 miles) to Traben-Trarbach.

❷ Traben-Trarbach, Rheinland-Pfalz
A trip to the ruins of the fortress Grevenburg above Traben-Trarbach offers rewarding views over the town and the picturesque Mosel Valley. Between 1520 and 1734 the fortress was besieged six times and then blown up, so it is small wonder that only a fragment of a wall with window holes is left.

The little town of Zell, on the other side of the river, should not be missed. It appears to be built into the landscape with vineyards all around it. The castle is open to visitors. Emperor Maximilian lived here at one time and it contains many treasures. Zeller Schwarze Katz (Black Cat) is a popular wine from the local grapes.

Continue on the B53, then the B49 to Cochem.

❸ Cochem, Rheinland-Pfalz
A real centre for tourism in the Mosel Valley is Cochem, which also lies in an important wine-growing area. The former Reichsburg, now the Burg (castle), was rebuilt in 1874, using plans from 1576. It affords splendid views over the Mosel Valley and its vineyards, which stretch from the river's edge up into the hills.

From Cochem continue on the B49/B416 and turn left at Moselkern for Burg Eltz.

❹ Burg Eltz, Rheinland-Pfalz
High above the wine-producing village of Moselkern stands the burg or fortress of Eltz, one of the most rewarding attractions in the area. Numerous oriels and towers and a

Cochem, with its romantic castle, the former Reichsburg, overlooking the Mosel

superb position made this superb fortress unconquerable for centuries. Even now, cars find the ascent difficult. The road stops at the Antonius Chapel, and the last few hundred metres have to be covered on foot or by shuttle bus. The knights of Eltz were called the Eisenköpfe (Iron Heads), a tribute to their stubbornness as well as to the numerous skirmishes in which they took part. The guided tour around the fortress is accompanied by many entertaining stories and anecdotes.

From Burg Eltz return to Moselkern, then turn left on the B416 to Koblenz.

❺ Koblenz, Rheinland-Pfalz
Where the Mosel enters the mighty Rhine lies Koblenz. Its unique situation has made it a place of great importance from Roman times. Koblenz's name is derived from the Roman *castrum ad confluentes*, the 'camp at the confluence'. It is not known when the Romans actually established their outpost

here, but it must have been before the reign of Emperor Tiberius (AD 14–37).

After almost total wartime destruction, part of the old centre of Koblenz has been meticulously restored. The actual point of land where the Mosel and Rhine meet is called the Deutsches Eck (German Corner), marked by a monument to German unity.

The Felsenfestung Ehrenbreitstein (Rock Fortress) dominates the Rhine and Mosel and is supposedly the largest fortress in Europe. It is best reached by chair-lift. The view from the terrace is spectacular, down to Koblenz and in the distance to the Eifel and Hunsrück mountain ranges. The fortress was always a thorn in the flesh of the French, and Napoleon destroyed it in 1801. It was subsequently rebuilt, but a clause in the Treaty of Versailles after World War I stated it must never again be used for military purposes. It now houses the Rhine Museum.

The former Kurfürstliches Schloss, or Residenzschloss as it is also known, was once the seat of Prince Wilhelm von Preussen and until 1918 it was owned by the Prussian kings. It now belongs to the state and is used for administrative purposes.

A terraced café on the vine-covered slopes around the spa town of Boppard

Burg Stolzenfels, built in 1242, is a former royal castle. It was destroyed by the French in 1688 and rebuilt after 1836. Its interior is worth seeing, especially the large Rittersaal (Knights' Hall) and the King's quarters.

From Koblenz take the B9 south for 22km (14 miles) to Boppard.

❻ **Boppard,** Rheinland-Pfalz

At a bend in the Rhine lies Boppard, a very old settlement which the Celts called Bandobriga. Later the Romans erected fortifications here around AD 400, and parts of the 8m (26-foot) high walls can still be seen. St Severuskirche (Church of St Severus) is late Romanesque. The Karmeliter-kirche is interesting; it has no tower, which is very rare for a Gothic church. The Alte Burg (Old Castle), dating from the 14th century, now houses the Museum der Stadt Boppard.

Castle ruins on the hillside above the village of St Goar

Continue south on the B9 for 15km (9 miles) to St Goar.

❼ St Goar, Rheinland-Pfalz
In the Middle Ages, many knights living in fortresses on narrow stretches of river supplemented their incomes by collecting tolls from passing ships – or just simply robbing them. They were the so-called Raubritter (robbing knights). One such fortress was 13th-century Schloss Rheinfels, just before St Goar. This former royal castle is now open to the public. The Stiftskirche in St Goar is a delightful mixture of styles. The church itself is 15th century, the crypt is Romanesque and the marble tombs are from the 16th and 17th centuries.

From St Goar continue south on the B9 to Bingen, 34km (21 miles).

❽ Bingen, Rheinland-Pfalz
The Burg Klopp fortress, which overlooks Bingen, was built on a Roman site with a deep well of 52m (170 feet), which probably goes back to the same period. The fortress was destroyed in 1689, and the remnants blown up in 1711, but between 1875 and 1879, it was totally rebuilt. The town has an interesting Heimatmuseum (local museum) which contains pre-historic exhibits.

On an island in the river stands the Mäuseturm (Mice Tower). This stone construction dates from 1208 and replaced a wooden Roman tower erected in 8 BC under the Roman military leader Drusus. Legend has it that when Bishop Hatto was thrown into the tower as a punishment for his cruelties, he was eaten alive by mice.

From Bingen continue due south on the B48 to Bad Kreuznach, 13km (8 miles).

❾ Bad Kreuznach, Rheinland-Pfalz
This sizeable spa lies on the River Nahe, and its thermal springs are used as the basis for well-organised treatments for rheumatism, gout and similar ailments. Unique to the town are the well-preserved Brücken-hauser (Bridge Houses). These date from the 15th century, and have been chosen as the town emblem. In the Römerhalle Museum, Roman mosaics and remains from the military camp are on view.

From Bad Kreuznach take the B48, then the B420 south to Kusel. Join the A62 and travel northwest towards Nonnweiler. Continue on the A1/E422 north to exit Moseltal, then southwest to Trier on the A602/B49, 155km (96 miles).

Opposite: The colourful main market square in Trier, probably the oldest city in Germany

UGENOPTIK
FRERE

Cotswold Wool & Stone

This is mainly a circuit of Cotswold countryside – a landscape of stone walls surrounding fertile fields and distinctive village architecture. The villages contain many fine churches, but the best known structure is the cross in the centre of Banbury. The family homes of two great men can be seen; one Englishman in Blenheim and one American in Sulgrave.

2 days 99 miles (159km)

ITINERARY

OXFORD • Woodstock (10m/16km)

WOODSTOCK • Chipping Norton (13m/21km)

CHIPPING NORTON • Rollright Stones (5m/8km)

ROLLRIGHT STONES • Broughton (14m/23km)

BROUGHTON • Banbury (3m/5km)

BANBURY • Sulgrave (7m/11km)

SULGRAVE • Aynho (13m/21km)

AYNHO • Deddington (3m/5km)

DEDDINGTON • Steeple Aston (5m/8km)

STEEPLE ASTON • Bicester (9m/14km)

BICESTER • Boarstall (7m/11km)

BOARSTALL • Oxford (10m/16km)

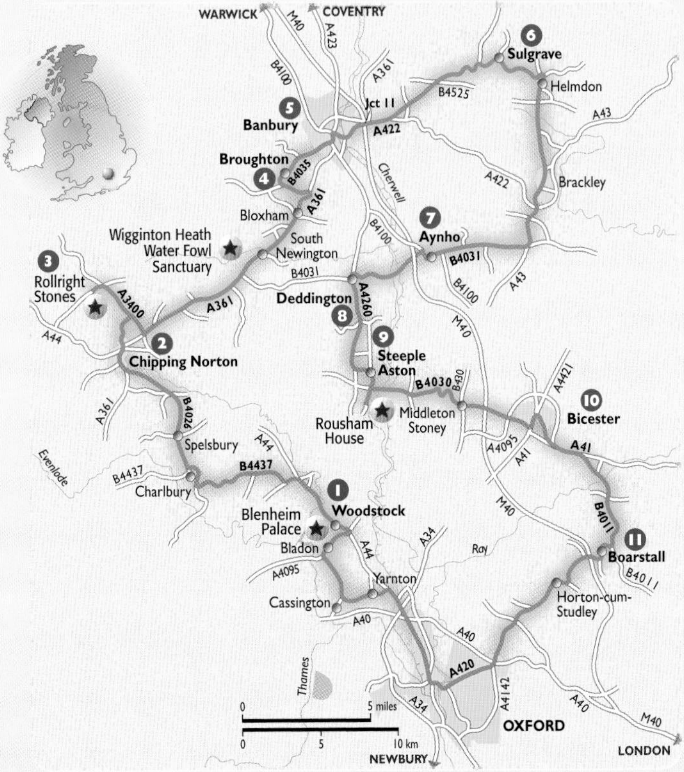

Blenheim Palace sits in grounds landscaped by 'Capability' Brown

Leave Oxford on the A44 and turn left along an unclassified road towards Cassington. Turn right to Bladon on the A4095, then left on the A44 to Woodstock.

❶ **Woodstock,** Oxfordshire
You can stop off in Bladon, to visit the churchyard where Sir Winston Churchill, his wife and parents are buried, before continuing along the road to Blenheim, where he was born. Blenheim Palace was given to the Marlborough family by Queen Anne as a reward for the 1st Duke of Marlborough's victory over the French at Blenheim in 1704.

Just outside the park is the town of Woodstock, with its mellow stone buildings. Kings of England came here for the excellent hunting in the Forest of Wychwood, but modern visitors have gentler interests. A quiet hour can be spent in the Oxfordshire County Museum, in the town centre, where the history of the people and the changing landscape is conveyed in exhibitions ranging from the Stone Age to the present time.

From Woodstock take the A44 turning left on to the B4437 to Charlbury and then the B4026 to Chipping Norton.

❷ **Chipping Norton,** Oxfordshire
Gateway to the Cotswolds and historic market town, this was the market for the sheep farmers of the area, and the wide main street is a relic of those days (the name 'chipping' means market). There are many fine old stone buildings, including the church, market hall, pubs and big houses, but it is the fine wool church which dominates the town, one of over 40 in the Cotswolds. Paid for by the proceeds from sheep farming, it dates mainly from the 14th and 15th centuries, but much of its stonework has been restored. Another of the town's landmarks is the chimney of Bliss Tweed Mill which is an important reminder of local industrial history.

Take the B4026, then go north along the A3400 for just over a mile (1.6km) and turn left along an unclassified road signed Little Rollright.

❸ **Rollright Stones,** Oxfordshire
This Bronze Age circle, which dates from earlier than 1000 BC, was nearly as important as Stonehenge in the neolithic period. Nicknamed the 'King's Men', it measures a full 100 feet (30m) across. Over the road is the King Stone, a monolith, and near by, just along the road, is the group of stones called the Whispering Knights, at the site of a prehistoric burial chamber. The surrounding countryside is patterned with stone walls of weathered limestone.

Return to the A3400 and turn south before branching left on to the A361, then turn left in Bloxham along unclassified roads to Broughton.

❹ **Broughton,** Oxfordshire
Broughton Castle is a fortified manor rather than a castle, turned into an Elizabethan house of style by the Fiennes family in about 1600. Surrounded by a great moat lake, it is set in gorgeous parkland, and has a stone church near by. The present owners, Lord and Lady Saye and Sele, are descendants of the family that has lived here for centuries. Celia Fiennes, the 17th-century traveller and diarist, was a member of this family. William de Wykeham, founder of Winchester School and New College, Oxford, acquired the manor and converted the manor house into a castle. In the medieval Great Hall there are suits of armour from the Civil War.

Drive 3 miles (5km) east along the B4035 to Banbury.

❺ **Banbury,** Oxfordshire
Banbury is a town of charm and character, with its interesting buildings and narrow medieval streets. Famous for the nursery rhyme 'Ride a cock horse to Banbury Cross', the town is also known for its spice cakes, which have been made here since the 16th century. The unusual church with its round tower replaced an older one demolished in the 18th century. There is still a weekly street market, which has been held regularly for over 800 years, and there used to be a livestock market, too, but nowadays the animals are taken to a permanent site on the edge of town, Europe's largest cattle market.

Head east along the A422. After 2 miles (3km) turn left on to the B4525, then to the unclassified road to Sulgrave.

❻ **Sulgrave,** Northamptonshire
The old manor in this attractive stone village was the home of ancestors of George Washington from 1539 to 1659, having been bought by Lawrence Washington, wool merchant and twice Mayor of Northampton. Not to be missed is the family coat of arms with its stars and stripes carved above the entrance porch, and the most treasured possession inside is an original oil painting of George Washington.

Take the unclassified road through Helmdon, heading south to Brackley to join the A43, then shortly right on to the B4031 to Aynho.

❼ **Aynho,** Northamptonshire
This village contains apricot trees from which, legend has it, fruit was paid as a toll to the Cartwrights, Lords of the Manor. They lived in the mansion in Aynhoe Park, and there are several memorials to them, including a Victorian marble cross in the church.

From Aynho go west along the B4031 to Deddington.

❽ **Deddington,** Oxfordshire
Dominating this village, which is built out of the honey-coloured local stone, is the church, with each of its eight pinnacles topped with gilded vanes. Adjacent Castle House was formerly the rectory, and parts of the building date from the 14th century. The area has many links with the days of the Civil War, and Charles I is believed to have slept at the 16th-century Castle Farm near by.

Drive southwards for 5 miles (8km) along the A4260 and then left on to an unclassified road to Steeple Aston.

Broughton Castle is a fine example of a gracious Elizabethan Manor

❾ Steeple Aston, Oxfordshire

Steeple Aston was winner of the Oxfordshire Best Kept Village Award in 1981 and 1983, and is still an eye-catching village. The village inn, Hopcroft's Holt, had associations with Claude Duval, a French highwayman who worked in these parts. Just beyond Steeple Aston is the Jacobean mansion of Rousham House, built by Sir Robert Dormer in 1635 and still owned by the same family. William Kent improved the house in the 18th century by adding the wings and stable block. In the magnificent garden, the complete Kent layout has survived. There is a fine herd of rare Longhorn cattle in the park, and the walled garden is a treat not to be missed.

Another unclassified road leads south on to the B4030 in turn leading to the A4095 for the 9 miles (14km) to Bicester.

❿ Bicester, Oxfordshire

Little can be seen of the Roman town at Alchester, to the south of Bicester, but excavations show that people lived here from about the middle of the 1st century AD until the late Roman period. Bicester itself is an market town with many old streets to explore. Its church contains elements of a 13th-century building, and there was once a 12th-century priory near by.

Take the A41 following the line of an old Roman road and then the B4011 towards Thame before turning sharp right to Boarstall.

⓫ Boarstall, Buckinghamshire

This tiny hamlet is the location of Boarstall Tower, an amazing stone gatehouse which was originally part of a massive fortified house. It dates from the 14th century and is now looked after by the National Trust, who also own Boarstall Duck Decoy. This 18th-century decoy is in 13 acres (5 hectares) of natural old woodland. Attractions include a small exhibition hall, nature trail and bird hide.

Take unclassified roads via Horton-cum-Studley along the edge of Otmoor for the return to Oxford.

The Causeway Coast

Larne is a busy port, the terminus for the shortest sea-crossing between Ireland and Britain. To the north is Carnfunnock Park, which has a maze in the shape of Northern Ireland. Larne marks the start of the scenic Antrim Coast Road, which was constructed in the 1830s to link the remote Glens of Antrim to the rest of Ulster.

2/3 days 163 miles (263km)

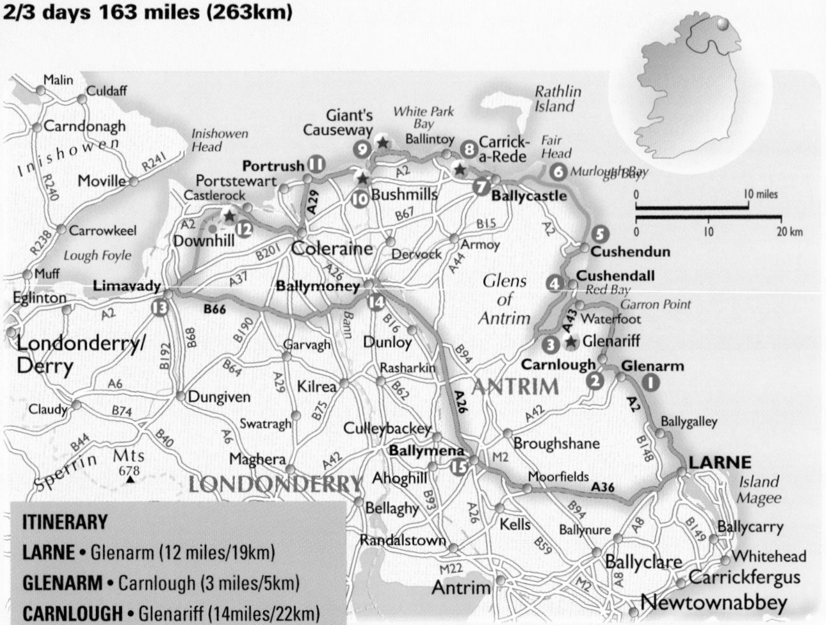

ITINERARY

LARNE • Glenarm (12 miles/19km)
GLENARM • Carnlough (3 miles/5km)
CARNLOUGH • Glenariff (14miles/22km)
GLENARIFF • Cushendall (7 miles/11km)
CUSHENDALL • Cushendun (6 miles/10km)
CUSHENDUN • Fair Head (10 miles/16km)
FAIR HEAD • Ballycastle (6 miles/10km)
BALLYCASTLE • Carrick-a-Rede (6 miles/10km)
CARRICK-A-REDE • Giant's Causeway (8 miles/13km)
GIANT'S CAUSEWAY • Bushmills (2 miles/3km)
BUSHMILLS • Portrush (6 miles/10km)
PORTRUSH • Downhill (12 miles/19km)
DOWNHILL • Limavady (11 miles/18km)
LIMAVADY • Ballymoney (20 miles/32km)
BALLYMONEY • Ballymena (19 miles/31km)
BALLYMENA • Larne (21 miles/34km)

Take the A2 coastal road north for 12 miles (19km) to Glenarm.

❶ Glenarm, Co Antrim

The Antrim Coast Road is so attractive that it is difficult to resist its magnetic lure, but leave it for a moment to sample the charm of Glenarm, a village that clings to the glen rather than to the coast. The neo-Tudor Glenarm Castle is the seat of the Earls of Antrim; its barbican and battlemented, buttressed walls of 1825 rise above the river just as it approaches the sea. The village has twisting streets (Thackeray apparently enjoyed their names), pavements patterned in limestone and basalt, a market house with an Italianate campanile and good, modest Georgian houses and shops.

All along the Antrim Coast Road, wonderful views unfold to delight the visitor

The forest, through the gateway at the top of the village, gives the first opportunity to walk up a delectable Antrim glen. This one is narrow, leafy and dense with pathways and abundant waterfalls.

Take the A2 to Carnlough.

❷ Carnlough, Co Antrim
Carnlough, at the foot of Glencloy, the least dramatic of the glens, has a good, safe beach. A railway used to carry lime from the kilns above the village to the harbour, over the bridge that spans the coast road. The bridge, the clock tower and the former town hall are made from great chunks of limestone. Frances Anne Vane Tempest Stewart, Countess of Antrim and Marchioness of Londonderry, was responsible for many major works, including Garron Tower, built in 1848, once a family home, now a boarding school. She is remembered in the town's main hotel, the Londonderry Arms, which was built in 1854 and has the feel of a coaching inn.

Take the A2, following signposts for Cushendall for 9 miles (14km) to Waterfoot. Turn left on to the A43 for 5 miles (8km) to Glenariff Forest Park.

❸ Glenariff, Co Antrim
The road obligingly provides a perfect route along this magnificent glen. The bay at its foot is 1 mile (1.6km) long and the chiselled sides draw in the fertile valley symmetrically to the head of the glen. There, the Forest Park allows easy exploration of the deep, wooded gorge with its cascades, 'Ess-na-crub' (Fall of the Hoof), 'Ess-na-laragh' (Fall of the Mare) and Tears of the Mountain.

Waterfoot, the little village at the foot of the glen, hosts The Glens of Antrim Feis (pronounced 'fesh') in July, a major festival of traditional music and dancing.

Between Red Bay and the pier are three caves. Nanny's Cave was inhabited by Ann Murray until her death, aged 100, in 1847. She supported herself by knitting and by selling poteen (an illicit distillation, pronounced potcheen).

Turn right to follow the B14 to Cushendall.

❹ Cushendall, Co Antrim
'The Capital of the Glens', Cushendall sits on a pleasant, sandy bay below Glenballyemon, Glenaan and Glencorp and in the curve of the River Dall. The rugged peak of Lurigethan broods over the village, while the softer Tieveragh Hill is supposedly the capital of the fairies. Cushendall owes much to an East Indian nabob, Francis Turnley, who built the Curfew Tower in the centre as a 'place for the confinement of idlers and rioters'.

In a tranquil valley by the sea just north of the village is the 13th-century church of Layde. The MacDonnells of Antrim are buried here, as are Englishmen stationed in these lonely posts as coastguards, and one memorial stone mourns an emigré killed in the American Civil War in 1865 when he was only 18 years old.

Continue on the A2 for 3 miles (5km), then turn right on to the B92 for Cushendun.

❺ Cushendun, Co Antrim
The very decided character of Cushendun is a surprise. This is a black-and-white village, with an orderly square and terraces of houses that were designed to look Cornish. Lord Cushendun married a Cornish wife, Maud, and commissioned the distinguished architect Clough Williams-Ellis to create a street-scape with style.

A little salmon fishery stands at the mouth of the River Dun, the 'dark brown water'. To the south is Cave House, locked in cliffs and approachable only through a long, natural cave. Castle Carra is to the north, the place where the clan quarrel between the O'Neills and the MacDonnells caused the treacherous murder of the great Shane O'Neill during a banquet in 1567.

At the north end of the village turn on to the road signposted 'scenic route' for Ballycastle by Torr Head. After 9 miles (14km) turn right to Murlough Bay.

❻ Fair Head and Murlough Bay, Co Antrim
Paths from the cluster of houses known as Coolanlough cross the barren headland broken by three dark lakes – Lough Doo, Lough Fadden and Lough na Cranagh, which has a crannóg or lake dwelling. Fair Head itself is exposed and barren, a place inhabited by wild goats and choughs (red-legged crows). The careful walker can descend the cliff using the Grey Man's Path, which follows a dramatic plunging fissure.

By contrast, Murlough Bay is green and fertile, generous in contours and abundantly wooded. Tradition has it that the Children of Lir were transformed into swans to spend 300 years here. At the top of the road is a monument to the Republican leader Sir Roger Casement, and a row of lime kilns, which would have burned the stone for use in fertiliser, whitewash or mortar.

After 1 mile (2km) turn right for Ballycastle, then right again on to the A2 to Ballycastle.

❼ Ballycastle, Co Antrim
There are two parts to Ballycastle – the winding main street which carries you up to the heart of the town, and Ballycastle by the sea, with its fine beach and tennis courts.

At the foot of the Margy River is Bonamargy Friary, founded by the Franciscans as late as 1500. The notorious Sorley Boy MacDonald is buried here. Elizabeth I found that he eluded all her attempts at capture, but in 1575, when he had sent his children to Rathlin Island for safety, he had to stand on the mainland helpless while they were murdered.

Ballycastle's museum illustrates the folk and social history of the Glens of Antrim.

At the harbour is a memorial to Gugliemo Marconi, who carried out the first practical test on radio signals between White Lodge, on the clifftop at Ballycastle, and Rathlin Island in 1898. You can travel by boat to Rathlin and savour the life of the 30 or so families who live and farm here. The island is a mecca for divers and birders. Robert the

Bruce hid in a cave on Rathlin after his defeat in 1306. Watching a spider repeatedly trying to climb a thread to the roof, he was encouraged to 'try, and try again'. He returned to Scotland to fight on, and was successful at the Battle of Bannockburn.

From the shore follow the B15 coastal route west for Ballintoy, then turn right, following the signpost to Carrick-a-Rede and Larry Bane.

8 Carrick-a-Rede, Co Antrim
A swinging rope bridge spans the deep chasm between the mainland and the rocky island of Carrick-a-Rede, and if you have a very strong heart and a good head, you can cross it. The bridge is put up each year by salmon fishermen, who use Carrick-a-Rede, 'the Rock in the Road', as a good place to net the fish in their path to the Bush and Bann rivers. The rope bridge is approached from Larry Bane, a limestone head which had once been quarried. Some of the quarry workings remain, and the quarry access to the magnificent seascape provides some guaranteed birding. It is possible to sit in your car and spot kittiwakes, cormorants, guillemots, fulmars and razorbills, though you might have to use binoculars to catch sight of the puffins on Sheep Island further out to sea.

Just to the west is Ballintoy, a very pretty little limestone harbour, at the foot of a corkscrew road. A little further west is the breathtaking sandy sweep of White Park Bay, accessible only on foot, and worth every step. Among the few houses that fringe the west end of the beach, tucked into the cliff, is Ireland's smallest church, dedicated to St Gobhan, patron saint of builders.

Take the B15 to join the A2 for Portrush, then turn right on to the B146 for the Giant's Causeway.

9 Giant's Causeway, Co Antrim
Sixty million years ago, or thereabouts, intensely hot volcanic lava erupted through narrow vents and, in cooling rapidly over the white chalk, formed into about 37,000 extraordinary geometric columns and shapes – mostly hexagonal, but also with four, five, seven or eight sides. That is one story. The other is that the giant, Finn MacCool, fashioned it so that he could cross dry-shod to Scotland.

The most famous sight in Ireland, the Giant's Causeway never fails to amaze and delight

Generations of guides have embroidered stories and created names for the remarkable formations – the Giant's Organ, the Giant's Harp, the Wishing Chair, and Lord Antrim's Parlour. The Visitor Centre tells the full story of the fact and fiction, the folklore and traditions, and provides a bus service down the steep road to the Causeway.

One story absolutely based on fact is of the Girona, a fleeing Spanish Armada galleon, wrecked in a storm on the night of 26 October 1588. A diving team retrieved a treasure hoard from the wreck in 1967, now on display in the Ulster Museum in Belfast. The wreck still lies under cliffs in Port na Spaniagh, one of a magnificent march of bays and headlands on the Causeway.

The 'water of life', patiently maturing in oak barrels at the Bushmills Distillery

Near the Visitor Centre is the Causeway School Museum, a reconstructed 1920s schoolroom, complete with learning aids and toys of the era.

Take the A2 to Bushmills.

⑩ Bushmills, Co Antrim
This neat village is the home of the world's oldest legal distillery, which was granted its licence in 1608. The water from St Columb's rill, or stream, is said to give the whiskey its special quality, and visitors can discover something of its flavour on tours of the distillery.

The River Bush is rich in trout and salmon, and its fast-flowing waters not only supported the mills that gave the town its name, but generated electricity for the world's first hydroelectric tramway, which carried passengers to the Giant's Causeway between 1893 and 1949.

Follow the A2 west to Portrush.

⑪ Portrush, Co Antrim
Portrush is a typical seaside resort, which flourished with the rise of the railways. It has three good bays, with broad stretches of sand, ranges of dunes, rock pools, white cliffs and a busy harbour.

Nearby Dunluce is one of the most romantic of castles, where a sprawling ruin clings perilously to the clifftop, presenting a splendid profile. The castle was a MacDonnell stronghold until half the kitchen fell into the sea on a stormy night in 1639. The Dunluce Centre is a high-tech entertainment complex.

Take the A29 for Coleraine, then follow the A2 for Castlerock, then on to Downhill, a distance of 12 miles (19km).

⑫ Downhill, Co Londonderry
The feast of magnificent coastal scenery is given a different face at Downhill. Here Frederick Hervey, who was Earl of Bristol and Bishop of Derry, decided to adorn nature with man's art, by creating a landscape with eyecatching buildings, artificial ponds and cascades, in keeping with the taste of the time. He was a great 18th-century eccentric, collector and traveller, who gave his name to the Bristol hotels throughout Europe. Although nature has won back much of the Earl Bishop's ambitious scheme, the spirit of the place is strongly felt, and Mussenden Temple, a perfect classical rotunda, sits on a wonderful headland.

Near by is 20th-century man's idea of seaside recreation, at Benone Tourist Complex, beside the 7 mile (11km) Benone Strand, one of the cleanest beaches in Europe, backed by a duneland park.

From the A2 turn left on Bishop's Road for Gortmore, then after 8 miles (13km) turn right on to the B201, then left on to the A2 for Limavady.

⑬ Limavady, Co Londonderry
The Roe Valley was the territory of the O'Cahans, and O'Cahan's Rock is one of the landmarks of the nearby Roe Valley Country

Farming the old-fashioned way at the Leslie Hill Open Farm in northern County Antrim

Park. One story says that it was here a dog made a mighty leap with a message to help relieve a besieged castle, giving this pleasant market town its name, 'The Leap of the Dog'.

The Londonderry Air was first written down here by Jane Ross, when she heard it being played by a street fiddler. Limavady was the birthplace of William Massey (1856–1925), Prime Minister of New Zealand from 1912 to 1925.

Take the A37 for Coleraine, then turn right on to the B66; follow signs for the B66 to Ballymoney.

⓮ Ballymoney, Co Antrim
A bustling town, Ballymoney recalls its farming past at Leslie Hill Open Farm, where visitors can travel through the park by horse and trap. Drumaheglis Marina provides access to the River Bann, elsewhere a fairly secluded river, and offers waterbus cruises. Three miles (5km) northeast, in Conagher, off the road to Dervock, is the birthplace of the 25th President of the US, William McKinley (1843–1901).

Take the A26 to Ballymena.

⓯ Ballymena, Co Antrim
Ballymena, the county town of Antrim, boasts as one of its sons Timothy Eaton, who founded the now defunct Eaton's Stores in Canada. To the east the hump of Slemish Mountain rises abruptly from the ground. It was here that St Patrick worked when he was first brought to Ireland as a slave. In the southern suburbs is the 40-foot (12m) high Harryville motte and bailey – one of the finest surviving Anglo-Norman earthworks in Ulster.

Just to the west is 17th-century Galgorm Castle, a Plantation castle built by Sir Faithful Fortescue in 1618. Beyond is the charming village of Gracehill, founded by the Moravians in the 18th century.

Take the A36 for 21 miles (34km) and return to Larne.

Of Alps, Lakes & Plain

Lombardy is crossed by the huge River Po and studded with great lakes – Maggiore, Garda, Como, Iseo and Lugano. Since the Middle Ages it has been a prosperous commercial region. Milano (Milan) nowadays is the thriving economic capital of Italy but the traces of its cultural past are everywhere.

4 days 728km (452 miles)

DRIVE ITINERARY

MILANO • Sacro Monte Varese (65km/40m)

SACRO MONTE VARESE • Lago Maggiore (32km/20m)

LAGO MAGGIORE • Como (76km/47m)

COMO • Lecco – around Lake Como (109km/68m)

LECCO • Bellagio (22km/14m)

BELLAGIO • Bergamo (61km/38m)

BERGAMO • Lago di Garda (78km/48m)

LAGO DI GARDA • Mantova (48km-30m)

MANTOVA • Cremona (66km/41m)

CREMONA • Pavia (136km/84m)

PAVIA • Milano (35km/22m)

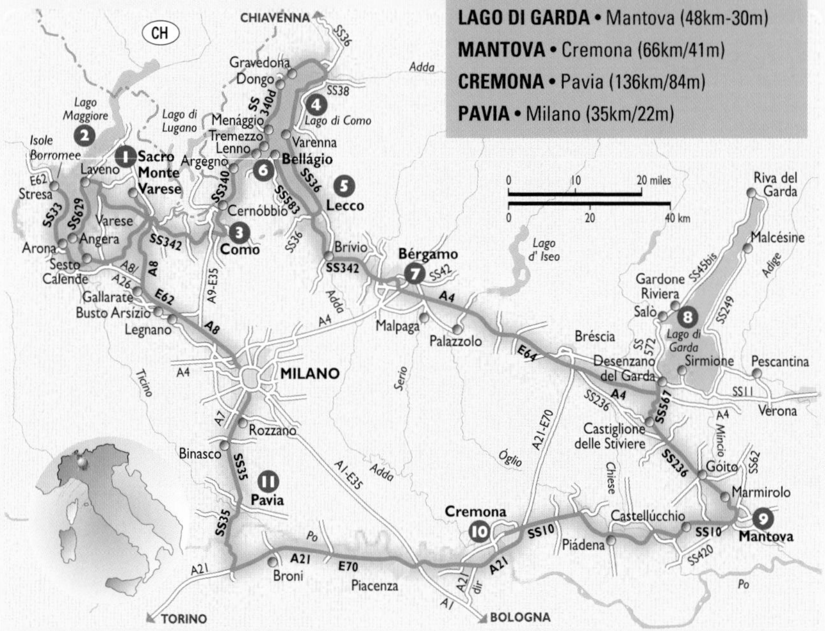

From Milano, take the A8 going north (via Legnano and Gallarate) – the latter about 38km (24 miles) – to Varese, about another 17km (10 miles). About 10km (6 miles) north of Varese lies Sacro Monte Varese.

❶ Sacro Monte Varese, Lombardia

The 'Sacred Mountain of Varese', with its narrow passages and ancient covered alleys, is only the backdrop for a pilgrimage route more famous nowadays for its art than for its saintly connections. It is supposed to have been founded by St Ambrose in thanks for Lombardy's deliverance from the Arian heresy (the doctrine put forward by the 4th-century theologian Arius, that Christ is not one body with God).

From the bottom of the Sacro Monte to the top, about 800m (2,625 feet), is a cobbled route with 14 chapels at intervals along the Sacred Way, each one dedicated to the Mystery of the Rosary. The shrines are the work of Bernascone and each is filled with life-size terracotta figures, by Bussola, acting out some religious episode. At the top is the lavishly decorated Church of Santa Maria del Monte. The views from the Sacro Monte are wonderful and, to restore you after the climb, you will find cafés and restaurants in the town.

From Sacro Monte Varese, go back to Varese, then continue on the SS342 to Lago Maggiore, about 22km (14 miles).

❷ Lago Maggiore, Lombardia
Only the eastern shore of Lago Maggiore (Lake Maggiore) is in Lombardia. Its western shore is in Piedmont and its northern part in Switzerland. It would take days to drive around the lake seeing all that there is to look at. These are the highlights.

At Angera is the Borromeo fortress (open to the public), which contains well-preserved 14th-century frescoes, a doll museum and a museum of children's clothing from the 18th century to the 1950s.

At Arona is another castle, this time ruined. Visit the Church of Santa Maria with, in the Borromeo Chapel, an altarpiece of 1511 by Ferrari.

Stresa is the largest resort on the lake. Full of Victorian-style hotels, it is also dotted with old-fashioned villas and luxurious gardens running down to the water's edge. Some gardens are open, including the Villa Pallavicino.

But the real gem of Maggiore is the Borromean islands. Isola Bella, perhaps the best known, is a huge private garden surrounding a palace (Palazzo Borromeo) – both open to the public. The gardens were laid out for Count Carlo III Borromeo in the 17th century by Angelo Crivelli. The elaborate complex includes white peacocks, grottoes, fountains and statuary. Isola Madre is another of the islands, famous for its large botanical garden which, with its palace, is well worth a visit.

Make for Varese from Stresa, take the SS33 to Sesto Calende at the foot of the lake, about 25km (16 miles), then follow signs to Varese, about 23km (14 miles). From Varese, take the SS342 to Como.

❸ Como, Lombardia
Como was the birthplace of the Roman writer Pliny the Elder. In fact you will see signs dotted around Lago di Como (Lake Como) pointing to the sites of the various villas the Pliny family owned here. One of the most elegant towns on the lake, Como is a centre for the production of fine fabrics, and it has an interesting silk museum. There is a waterfront promenade, busy cafés, palm trees and parks. The Duomo (cathedral) dates mainly from the 15th century. The rose window on the façade is Gothic in style and there is excellent carving by the Rodari brothers of Maroggia, from about 1500.

Other relics of old Como include the churches of San Abbondio, San Fedele, which was once the cathedral, and the Porta Vittoria, the late 12th-century city gate. The Museum of Archaeology contains an enormous collection of pre-Roman and Roman finds. The History Museum shares the same building.

Como also has a good art gallery, with classical, abstractionist and futurist works. See also the Temple of Alessandro Volta, which has equipment used by the man who gave his name to the electric volt.

From Como, drive around Lago di Como, starting on the SS340 up the left-hand side of the lake.

❹ Lago di Como, Lombardia
All around the lake you will see vast villas and castles overlooking the water. Cernóbbio is a pretty town about 7km (4.5 miles) from Como. Here is the grand Hotel Villa D'Este, once the home of the English Queen Caroline.

At Tremezzo is the Villa Carlotta, once lived in by Princess Carlotta of Prussia, who laid out its gardens in the 1850s. You can visit this as well as the Villa Arconati, just a few kilometres outside Tremezzo, at Lenno. Further on around the lake are Menaggio and Gravedona.

At nearby Dongo, Mussolini was captured by the partisans in 1945. On the other side of the lake, at Varenna, visit the Villa Monastero with its formal gardens and the Romanesque

Church of San Giorgio. One really good way to see the lake – and admire the towns from a distance – is to take a boat trip around it. It is possible to take one that stops at a number of places, using it like a bus.

Lecco lies at the foot of the eastern arm of Lake Como, from Como itself a direct distance of 29km (18 miles).

❺ Lecco, Lombardia

Lecco is in direct contrast to its illustrious neighbour Como. More industrial than prettier Como, Lecco's claim to fame is that it was the birthplace of Alessandro Manzoni, the great 19th-century Italian novelist. The Villa Manzoni, his former home, is now a museum – you will find it in Via Promessi Sposi, named after the writer's most famous novel which, translated, means 'The Betrothed' (the street is also known as Via Amendola). While you are in town, visit the Duomo, with its 14th-century frescos in the style of Giotto, and the Ponte Azzone Visconti, a medieval bridge over the Adda river. Although much altered (it no longer has any towers) and enlarged, it still has much of its early character.

From Lecco, take the SS583 up the western edge of Lecco's portion of Lake Como to Bellagio.

❻ Bellagio, Lombardia

Bellagio is one of the most beautiful points on Lake Como. Not only is it an interesting old town, but it is splendidly sited on a promontory overlooking the three arms of the lake. There is plenty to do here apart from just sitting in the sun enjoying the view. The 12th-century Basilica of San Giacomo has good carving in the apse. There is Villa Serbelloni, whose gardens can be visited, and Villa Melzi d'Eril, the gardens of which are open to the public. If time is short, the Villa Sebelloni gardens, supposed to stand on the site of the younger Pliny's villa 'Tragedia', are the more interesting.

Gaily painted boats along the quayside in the resort of Sirmione on Lake Garda

Return to Lecco, then take the SS36 going south for about 15km (9 miles) until it cuts the SS342. Take the latter to Bergamo, about 24km (15 miles).

❼ Bergamo, Lombardia

Bergamo is divided into the Città Alta and the Città Bassa, the Upper City and the Lower City. The former is the more interesting, as well as being the older. Its best monuments are in the Piazza Vecchia. In it is the late 16th-century Biblioteca Civica (Civic Library), modelled on Venice's great library building, designed by Sansovino. Across the square, past Contarini's fountain surrounded by stone lions, is the 12th-century Torre Civica with its 15th-century clock that still tolls the curfew hour (10pm). Behind the 12th-century Palazzo della Ragione are the Duomo and the ornate Colleoni Chapel. You can just see the base of the latter through the pointed arched loggia beneath the Palazzo della Ragione. Built in 1476, the façade of the Colleoni Chapel is a mass of sculptured decoration and coloured marble. Inside is the tomb and a statue of Bartolomeo Colleoni, who controlled Venice's armed forces in the 15th century. The ceiling fresco is by Tiepolo.

The elegant buildings lining the quayside at Bellagio, left, one of the most attractive of the lakeside resorts, are best viewed on a tour by boat

The Church of Santa Maria Maggiore, in Piazza Duomo, is a fine Romanesque building with a sumptuous interior. Also in the Upper City is the Cittadella (citadel), which contains the Natural History Museum, and the Museo Donizetti – this great composer was born in Bergamo, and you can visit the Teatro Donizetti in the Lower City. Between the Upper and Lower Cities is the Galleria dell'Accademia Carrara, a first-class collection of art, well worth taking in.

From Bergamo, take the A4 via Brescia to Lago di Garda, about 78km (48 miles) – at Desenzano del Garda at the foot of the lake.

❽ Lago di Garda, Lombardia

The most interesting ports of call around Lago (Lake) di Garda are Salò, Gardone Riviera, Riva del Garda, Malcesine and Sirmione. All are accessible by the steamer, and rather than drive around the lake, you could leave the car at Desenzano del Garda and go by boat. Salò has a fine Gothic Duomo (cathedral) with a noteworthy Renaissance portal. At Gardone Riviera, most things to visit have something to do with Gabriele d'Annunzio (1863–1938), one of the greatest writers and poets of his generation. His villa, Vittoriale degli Italiani was specially built for him and can be visited. The villa and grounds are filled with an extraordinary array of bits and pieces, like the great ornate organs in the music room, among which the writer chose to live. There is also a museum and a mausoleum in the villa's grounds.

At Riva del Garda, right at the northern tip of the lake, about 95 breathtaking kilometres (60 miles) away from Desenzano del Garda up the western edge of the lake, and actually in the Trentino region, is a 13th-century tower, the Torre Apponale, and a clutter of other ancient edifices of which the Palazzo Pretorio and the 12th-century Rocca (fortress) are the most interesting. The town's Museo Civico (Civic Museum) contains an interesting collection of armour and archaeological finds from the area, housed in the Rocca.

Malcesine, halfway down the eastern edge of the lake, is the proud possessor of the magnificent Castello Scaligero (Scaliger Castle) dramatically situated at the water's edge. But the castle at Sirmione is more remarkable. Also from the 13th century and one of the Scaligeri castles, its battlements and its dramatic situation half in the water make it possibly the most memorable sight on the Lago di Garda.

From Desenzano del Garda, take the SS567 for 11km (7 miles) to Castiglione delle Stiviere, at which branch on to the SS236 and continue on to Mantova, about 37km (23 miles).

❾ Mantova, Lombardia
Mantova (Mantua) sits on a swampy, marshy bend in the Mincio River. Its claim to fame is that it was the seat of one of the most intellectually active and refined courts of the Italian Renaissance. The Gonzaga family were the rulers and they embellished the town with a remarkable Palazzo Ducale (Ducal Palace) that still contains some of their art collection. The neo-classical rooms have a set of early 16th-century Flemish tapestries and the duke's apartments have a fine collection of classical statuary. Here you will see Rubens' vast portrait of the Gonzaga family. The Camera degli Sposi in the Castel di San Giorgio is world famous for its brilliant frescos by Mantegna, finished in 1474. Apart from a series of portraits of the family, there are others of their favourite dwarfs. In the Casetta dei Nani, the House of the Dwarfs, you can see the miniature rooms where the latter were once thought to have lived. The Palazzo del Té is another Gonzaga palace built by Giulio Romano in 1527 for Federico II Gonzaga's mistress. The Sala dei Giganti, the Room of the Giants, is its masterpiece: huge frescoed fighting giants seem to bring down the ceiling. The Basilica of Sant'Andrea, designed by Leon Battista (1472), houses a chalice of Christ's blood, a relic once much venerated by the Gonzaga.

Take the SS10 for 66km (41 miles) to Cremona.

❿ Cremona, Lombardia
You cannot come to Cremona and not visit the Museo Stradivariano (Stradivarian Museum). The modern violin was developed in this city in 1566, and one of the great masters of violin-making here – though much later – was Antonio Stradivarius. The Town Hall has a valuable collection of violins, including instruments by Stradivari, Amati and Guarneri. There is also the Museo Civico (Civic Museum) in which much space is devoted to Roman Cremona. The Duomo (cathedral) has five wonderful 17th-century Brussels tapestries as well as a series of frescos by local artists. The tall bell tower of the cathedral can also be visited, and there are fine views from the top. Among the town's most interesting churches is Sant' Agostino with a Madonna and Saints by Perugino, who was once Raphael's teacher.

From Cremona, take the A21 via Piacenza for 33km (20 miles) as far as the Casteggio turning, 82km (51 miles), for the SS35 to Pavia, a further 21km (13 miles).

⓫ Pavia, Lombardia
Pavia was at one time an important Roman city (*Ticinum*). Little remains today, though the municipal museums in Castello Visconteo contain finds from Roman times and early Pavia. On an upper floor you will find the picture gallery with works by, among others, Bellini and Van der Goes, the latter one of the most important of the Flemish Renaissance painters.

The most noteworthy monument to visit is the Certosa di Pavia, a remarkable, highly decorative Renaissance monastery complex, situated just on the outskirts of town. A tour will take in the vestibule, the cloisters and the church with Gothic, Renaissance and baroque decoration.

Back in the town, Leonardo was partially responsible for the design of the Duomo, begun in 1488, and in addition to the cathedral, there are about six other churches worth seeing.

Take the SS35 back to Milano, about 35km (22 miles).

Roman Relics & Golden Beaches

Barcelona's hills, Montjuïc and Tibidabo, are great places for entertainment. Museums, from modern to Romanesque art, and the Olympic Stadium are on Montjuïc, which rises above the city's brilliantly redeveloped seafront. Tibidabo has a funfair and stunning panoramic views. Below lies the amazing Gaudí creation of Parc Güell.

2/3 days 597km (373 miles)

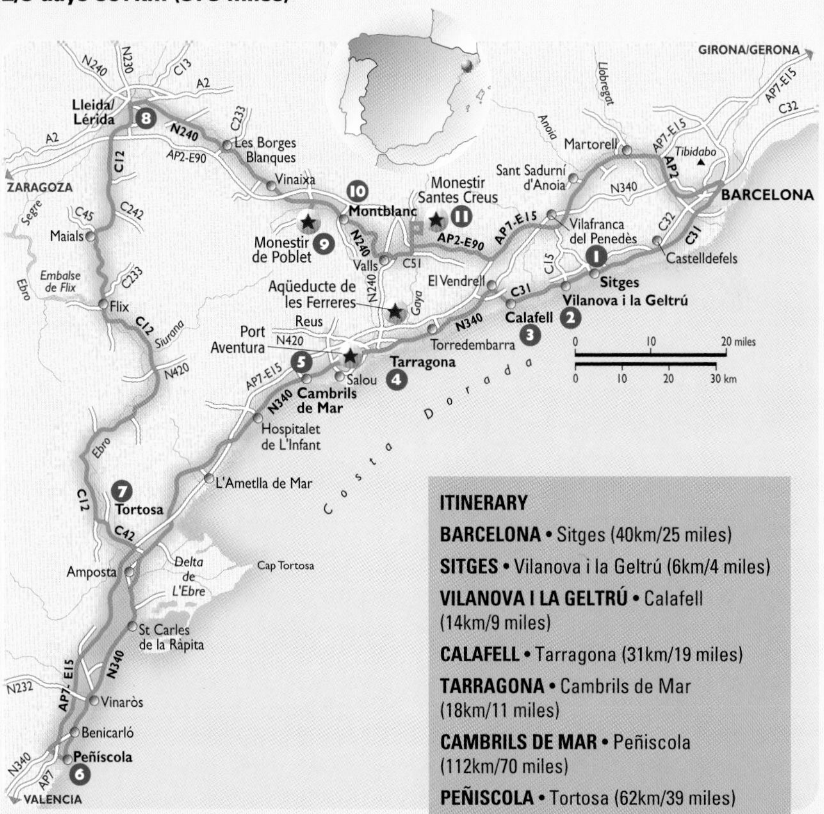

ITINERARY

BARCELONA • Sitges (40km/25 miles)

SITGES • Vilanova i la Geltrú (6km/4 miles)

VILANOVA I LA GELTRÚ • Calafell (14km/9 miles)

CALAFELL • Tarragona (31km/19 miles)

TARRAGONA • Cambrils de Mar (18km/11 miles)

CAMBRILS DE MAR • Peñíscola (112km/70 miles)

PEÑÍSCOLA • Tortosa (62km/39 miles)

TORTOSA • Lleida (128km/80 miles)

LLEIDA • Monestir de Poblet (53km/33 miles)

MONESTIR DE POBLET • Montblanc (8km/5 miles)

MONTBLANC • Monestir Santes Creus (35km/22 miles)

MONESTIR SANTES CREUS • Barcelona (90km/56 miles)

Leave Barcelona from the Plaça Espanya and take the C31 southwest to Sitges.

❶ Sitges, Barcelona

Sitges is a traditional resort that lured Spanish families long before it became an international tourist centre. As well as its splendid sandy beach and shallow waters, Sitges is a picturesque little town with great charm. The local church, with its rose-

Situated on the outskirts of Tarragona, on the road to Valls, are the impressive remains of the Roman aqueduct Les Ferreres

coloured façade, adds to the picture. The Cau Ferrat Museum, once home of the writer and artist Santiago Rusinyol (1861–1931), houses a collection of his paintings, together with works by El Greco, Picasso, Utrillo and others.

Take a minor road southwest for 6km (4 miles) to Vilanova i la Geltrú (Vilanueva y Geltrú).

❷ Vilanova i la Geltrú, Barcelona
This is an industrial town and a resort, with a fine sandy beach and picturesque fishing harbour. It has two museums of interest: the Museu Romàntic Casa Papiol, which is housed in an elegantly furnished town house and devoted to life in the early 1800s; and the Biblioteca Museu Balaguer, which is noted for its fine collection of antiquities and Catalan paintings.

Continue down the C31 coast road to Calafell, 14km (9 miles).

❸ Calafell, Barcelona
The small fishing village of Calafell is another favourite summer resort with a long sandy beach, suitable for a quiet stop and a look at the Romanesque parish church and the ruins of the 12th-century castle.

Continue on the C31 to El Vendrell and join the N340 to Tarragona.

❹ Tarragona, Tarragona
The route passes through El Vendrell, the birthplace of the famous Spanish cellist, Pablo Casals (1876–1973).

The old Roman town of Tarragona was founded by Publius Cornelius Scipio during the Second Punic War of 218 BC. A stroll along the attractive tree-lined Rambla Nova leads to the observation platform '*Balcó del Mediterrani*', which offers a sweeping view of the coast. Below is the harbour and the Parc del Miracle, where you can see the remnants of a 2nd- or 3rd-century BC Roman amphitheatre, once the venue for combats between man and beast. The Museu

This quiet corner in Tortosa is typical of the historic towns in the region

National Arqueològic has mosaics, ceramics and antiquities from the region. A climb from the centre of town takes you to the cathedral, which was built between the 12th and 14th centuries. It shows a harmonious blending of Romanesque and Gothic styles, with a fine façade and lovely rose window in the centre. The Passeig Arqueologic is a pleasant shaded walk along the foot of the massive city ramparts, which extend for some 1,000m (1,100 yards) and up to 10m (33 feet) in parts.

The Museu y Necrópolis Paleocristina, on the outskirts of the town, has a fine display of tombs, mosaics and jewellery. Adjoining it is an old Christian cemetery dating back to the 3rd century.

Continue on the N340 south to Cambrils de Mar.

❺ Cambrils de Mar, Tarragona
Cambrils de Mar is a picturesque little port with a maritime tradition. The harbour is dominated by an ancient church tower, originally a Roman defence fortification. The port becomes a hive of activity when the fishing fleet comes in, and has a reputation for good eating.

Continue south down the coastal road (N340) for 112km (70 miles) to Peñiscola.

❻ Peñiscola, Castellón
This is a veritable jewel of a place, rising like a fortress from a rocky peninsula that juts out to sea. The town was taken from the Moors in 1233 by King Jaime I. Its main feature is the castle, an impressive structure built by the Knights Templars. Later, the deposed antipope, Benedict XIII (Pope Luna), took refuge in the castle and spent his last years here until his death in 1422. The castle offers magnificent views of the coastline. Within the surrounding walls is the old town, a labyrinth of tiny winding streets – strictly for pedestrians only.

Drive inland to join the AP7 north, turning off after 46km (29 miles) on the C42 to Tortosa.

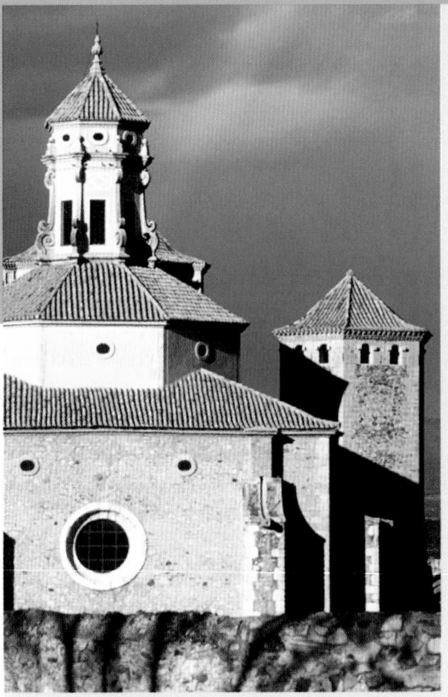

The Monestir de Poblet is one of the largest Cistercian abbeys in Spain

❼ Tortosa, Tarragona
The episcopal town of Tortosa holds a commanding position over the delta of the River Ebre. The cathedral was begun in 1347 and built over a long period of time. The naves are 14th-century Gothic, while the façade and the chapel to the Mare de Deu de la Cinta (the Virgin), patron saint of the city, are baroque.

Other buildings of note in the town are the 14th-century Palau Episcopal and the Colegio de Sant Lluis, which was founded i n 1544 by Emperor Charles V for converts from the Moorish faith, and has an elegant courtyard with some fine decoration. Many splendid old palaces from the 15th and 16th centuries can be seen, as well as remains of the city walls.

Take the C12 north to Maials, then the C12 to Lleida (Lérida).

❽ Lleida, Lleida/Lérida
Originally an Iberian settlement, Lleida came under the Romans in the 2nd century BC and was the scene of numerous battles and sieges over the years. It was the birthplace of Enrique Granados (1867–1916), famed for his classical guitar compositions.

Enclosed within the city walls is the Seu Vella (old cathedral), which is dominated by a tall 14th-century octagonal tower. Built between the 12th and 15th centuries, it shows the transition from Romanesque to Gothic. During the 18th century the cathedral was used as a garrison and has been undergoing restoration for some years. It has a fine Gothic cloister, noted for its tall, graceful arches.

Lleida also has a new cathedral. The Seu Nova was built in the 18th century in neo-classical style, and was the first of its kind in Catalunya. Other sights of interest include the 13th-century town hall; the Palau de la Paería, which is noted for its fine façade; and the churches of Sant Llorenc and Sant Martín. The 15th-century hospital of Santa María houses the Museu Arqueològic, with Iberian and Roman relics from the area. Lleida is an excellent centre for excursions into the Pyrenees.

Take the N240 southeast towards Tarragona. Shortly after going under the AP2 (motorway) turn right to the Monestir de Poblet.

❾ Monestir de Poblet, Tarragona
Tucked away on the lower slopes of the Prades Mountains, the Monastery of Santa María de Poblet was founded in 1149 by Ramón Berenguer IV as a token of thanks to God for the regaining of Catalunya from the Moors. The following year 12 Cistercian monks, sent from Fontfroide (near Narbonne in France), began building the monastery which is a fine example of Cistercian art.

The monks benefited from the patronage of the Aragón kings, for whom the

The Church of Santa María, in the superb medieval town of Montblanc

monastery became a favourite stopping place for royal journeys. The lovely Gothic cloister and adjoining chapter house contain a number of abbots' tombstones in the pavement.

Rejoin the N240 and continue for 8km (5 miles) to Montblanc.

⑩ Montblanc, Tarragona

Montblanc is an impressive sight, with its massive medieval ramparts and towers and narrow entrance gates. Overlooking the town is the Church of Santa María begun in the 14th century and never fully completed.

Continue on the N240 southeast to Valls. Turn left on to the C51, then left again on a minor road, crossing the AP2 to Santes Creus.

⑪ Monestir Santes Creus, Tarragona

The Santes Creus monastery rises grandly over the forest around it. It is a fine example of the Cistercian style and is, like Poblet, among Catalunya's most important monasteries.

Founded in 1157, the monastery was occupied by Cistercian monks from France. It long enjoyed the favour of the Kings of Aragón but, like Poblet, it suffered damage during the wars of the 19th century, and is also under restoration. The church is 12th-century Romanesque and contains the royal tombs of former kings of Catalunya including that of Pedro III.

Return south to the AP2 and join the AP7 back to Barcelona, 90km (56 miles).

N1
LE T
LO

Part 4

Useful words and phrases

Dutch
Words and phrases

For clarity we have put the English phrase in light type, foreign language terms in dark type and their phonetic pronunciation in light italic.

Asking for directions

Excuse me, could I ask you something?
Pardon, mag ik u iets vragen?
Pardon, makh ik oo eets frakhen?

I've lost my way
Ik ben de weg kwijt
Ik ben de vekh kwayet

Is there a...around here?
Weet u een...in de buurt?
Vayt oo an...in de boo-ert

Is this the way to...?
Is dit de weg naar...?
Is dit de vekh naar...?

Could you tell me how to get to...by car/on foot?
Kunt u me zeggen hoe ik naar...moet rijden/lopen?
Kunt-oo me zekhen hoo ik naar...moot rayeden/loapen?

What's the quickest way to...?
Hoe kom ik het snelst in...?
Hoo kom ik het snel-ste in...?

How many kilometers is it to...?
Hoeveel kilometer is het nog naar...?
Hoofayl keelomayter is het nokh naar...?

Could you point it out on the map?
Kunt u het op de kaart aanwijzen?
Kunt oo het op de kaart aan-wayezen?

Ask the speaker to point to what they are saying

Ik weet het niet, ik ben hier niet bekend
I don't know, I don't know these parts

U zit verkeerd
You're going the wrong way

U moet terug naar...
You have to go back to...

Daar wijzen de borden u verder
From there on just follow the signs

Daar moet u het opnieuw vragen
When you get there, ask again

Useful words

rechtdoor
straight on
linksaf
turn left
rechtsaf
turn right
afslaan
turn
volgen
follow
oversteken
cross
de kruising
intersection
de straat
the street
het verkeerslicht
the traffic light
de tunnel
the tunnel/underpass
het verkeersbord 'voorrangskruising'
the 'give way' sign
het gebouw
the building
op de hoek
at the corner
de rivier
the river
het viaduct
the fly-over
de brug
the bridge
de spoorwegovergang/de spoorbomen
the level crossing/the crossing barriers
het bord richting...
the sign pointing to...
de pijl
the arrow

Road traffic signs

afrit
exit

alle richtingen
all directions

andere richtingen
other directions

centrum
town centre

doodlopende weg
dead end (cul-de-sac)

doorgaand verkeer gestremd
road closed

doorgaand verkeer
through traffic

eenrichtingsverkeer
one-way traffic

einde snelheidsbeperking
end of speed limit

fabrieksuitgang
works exit

fietsers
cyclists

fietspad
cycle path

gevaar
danger

gevaarlijke bochten
dangerous bends

helling
incline

ijzel
black ice

inrijden verboden
no entry

kruising
junction

langzaam
slow

links houden
keep left

maximum snelheid
maximum speed

ondergrondse parkeergarage
underground car park

ontsteek uw lichten
switch on lights

oversteekplaats voetgangers
pedestrian crossing

overweg
level crossing

parkeerplaats
parking/layby (out of town)

parkeerzone (parkeerschijf verplicht)
zone parking (disc must be shown)

rechts houden
keep right

rijbaan voor bus
bus lane

slecht wegdek
irregular road surface

slipgevaar
slippery road

snelheid verminderen
reduce speed

snelweg
motorway

stapvoets
drive at walking pace

steenslag
loose chippings

tegenliggers
oncoming traffic

uitgang
exit/way out

uitrit
exit

uitrit vrijlaten
keep exit free

verboden in te halen
no overtaking

verboden linksaf te slaan
no left turn

verboden rechtsaf te slaan
no right turn

verminder snelheid
reduce speed

verplichte rijrichting
compulsory route

voetgangers
pedestrians

voorangsweg
major road

voorrang verlenen
give way

voorsorteren
get in lane

wachtverbod
no waiting

weg afgesloten
road closed

wegomlegging
diversion

wegversmalling
road narrows

werk in uitvoering
roadworks

zachte berm
soft verge

ziekenhuis
hospital

French
Words and phrases

For clarity we have put the English phrase in light type, foreign language terms in dark type and their phonetic pronunciation in light italic.

Asking for directions

Excuse me, could I ask you something?
Pardon, puis-je vous demander quelque chose?
pahrdawn, pwee jhuh voo duhmohnday kehlkuh shoaz?

I've lost my way
Je me suis égaré(e)
jhuh muh swee zaygahray

Is there an... around here?
Connaissez-vous un...dans les environs?
konehssay voo zuhn... dohn lay zohnveerawn?

Is this the way to...?
Est-ce la route vers...?
ehs lah root vehr...?

Could you tell me how to get to...?
Pouvez-vous me dire comment aller à...?
poovay voo muh deer komohn tahlay ah...?

What's the quickest way to...?
Comment puis-je arriver le plus vite possible à...?
komohn pwee jhuh ahreevay luh plew veet pohseebl ah...?

How many kilometres is it to...?
Il y a encore combien de kilomètres jusqu'à...?
eel ee yah ohnkor kohnbyahn duh keeloamehtr jhewskah...?

Could you point it out on the map?
Pouvez-vous me l'indiquer sur la carte?
poovay voo muh lahndeekay sewr lah kahrt?

Ask the speaker to point to what they are saying

Je ne sais pas, je ne suis pas d'ici
I don't know, I don't know my way around here

Vous vous êtes trompé
You have to go back to...

Vous devez retourner à...
You're going the wrong way

Là-bas les panneaux vous indiqueront la route
From there on just follow the signs

Là-bas vous demanderez à nouveau votre route
When you get there, ask again

Useful words

tout droit
straight ahead
à gauche
left
à droite
right
tourner
turn
suivre
follow
traverser
cross
le carrefour
the intersection
la rue
the street
le feu (de signalisation)
the traffic light
le tunnel
the tunnel
le panneau 'cédez lapriorité'
the 'give way' sign
l'immeuble
the building
à l'angle, au coin
at the corner
la rivière, le fleuve
the river
l'autopont
the fly-over
le pont
the bridge
le passage à niveau
the level crossing
la barrière
boom
le panneau direction...
the sign pointing to...
la flèche
the arrow

Road traffic signs

chaussée à gravillons
loose chippings

chaussée déformée
uneven road surface

chaussée glissante
slippery road

circulation alternée
alternate priority

danger
danger

carrefour dangereux
dangerous crossing

danger priorité à droite
priority to vehicles from right

descente dangereuse
steep hill

déviation
diversion

fin de...
end of...

fin d'allumage des feux
end of need for lights

fin de chantier
end of roadworks

interdiction de dépasser
no overtaking

interdiction de klaxonner
no horns

interdiction sauf riverains
access only

limite de vitesse
speed limit

passage à niveau
level crossing

passage d'animaux
animals crossing

passage pour piétons
pedestrian crossing

péage
toll

poids lourds
heavy goods vehicles

rappel
reminder

remorques et semi-remorques
lorries and articulated lorries

sens unique
one-way traffic

serrez à droite
keep right

sortie
exit

sortie de camions
factory/works exit

interdiction de stationner
no parking

taxis
taxi rank

travaux (sur...km)
roadworks ahead

véhicules lents
slow traffic

véhicules transportant des matières dangereuses
vehicles transporting dangerous substances

verglas fréquent
ice on road

virages sur...km
bends for...km

vitesse limite
maximum speed

zone bleue
parking disc required

zone piétonne
pedestrian zone

German
Words and phrases

For clarity we have put the English phrase in light type, foreign language terms in dark type and their phonetic pronunciation in light italic.

Asking for directions

Excuse me, could I ask you something?
Verzeihung, dürfte ich Sie etwas fragen?
fair tsaioong, duerfter ikh zee etvass frargen?

I've lost my way
Ich habe mich verlaufen/(with car) mich verfahren
ikh harber mikh fairlowfen/mikh fairfahren

Is there a(n)... around here?
Wissen Sie, wo hier in der Nähe ein(e)...ist?
vissen zee, vo heer in dayr nayher ain(er)...ist?

Is this the way to...?
Ist dies die Strasse nach...?
ist dees dee shtrasser nakh...?

Could you tell me how to get to the... (name of place) by car/on foot?
Können Sie mir sagen, wie ich nach... (name of the place) fahren/gehen muss?
koenen zee meer zargen, vee ikh nakh ... fahren/gayhen muss?

What's the quickest way to...?
Wie komme ich am schnellsten nach...?
vee kommer ikh am shnellsten nakh...?

How many kilometres is it to...?
Wieviel Kilometer sind es noch bis...?
veefeel kilomayter zint ez nokh biss...?

Could you point it out on the map?
Können Sie es mir auf der Karte zeigen?
koennen zee ez meer owf dayr karter tsaigen?

Ask the speaker to point to what they are saying

Ich weiss nicht, ich kenne mich hier nicht aus
I don't know, I don't know my way around here

Da sind Sie hier nicht richtig
You're going the wrong way

Sie müssen zurück nach...
You have to go back to...

Sie fahren über die...Strasse
You take...Street

Sie fahren über die...Strasse drüber
You cross over...Street

Da sehen Sie schon die Schilder
From there on you will see the signs

Da müssen Sie noch mal fragen
When you get there, you will have to ask again

Useful words

geradeaus
straight
nach links/links abbiegen
left/turn left
nach rechts/ rechts abbiegen
right/turn right
abbiegen
turn
folgen
follow
überqueren
cross
die Kreuzung
the intersection
die Strasse
the street
die (Verkehrs)ampel
the traffic light
das Gebäude
the building
an der Ecke
at the corner
der Fluss
the river
die Brücke
the bridge
die (Bahn)schranken
the level crossing/the boomgates
das Schild Richtung...
the sign pointing to...
der Pfeil
the arrow

Road traffic signs

abbiegen
turn

Anlieger frei
residents only

Auffahrt
slip road/approach to house

Auflieger schwenkt aus
trailer may swing out

Ausfahrt
exit

Autobahndreieck
motorway merging point

Baustelle
roadworks ahead

bei Nässe/Glätte
in wet/icy conditions

Durchgangsverkehr (verboten)
(no) throughway

Einbahnstrasse
one-way street

Einfahrt
entry/access

Ende der Autobahn
end of motorway

Frostaufbrüche
frost damage

Gefahr
danger

gefährlich
dangerous

Gegenverkehr
oncoming traffic

gesperrt (für alle Fahrzeuge)
closed (for all vehicles)

Glatteis
ice on road

Kurve(nreiche Strecke)
bend/dangerous bends

Licht einschalten/ ausschalten
switch on lights/end needs for lights

LKW
heavy goods vehicle

Naturschutzgebiet
nature reserve

Nebel
beware fog

Parkscheibe
parking disk

PKW
motorcar

Radfahrer kreuzen
cyclists crossing

Rasthof-stätte
services

Rastplatz bitte sauberhalten
please keep picnic area tidy

Rollsplit
loose chippings

Schleudergefahr
danger of skidding

Seitenstreifen nicht befahrbar
soft verges

Seitenwind
cross wind

Spurrillen
irregular road surface

Standstreifen
hard shoulder

Starkes Gefälle
steep hill

Stau
traffic jam

Stauwarnanlage
hazard lights

Steinschlag
falling stones

Talbrücke
bridge over a valley

Überholverbot
no overtaking

Umleitung
diversion

Unbeschränkter Bahnübergang
unguarded level crossing/dangerous crossing

Verengte Fahrbahn
narrow lane

Vorfahrt beachten
give way

Vorfahrtsstrasse
major road

Wasserschutzgebiet
protected reservoir area

zurückschalten
to change back

Greek
Words and phrases

For clarity we have put the English phrase in light type, foreign language terms in dark type and their phonetic pronunciation in light italic.

Asking for directions

Excuse me, could I ask you something?
Συγγνώμη, μπορώ να σας ρωτήσω κάτι;
sighnómi, boró na sas rotíso káti?

I've lost my way
'Εχασα το δρόμο
échasa to dhrómo

Is there a(n)...around here?
Ξέρετε κανένα...εδώ κοντά;
xérete kanéna...edhó kondá?

Is this the way to...?
Αυτός είναι ο δρόμος για..;
aftós íne o dhrómos ya...?

Could you tell me how to get to... (name of place)
Μπορείτε να μου πείτε πώς μπορώ να πάω σε... ;
boríte na moo píte pos boró na páo se...?

What's the quickest way to...?
Ποιός είναι ο πιο σύντομος δρόμος για... ;
pyos íne o pyo síndomos dhrómos ya ...?

How many kilometres is it to...?
Πόσα χιλιόμετρα είναι ακόμα ως...;
pósa hilyómetra íne akóma os...?

Could you point it out on the map?
Μπορείτε να το δείξετε στο χάρτη;
boríte na to dhíxete sto chartí?

Ask the speaker to point to what they are saying

Δεν ξέρω, δεν είμαι από δω
I don't know, I don't know my way around here

Πήρατε λάθος δρόμο
You're going the wrong way

Πρέπει να γυρίσετε σε...
You have to go back to...

Εκεί θ' ακολουθήσετε τις πινακίδες
From there on just follow the signs

Εκεί θα ξαναρωτήσετε
When you get there, ask again

Useful words

ίσια
straight ahead

αριστερά
left

δεξιά
right

στρίβω
turn

ακολουθώ
follow

περνάω το δρόμο
cross the road

η διασταύρωση
the intersection

ο δρόμος/η οδός
the street

το φανάρι
the traffic light

το τούνελ
the tunnel

η πινακίδα διασταύρωση προτεραιότητας
the 'give way' sign

το κτίριο
the building

στη γωνιά
at the corner

το ποτάμι
the river

η ανισόπεδη διασταύρωση
the flyover

Road traffic signs

ΑΠΑΓΟΡΕΥΕΤΑΙ Η ΠΡΟΣΠΕΡΑΣΗ
no overtaking

ΑΠΑΓΟΡΕΥΕΤΑΙ Η ΣΤΑΘΜΕΥΣΗ
no parking

ΑΡΓΑ slow
ΑΥΤΟΚΙΝΗΤΟΔΡΟΜΟΣ
road suitable for cars

ΑΦΥΛΑΚΤΗ ΔΙΑΒΑΣΗ
unmanned crossing

ΔΕΥΤΕΡΕΥΩΝ ΔΡΟΜΟΣ
minor road

ΔΙΑΧΩΡΙΣΜΟΣ
road divides

ΔΙΟΔΙΑ toll
ΔΩΣΕΤΕ ΠΡΟΤΕΡΑΙΟΤΗΤΑ
give way

ΕΘΝΙΚΗ ΟΔΟΣ
(ΜΕ ΔΙΟΔΙΑ)
motorway (with toll)

ΕΙΣΟΔΟΣ
entrance

ΕΛΑΤΤΩΣΑΤΕ ΤΑΧΥΤΗΤΑ
reduce speed

ΕΛΕΥΘΕΡΗ ΚΥΚΛΟΦΟΡΙΑ
clearway

ΕΠΑΡΧΙΑΚΗ ΟΔΟΣ
minor road

ΕΠΙΚΙΝΔΥΝΗ ΔΙΑΣΤΑΥΡΩΣΗ
dangerous junction

ΕΠΙΚΙΝΔΥΝΗ ΚΑΤΩΦΕΡΕΙΑ
steep hill

ΕΠΙΚΙΝΔΥΝΗ ΣΤΡΟΦΗ
dangerous bend

ΕΞΟΔΟΣ exit
ΕΞΟΔΟΣ ΟΧΗΜΑΤΩΝ
exit for heavy goods vehicles

Η ΤΑΧΥΤΗΤΑ ΕΛΕΓΧΕΤΑΙ ΜΕ ΡΑΝΤΑΡ
radar speed checks

ΚΑΤΟΛΙΣΘΗΣΕΙΣ
loose chippings

ΚΕΝΤΡΟ
centre

ΚΙΝΔΥΝΟΣ
danger

ΚΛΕΙΣΤΗ ΟΔΟΣ
road closed

ΚΥΚΛΟΦΟΡΙΑ ΑΠΟ ΑΝΤΙΘΕΤΗ ΚΑΤΕΥΘΥΝΣΗ
oncoming traffic

ΜΟΝΟΔΡΟΜΟΣ
one-way street

ΝΟΣΟΚΟΜΕΙΟ
hospital

ΟΔΟΣ ΠΡΟΤΕΡΑΙΟΤΗΤΑΣ
road with priority over vehicles entering from side roads

ΠΑΡΑΚΑΜΠΤΗΡΙΟΣ
diversion

ΠΕΖΟΔΡΟΜΟΣ
pavement

ΠΕΡΙΜΕΝΕΤΕ wait
ΠΡΟΣΟΧΗ
look out!

ΠΡΟΣ ΠΑΡΑΛΙΑ
to the beach

ΣΤΑΘΜΟΣ ΠΡΩΤΩΝ ΒΟΗΘΕΙΩΝ
first-aid post

ΣΤΕΝΩΜΑ ΟΔΟΣΤΡΩΜΑΤΟΣ
road narrows

ΣΤΡΟΦΕΣ bends
ΤΕΛΟΣ ΑΠΑΓΟΡΕΥΜΕΝΗΣ ΖΩΝΗΣ
end of forbidden zone

ΥΨΟΣ ΠΕΡΙΟΡΙΣΜΕΝΟ
restricted height

ΧΩΜΑΤΟΔΡΟΜΟΣ
packed-earth road

Italian
Words and phrases

For clarity we have put the English phrase in light type, foreign language terms in dark type and their phonetic pronunciation in light italic.

Asking for directions

Excuse me, could I ask you something?
Mi scusi, potrei chiederLe una cosa?
Mee skoozee potray keeaydayrlay oonah kozah?

I've lost my way
Mi sono perso/a
Mee sono payrso/ah

Is there a(n)...around here?
Sa se c'è un/una... da queste parti?
Sah say chay oon/oonah...dah kwaystay pahrtee?

Is this the way to...?
E' questa la strada per...?
Ay kwaystah lah strahdah payr...

Could you tell me how to get to....?
Mi può indicare la strada per...?
Mee pwo eendeekahray lah strahdah payr...?

What's the quickest way to...?
Qual'è la strada più diretta per...?
Kwahlay ay lah strahdah peeoo deerayttah payr...?

How many kilometres is it to...?
A quanti chilometri è...?
Ah qwahntee keelomaytreeay....?

Could you point it out on the map?
Me lo può indicare sulla mappa?
May lo pwo eendeekahray soollah mahppah?

Ask the speaker to point to what they are saying

Non lo so, non sono di questa città/regione
I don't know, I don't know my way around here

Ha sbagliato strada
You're going the wrong way

Deve ritornare a...
You have to go back to...

Là, deve seguire le indicazioni
From there on just follow the signs

Là, chieda di nuovo
When you get there, ask again

Useful words

Vada dritto
Go straight ahead
Giri a sinistra
Turn left
Giri a destra
Turn right
Volti a destra/sinistra
Turn right/left
Segua
Follow
Attraversi
Cross
l'incrocio
the intersection/crossroads
la strada
the road/street
il semaforo
the traffic light
la galleria
the tunnel
il cartello/segnale stradale di 'dare la precedenza'
the 'give way' sign
il palazzo
the building
all'angolo
at the corner
il fiume
the river
il viadotto
the flyover
il ponte
the bridge
il passaggio a livello
the level crossing
le indicazioni per...
the signs pointing to....
la freccia
the arrow

Road traffic signs

accendere i fari (in galleria)
switch on headlights (in the tunnel)

alt
stop

area/stazione di servizio
service station

attenzione
beware

autocarri
heavy goods vehicles

banchina non transitabile
impassable verge

caduta massi
beware, falling rocks

cambiare corsia
change lanes

chiuso al traffico
road closed

corsia di emergenza
emergency lane

curve
bends

deviazione
detour

disco orario (obbligatorio)
parking disk (compulsory)

divieto di accesso
no entry

divieto di sorpasso/di sosta
no overtaking/no parking

diritto di precedenza a fine strada
right of way at end of road

galleria
tunnel

incrocio
intersection/crossroads

(isola/zona) pedonale
traffic island/ pedestrian precinct

lasciare libero il passo/passaggio
do not obstruct

lavori in corso
roadworks

pagamento/ pedaggio
toll payment

parcheggio a pagamento/ riservato a...
paying car park/parking reserved for...

parcheggio custodito
supervised car park

passaggio a livello
level crossing

altezza limitata a...
maximum headroom...

passo carrabile
driveway

pericolo(so)
danger(ous)

pioggia o gelo per km....
rain or ice for...kms

precedenza
right of way

rallentare
slow down

senso unico
one way

senso vietato
no entry

soccorso stradale
road assistance (breakdown service)

sosta limitata
parking for a limited period

strada deformata/in dissesto
broken/uneven surface

strada interrotta
road closed

strettoia
narrowing in the road

tenere la destra/sinistra
keep right/left

traffico interrotto
road blocked

transito con catene
snow chains required

uscita
exit

velocità massima
maximum speed

vietato l'accesso/ai pedoni
no access/no pedestrian access

vietato l'autostop
no hitch-hiking

vietato svoltare a destra/sinistra
no right/left turn

zona disco
disk zone

zona rimozione (ambo i lati)
tow-away area (both sides of the road)

Portuguese Words and phrases

For clarity we have put the English phrase in light type, foreign language terms in dark type and their phonetic pronunciation in light italic.

Asking for directions

Excuse me, could I ask you something?
Desculpe, posso-lhe fazer uma pergunta?
deshcoolp possoo lher fazair ooma pergoonta?

I've lost my way
Perdi-me
perdee muh

Is there a...around here?
Conhece um...perto daqui?
coonyes oom...pairtoo dakee?

Is this the way to...?
É este o caminho para...?
eh esht oo cameenyoo parra...?

Could you tell me how to get to the... (name of place) by car/on foot?
Poderia dizer-me como devo fazer para ir para...a pé/de carro?
pooderia dizair muh como dayvoo fazair parra eer parra...ah peh/duh cahroo?

What's the quickest way to...?
Como é que chego o mais depressa possível a...?
como eh kuh chaygoo oo mysh depressa posseevel ah...?

How many kilometres is it to...?
Quantos quilómetros faltam ainda para chegar a...?
cuarntoosh keelometroosh faltam ayeenda parra sheggar ah...?

Could you point it out on the map?
Poderia indicar-me aqui no mapa?
pooderiah eendiccar muh akee noo mappa?

Ask the speaker to point to what they are saying

Não sei, não conheço isto aqui
I don't know, I don't know my way around here

Está enganado
You're going the wrong way

Tem de voltar a...
You have to go back to...

Aí as placas indicam-lhe o caminho a seguir
From there on just follow the signs

Aí deve perguntar de novo
When you get there, ask again

Useful words

em frente
straight ahead
à esquerda
left
à direita
right
cortar
turn
seguir
follow
atravessar
cross
cruzamento
intersection
estrada
street
semáforo
traffic light
placa de trânsito `cruzamento com prioridade'
`give way' sign
rio
river
passagem de nível; cancelas
level crossing
placa indicando o caminho à...
sign pointing to...
ponte
bridge
seta
arrow

Road traffic signs

aberto
open

animais cruzando
animals crossing

auto-estrada (com portagem)
motorway (with tolls)

bermas baixas
low hard shoulder

bifurcação
road fork

centro da cidade
city centre

circule pela direita
keep right

circule pela esquerda
keep left

cruzamento perigoso
dangerous crossroads

cuidado
caution

curva a...quilómetros
road bends in... kms

curva perigosa
dangerous bend

dê passegem
give way

desvio
diversion

devagar
slow down

espere
wait

estacionamento
parking

estacionamento proibido
no parking

estrada em mau estado
irregular road surface

estrada interrompida
no through road

estrada nacional
main road

excepto
except

fechado
closed

fim de...
end of...

fim de obras
end of roadworks

gelo
ice on road

neve
snow

nevoeiro
fog

obras
roadworks

passagem de nivel (sem guarda)
level crossing (unmanned)

perigo
danger

portagem
toll

posto de primeiros socorros
First-Aid Post

saída
exit

sentido único
one-way street

vedado ao trânsito
road closed

veículos pesados
heavy vehicles

velocidade máxima
maximum speed

via de acesso
access only

Spanish
Words and phrases

For clarity we have put the English phrase in light type, foreign language terms in dark type and their phonetic pronunciation in light italic.

Asking for directons

Excuse me, could I ask you something?
Perdone, ¿podría preguntarle algo?
pehrdohneh, pohdreeah prehgoontahrleh ahlgoh?

I've lost my way
Me he perdido
meh eh pehrdeedoh

Is there a(n)...around here?
¿Sabe dónde hay un(a)...por aquí?
sahbeh dohndeh ay oon(ah)...pohr ahkee?

Is this the way to...?
¿Se va por aquí a...?
seh bah pohr ahkee ah...?

Could you tell me how to get to the... (name of place) by car/on foot?
¿Podría decirme cómo llegar a... (en coche/a pie)?
pohdreeah dehtheermeh kohmoh lyehgahr ah... (ehn kohcheh/ah pyeh)?

What's the quickest way to...?
¿Cómo hago para llegar lo antes posible a...?
kohmoh ahgoh pahrah lyehgahr loh ahntehs pohseebleh ah...?

How many kilometres is it to...?
¿Cuántos kilómetros faltan para llegar a...?
kwahntohs keelohmehtrohs fahltahn pahrah lyehgahr ah...?

Could you point it out on the map?
¿Podría señalarlo en el mapa?
pohdreeah sehnyahlahrloh ehn ehl mahpah?

Ask the speaker to point to what they are saying

No sé; no soy de aquí
I don't know, I don't know my way around here

Por aquí no es
You're going the wrong way

Tiene que volver a...
You have to go back to...

Allí los carteles le indicarán
From there on just follow the signs

Vuelva a preguntar allí
When you get there, ask again

Useful words

todo recto
straight ahead
a la izquierda
left
a la derecha
right
doblar
turn
seguir
follow
cruzar
cross
el cruce
the intersection
la calle
the street
el semáforo
the traffic light
el túnel
the tunnel
el stop
the `give way' sign
el edificio
the building
en la esquina
at the corner
el río
the river
el viaducto
the flyover
el puente
the bridge
el paso a nivel/las barreras
the level crossing/ the boom gates
el cartel en dirección de...
the sign pointing to...
la flecha
the arrow

Road traffic signs

a la derecha
right

a la izquierda
left

abierto
open

altura máxima
maximum height

arcenes sin afirmar
soft verges

žatención, peligro!
danger

autopista de peaje
toll road

autovía
motorway

bajada peligrosa
steep hill

calzada resbaladiza
slippery road

cambio de sentido
change of direction

cañada
animals crossing

carretera comarcal
secondary road

carretera cortada
road closed

carretera en mal estado
irregular road surface

carretera nacional
main road

ceda el paso
give way

cerrado
closed

cruce peligroso
dangerous crossing

curvas en...km
bends for...km

despacio
drive slowly

desprendimientos
loose rocks

desvío
diversion

dirección prohibida
no entry

dirección única
one-way traffic

encender las luces
switch on lights

espere
wait

estacionamiento reglamentado
limited parking zone

excepto...
except for...

fin de...
end of...

hielo
ice on road

niebla
beware fog

obras
roadworks ahead

paso a nivel (sin barreras)
level crossing (no gates)

paso de ganado
cattle crossing

peaje
toll

peatones
pedestrian crossing

precaución
caution

prohibido aparcar
no parking

prohibido adelantar
no overtaking

puesto de socorro
first aid

salida
exit

salida de camiones
factory/works exit

substancias peligrosas
dangerous substances

travesía peligrosa
dangerous crossing

zona peatonal
pedestrian zone

Turkish
Words and phrases

For clarity we have put the English phrase in light type, foreign language terms in dark type and their phonetic pronunciation in light italic.

Asking for directions

Excuse me, could I ask you something?
Özür dilerim, size bir şey sorabilir miyim?
urzewR dileRim, sizeh biR shey soRabiliR miyim?

I've lost my way
Yolumu kaybettim
yoloomoo kíbet-tim

Is there a(n)...around here?
Bu civarda bir...var mı?
boo jivaRda biR...vaR muh?

Is this the way to...?
...giden yol bu mu?
...giden yol boo moo?

Could you tell me how to get to the...(name of place) by car/on foot?
Bana...arabayla/yaya nasıl gidebileceğimi söyleyebilir misiniz?
bana...aRabíla/ya-ya nasuhl gidebileje:imi suhyleyebiliR misiniz?

What's the quickest way to...?
...en çabuk nasıl gidebilirim?
...en chabook nasuhl gidebiliRim?

How many kilometres is it to...?
...kaç kilometre kaldı?
...kach kilometReh kalduh?

Could you point it out on the map?
Haritada gösterebilir misiniz?
haRitada gursteRebiliR misiniz?

Opposite: Cave dwellings and surface houses in the Cappadocia village of Yaprakhisar

Ask the speaker to point to what they are saying

Bilmiyorum, buralı değilim
I don't know, I don't know my way around here

Yanlış yoldasınız
You're going the wrong way

...geri dönmelisiniz
You have to go back to...

Oradan levhaları takip ediniz
From there on just follow the signs

Oraya varınca tekrar sorun
When you get there, ask again

Useful words

doğru
straight ahead
sola
left
sağa
right
dönmek
turn
takip etmek
follow
karşıya geçmek
cross
kavşak
the intersection
sokak
the street
trafik ışıkları
the traffic lights
tünel
the tunnel
'yol ver' işareti
the `give way' sign
bina
the building
köşede
at the corner
ırmak/nehir
the river
bağlantı yolu
the flyover
köprü
the bridge
hemzemin geçit
the level crossing/the boom gates
...giden yolu gösteren levha
the sign pointing to...

Road traffic signs

Beklemek yasaktır
no waiting

Bozuk yol
poor road surface

D (durak)
D (bus stop)

Dikkat
caution

Dur
stop

Gümrük
customs

H (hastane)
H (hospital)

Havaalanı
airport

Jandarma
gendarmarie

Park etmek yasaktır
no parking

Polis
police

Şehir merkezi
city centre

Tamirat
roadworks

Tek yön
one way

Tünel
tunnel

Viraj
bend

Yangın tehlikesi
danger of fire

Yavaş
slow

200 Channel tunnel maps, road distance chart and mountain passes

Part 5

Channel tunnel maps, road distance chart and mountain passes

Channel tunnel maps

Travelling by high-speed train is a comfortable and reliable way to reach your destination

The Eurotunnel shuttle service for cars, cars towing caravans and trailers, motorcycles, coaches and HGV vehicles runs between terminals at Folkestone and Calais/ Coquelles in France.

It takes just over one hour to travel from the M20 motorway in Kent, via the Channel Tunnel, to the A16 autoroute in France. The service runs 24 hours a day, every day of the year.

For the latest ticket and travel information call the Eurotunnel Call Centre (**tel: 08705 353535**) or visit **www.eurotunnel.com**

There are up to four departures per hour at peak times, with the journey in the tunnel from platform to platform taking just 35 minutes (45 minutes at night). Travellers pass through British and French frontier controls on departure, saving time on the other side of the Channel.

Each terminal has plenty of parking, ATMs, bureaux de change, restaurants, toilet facilities, a 24-hour information point and a variety of shops. In Calais/Coquelles, the Cité de l'Europe contains numerous shops, restaurants and a hypermarket.

Folkestone Terminal

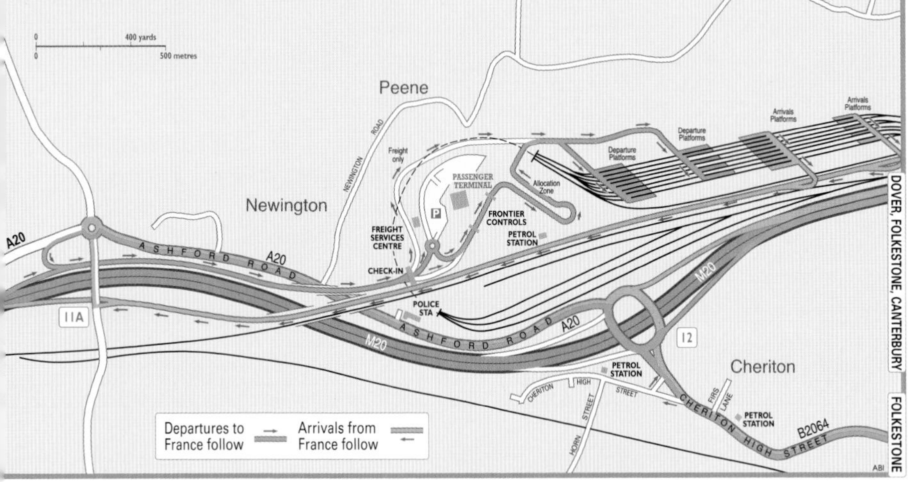

Calais / Coquelles Terminal

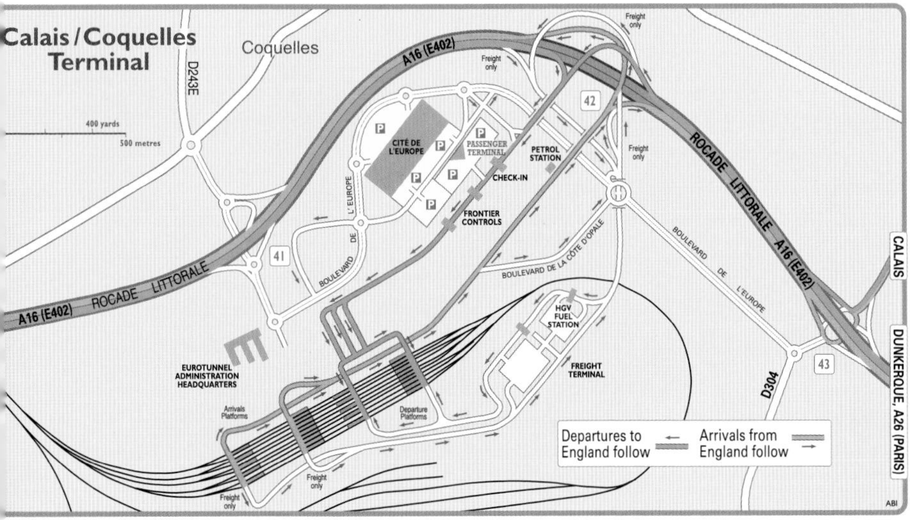

Road distance chart

Frankfurt am Main-Ljubljana = 804 km

Amsterdam	Athína	Barcelona	Belfast	Beograd	Berlin	Bern	Birmingham	Bordeaux	Bratislava	Brussel/Bruxelles	Bucureşti	Budapest	Dublin	Edinburgh	Frankfurt am Main	Genève	Göteborg	Hamburg	Helsinki/Helsingfors	İstanbul	København	Köln	Kyïv	Lisboa	Ljubljana
2760																									
1557	2520																								
1312	3520	2265																							
1718	1044	1981	2816																						
655	2288	1863	1868	1247																					
838	1971	944	1725	1363	922																				
738	3285	1691	582	2244	1295	1152																			
1091	3049	552	1815	2007	1634	852	1241																		
1225	1618	1866	2324	577	671	938	1750	1879																	
206	2568	1355	1148	1673	763	637	574	883	1181																
2181	1106	2597	3279	619	1646	1893	2706	2613	977	2136															
1398	1429	1897	2497	388	864	1111	1923	2053	194	1353	788														
1088	3455	2041	164	2594	1644	1502	358	1585	2101	925	3057	2274													
1190	3557	2143	305	2695	1746	1603	460	1686	2203	1026	3159	2376	468												
445	2323	1323	1545	1281	565	423	971	1150	788	400	1744	961	1321	1422											
908	2372	778	1683	1331	1072	165	1109	687	1088	706	1946	1261	1457	1561	573										
1178	3131	2479	2412	2090	823	1637	1839	2185	1514	1307	2490	1708	2187	2290	1214	1787									
463	2602	1763	1696	1561	294	910	1123	1470	985	591	1961	1178	1471	1574	487	1059	728								
2580	3590	3788	3792	2641	1959	2847	3220	3551	2208	2687	2483	2252	3567	3670	2489	2996	982	2192							
2649	1092	2913	3748	935	2179	2294	3175	2929	1509	2605	681	1320	3522	3626	2213	2261	3022	2493	3164						
920	2873	2220	2153	1832	564	1378	1580	1927	1255	1048	2231	1449	1928	2031	955	1528	269	469	1123	2764					
265	2506	1342	1352	1464	575	585	778	1062	972	208	1928	1145	1126	1230	192	735	1141	425	2500	2396	882				
2016	1994	3093	3228	1322	1398	2190	2655	2988	1251	2123	888	1123	3003	3106	1884	2340	2211	1681	1595	1569	1952	1935			
2296	3787	1237	3019	3188	2838	2150	2446	1202	3090	2095	3804	3103	2793	2897	2355	1989	3397	2681	4764	4119	3138	2273	4199		
1241	1572	1455	2294	530	999	836	1721	1471	435	1153	1146	443	2069	2173	804	803	1916	1203	2623	1462	1656	987	1565	2661	
533	2910	1486	766	2039	1090	947	193	1030	1546	370	2502	1719	541	645	766	905	1634	918	3015	2970	1375	574	2450	2243	1537
386	2355	1149	1355	1469	762	431	782	946	1010	213	1965	1183	1129	1233	240	500	1326	610	2687	2401	1066	188	2081	2159	956
1800	3145	614	2523	2573	2343	1535	1950	706	2458	1599	3189	2489	2298	2402	1859	1374	2901	2185	4268	3505	2642	1778	3684	619	2046
868	3415	1821	461	2374	1425	1282	138	1365	1881	705	2837	2054	310	339	1101	1240	1969	1253	3350	3305	1710	909	2785	2578	1872
1236	2567	505	2003	1526	1541	623	1429	654	1419	1034	2141	1441	1778	1881	1003	422	2158	1442	3467	2457	1899	1025	2564	1711	999
1077	1218	977	1963	1026	1033	350	1390	985	919	876	1642	942	1737	1841	662	317	1833	1120	2959	1958	1574	823	2064	2182	499
1742	2448	2878	2955	1513	1124	1938	2381	2714	1178	1850	1341	1125	2729	2833	1620	2088	1938	1408	1183	2023	1678	1662	557	3927	1593
2449	2864	3584	3661	2084	1830	2644	3088	3420	1885	2556	1758	1831	3435	3539	2326	2794	2643	2114	1116	2440	2385	2368	871	4364	2300
827	1990	1370	1880	949	585	442	1297	1278	466	739	1421	639	1655	1759	390	591	1502	789	2511	1880	1242	573	1718	2576	435
1859	597	1555	2746	1483	1693	1132	2173	1704	1376	1658	2099	1399	2521	2624	1444	1085	2586	1874	3563	2415	2327	1606	2521	2761	956
1490	3443	2790	2723	2402	1134	1949	2150	2497	1826	1618	2801	2019	2498	2601	1525	2098	315	1039	1030	3333	580	1446	2522	3710	2248
525	2465	1039	1248	1800	1068	592	659	583	1340	324	2295	1513	1023	1126	604	529	1626	910	2993	2732	1367	502	2428	1796	1287
2094	4028	1076	2818	2986	2637	1948	2244	1000	2889	1893	3602	2902	2592	2696	2153	1788	3196	2480	4563	3918	2936	2072	3997	300	2459
891	1946	1709	2045	904	341	769	1471	1601	328	902	1304	522	1820	1923	510	919	1186	657	2178	1836	927	693	1389	2814	664
1618	2807	2825	2830	1766	996	1885	2257	2590	1333	1725	1676	1378	2604	2708	1527	2035	1760	1230	962	2357	1501	1537	1029	3803	1748
1658	1190	1354	2545	1282	1493	932	1972	1503	1175	1457	1898	1198	2320	2423	1243	884	2386	1673	3363	2214	2126	1405	2321	2560	755
2180	3190	3388	3393	2241	1558	2447	2819	3152	1809	2288	2084	1853	3167	3271	2089	2597	2284	1793	387	2765	2063	2099	1196	4365	2223
1727	1121	1990	2826	303	1389	1372	2252	2007	707	1682	824	539	2600	2704	1290	1339	2402	1644	2791	1113	2143	1474	1601	3196	539
2277	3998	998	3000	2957	2838	1919	2427	1183	2842	2076	3573	2873	2775	2878	2299	1759	3378	2662	4763	3889	3119	2255	4068	403	2430
2139	654	2402	3237	424	1668	1783	2664	2418	998	2094	598	809	3012	3115	1702	1750	2512	1982	3061	781	2253	1885	1485	3608	951
2095	735	2358	3193	380	1624	1739	2620	2375	954	2050	372	765	2968	3071	1658	1707	2468	1938	2854	555	2209	1841	1259	3564	907
1534	3488	2835	2768	2446	1175	1993	2195	2541	1870	1663	2846	2064	2543	2646	1570	2143	481	1084	505	3378	624	1497	2566	3755	2293
1920	3105	3127	3132	2063	1298	2187	2559	2892	1631	2027	1973	1675	2907	3011	1829	2337	2062	1533	90	2654	1803	1839	1326	4105	2046
2333	454	2597	3432	619	1862	1978	2858	2613	1193	2288	656	1004	3207	3310	1896	1945	2707	2177	3139	642	2447	2080	1543	3802	1145
2103	735	2366	3201	606	1765	1748	2628	2383	1083	2058	886	915	2976	3163	1666	1715	2778	2020	3167	1069	2518	1849	1773	3572	915
3071	4692	4371	4304	3743	2715	3529	3731	4078	3311	3199	3586	3355	4114	4182	3106	3679	1949	2620	1360	4267	2160	3033	2698	5291	3829
1897	3363	363	2603	2322	2202	1283	2030	803	2206	1695	2937	2237	2378	2482	1663	1123	2819	2103	4128	3253	2560	1686	3433	894	1795
1636	2550	2776	2849	1509	1018	1836	2275	2608	1077	1744	1384	1121	2623	2727	1518	1986	1733	1203	1142	2066	1474	1555	738	3821	1492
1202	2097	2342	2414	1056	584	1402	1841	2174	643	1309	1240	668	2189	2293	1084	1552	1397	868	1566	1922	1138	1121	815	3387	1057
1148	1664	1789	2246	622	629	861	1673	1802	66	1103	1022	240	2021	2125	711	1010	1473	943	2246	1554	1214	895	1319	3016	378
1326	1435	1586	2424	394	988	968	1852	1603	417	1281	1009	347	2199	2302	889	936	2001	1243	2604	1325	1741	1073	1470	2793	135

Distances (in kilometres) are calculated by the shortest or quickest route and should be considered to be approximate.
The calculation includes any part of the journey taken by car ferry.

	Marseille	Milano	Minsk	Moskva	München	Napoli	Oslo	Paris	Porto	Praha	Rīga	Roma	Sankt-Peterburg	Sarajevo	Sevilla	Skopje	Sofiya	Stockholm	Tallinn	Thessaloniki	Tiranë	Tromsø	València	Vilnius	Warszawa	Wien
Milano	520																									
Minsk	2557	2048																								
Moskva	3264	2755	704																							
München	1044	502	1524	2231																						
Napoli	1099	779	2534	3240	1109																					
Oslo	2470	2144	2248	2954	1813	2898																				
Paris	799	874	2154	2861	852	1643	1937																			
Porto	1514	1981	3724	4430	2375	2559	3506	1589																		
Praha	1389	859	1149	1855	375	1483	1498	1031	2611																	
Rīga	2505	1996	472	931	1548	2655	2072	2016	3601	1260																
Roma	898	578	2333	3040	908	237	2697	1417	2358	1281	2456															
Sankt-Peterburg	3067	2558	784	716	2110	3164	2325	2574	4164	1778	562	2963														
Sarajevo	1534	1034	1664	2370	958	1492	2713	1779	2995	1046	1917	1291	2392													
Sevilla	1485	1952	3853	4559	2346	2530	3690	1771	650	2684	3802	2329	4364	2968												
Skopje	1946	1446	1934	2356	1370	1903	2823	2191	3406	1324	2187	936	2662	470	3377											
Sofiya	1902	1402	1713	2130	1326	1859	2779	2147	3363	1281	2047	1317	2455	558	3333	227										
Stockholm	2514	2189	2293	2656	1858	2943	537	1964	3551	1541	910	2743	906	2756	3736	2867	2823									
Tallinn	2807	2298	770	1043	1850	2957	2374	2314	3903	1562	302	2757	357	2214	4103	2484	2344	595								
Thessaloniki	2141	1641	1997	2414	1565	2098	3018	2385	3601	1519	2381	1164	2740	698	3572	228	284	3062	2678							
Tiranë	1910	1410	2040	2644	1334	640	3089	2155	3371	1422	2293	816	2768	385	3342	288	514	3133	2660	393						
Tromsø	4051	3725	2286	2219	3394	4479	1616	3500	5089	3077	2064	4279	1502	3894	5272	4164	3957	1605	1859	4242	4346					
València	849	1316	3217	3924	1710	1895	3130	1375	879	2048	3166	1694	3728	2328	644	2743	2699	3175	3538	2936	2706	4744				
Vilnius	2456	1947	181	863	1424	2432	2044	2030	3620	1046	291	2231	743	1660	3752	1929	1756	2089	658	2040	2111	2245	3116			
Warszawa	2022	1513	541	1247	990	1998	1709	1596	3185	612	692	1797	1167	1207	3317	1476	1433	1753	1059	1671	1659	2669	2682	435		
Wien	1361	861	1216	1923	388	1318	1784	1233	2814	285	1371	1117	1847	758	2765	1043	999	1829	1739	1237	1225	3398	2179	1115	681	
Zagreb	1130	632	1472	2178	554	1089	2312	1406	2591	645	1730	887	2205	400	2562	815	771	2356	2097	1008	862	3926	1926	1473	1039	359

Mountain passes

Snow-capped mountains tower above the town of Chamonix in France and the snaking road which carrries traffic to the Mont Blanc Tunnel to Courmayeur in Italy

It is best not to attempt to cross mountain passes at night, and daily schedules should make allowances for the comparatively slow speeds inevitable in mountainous areas.

Gravel surfaces (such as dirt and stone chips) vary considerably; they are dusty when dry, slippery when wet. Where known to exist, this type of surface has been noted.

Road repairs can be carried out only during the summer, and may interrupt traffic. Precipitous road sides are rarely, if ever, totally unguarded; on the older roads, stone pillars are placed at close intervals. Gradient figures take the mean figure on hairpin bends, and may be steeper on the inside of the curves, particularly on the older roads.

Gradients Conversion Table

All steep hill signs show the grade in percentage terms. The following conversion table may be used as a guide:

30% = 1 in 3	**14% = 1 in 7**
25% = 1 in 4	**12% = 1 in 8**
20% = 1 in 5	**11% = 1 in 9**
16% = 1 in 6	**10% = 1 in 10**

Before attempting late evening or early morning journeys across frontier passes, check the times of opening of the frontier controls. A number close at night; for example the Timmelsjoch border is closed 20.00 and 07.00hrs and during the winter.

Always engage a low gear before either ascending or descending steep gradients, and keep well to the right-hand side of the road and avoid cutting corners. Avoid excessive use of brakes. If the engine overheats, pull off the road, making sure that you do not cause an obstruction, leave the engine idling, and put the heater controls (including the fan) into the maximum heat position. Under no circumstances should you remove the radiator cap until the engine has cooled down. Do not fill the coolant system of a hot engine with cold water.

Always engage a lower gear before taking a hairpin bend, give priority to vehicles ascending and remember that as your altitude increases, so your engine power decreases. Always give priority to postal coaches travelling in either direction. Their route is usually signposted.

Caravans

Passes suitable for caravans are indicated in the table on the following pages. Those shown to be negotiable by caravans are best used only by experienced drivers in cars with ample power; the rest are probably best avoided. A correct power-to-load ratio is always essential.

Winter Conditions

Mountain passes – Key to abbreviations:
Winter conditions are given in italics in the last column. UO means 'usually open', although a severe fall of snow may temporarily obstruct the road for 24 to 48 hours, and wheel chains are often necessary; OC means 'occasionally closed', UC, usually closed, between the dates stated. Dates for opening and closing the passes are approximate only. Warning notices are usually posted at the foot of a pass if it is closed, or if chains or snow tyres should or must be used.

Wheel chains may be needed early and late in the season, and between short spells (a few hours) of obstruction. At these times, conditions are usually more difficult for caravans on the passes.

In fair weather, wheel chains or snow tyres are only necessary on the higher passes, but in severe weather you will probably need to use them (as a rough guide) at altitudes exceeding 610 metres (2000ft).

Pass name, height and country	From and to	Distances from summit and max gradient	Min width of road	Conditions (see page 207 for key to abbreviations)
***Albula** 2312 metres (7585ft) Switzerland	Tiefencastel 851 metres (2792ft) La Punt 1687 metres (5535ft)	30km 1 in 10 18.6 miles 9km 1 in 10 5.6 miles	3.5 metres 11ft 6in	UC Nov–early Jun. An inferior alternative to the Julier; tar and gravel, fine scenery. Alternative rail tunnel.
Allos 2250 metres (7382ft) France	Barcelonnette 1132 metres (3714ft) Colmars 1235 metres (4052ft)	20km 1 in 10 12.4 miles 24km 1 in 12 14.9 miles	4 metres 13ft 1n	UC early Nov–early Jun. Very winding, narrow mostly unguarded but not difficult otherwise; passing bays on southern slope, poor surface (maximum width vehicles 1.8 metres, 5ft 11in).
Aprica 1176 metres (3858ft) Italy	Tresenda 375 metres(1230ft) Edolo 699 metres (2293ft)	14km 1 in 11 8.7 miles 15km 1 in 16 9.3 miles	4 metres 13ft 1in	UO Fine scenery, good surface, well graded; suitable for caravans.
Aravis 1498 metres (4915ft) France	La Clusaz 1040 metres (3412ft) Flumet 917 metres (3009ft)	8km 1 in 11 5.0 miles 12km 1 in 11 7.4 miles	4 metres 13ft 1in	OC Dec–Mar. Outstanding scenery, and a fairly easy road.
Arlberg 1802 metres (5912ft) Austria	Bludenz 581 metres (1905ft) Landeck 816 metres (2677ft)	35km 1 in 8 21.7 miles 32km 1 in 7.5 20 miles	6 metres 19ft 8in	OC Dec–Apr. Modern road; short, steep stretch from west easing towards the summit; heavy traffic; parallel toll road tunnel. Suitable for caravans; using tunnel. Pass road closed to vehicles towing trailers.
Aubisque 1710 metres (5610ft) France	Eaux Bonnes 750 metres (2461ft) Argelés-Gazost 463 metres (1519ft)	12km 1 in 10 7 miles 30km 1 in 10 19 miles	3.5 metres 11ft 6in	UC mid Oct–Jun. A very winding road; continuous but easy ascent; the descent incorporates the Col de Soulor (1450 metres, 4757ft); 8km (5 miles) of very narrow, rough unguarded road, with a steep drop.
Ballon d'Alsace 1178 metres (3865ft) France	Giromagny 476metres (1562ft) St-Maurice-sur-Moselle 549 metres (1801ft)	17km 1 in 9 10.6 miles 9km 1 in 9 5.6 miles	4 metres 13ft 1in	OC Dec–Mar. A fairly straightforward ascent and descent, but numerous bends; negotiable by caravans.
Bayard 1248 metres (4094ft) France	Chauffayer 911 metres (2989ft) Gap 733 metres (2405ft)	18km 1 in 12 11.2 miles 8km 1 in 7 5.0 miles	6 metres 19ft 8in	UO Part of the Route Napoléon. Fairly easy, steepest on the southern side with several hairpin bends; negotiable by caravans from north to south.
***Bernina** 2330 metres (7644ft) Switzerland	Pontresina 1805 metres (5922ft) Poschiavo 1019 metres (3343ft)	15.5km 1 in 10 10.5 miles 18.5km 1 in 8 11.5 miles	5 metres 16ft 5in	OC Dec–Mar. A good road on both sides; negotiable by caravans.
Bonaigua 2072 metres (6797ft) Spain	Viella 974 metres (3195ft) Esterri d'Aneu 957 metres (3140ft)	23km 1 in 12 14 miles 23km 1 in 12 14 miles	4.3 metres 14ft 1in	UC Nov–Apr. A sinuous and narrow road with many hairpin bends and some precipitous drops; the alternative route to Lleida (Lérida) through the Viella tunnel is open in winter.
Bracco 613 metres (2011ft) Italy	Riva Trigoso 43 metres (141ft) Borghetto di Vara 104metres (341ft)	15km 1 in 7 9.3 miles 18km 1 in 7 11.2 miles	5 metres 16ft 5in	UO A two-lane road with continuous bends; passing usually difficult; negotiable by caravans; alternative toll motorway available.
Brenner 1374 metres (4508ft) Austria–Italy	Innsbruck 574 metres (1883ft) Vipiteno 948 metres (3110ft)	36km 1 in 12 22miles 15km 1 in 7 9.3 miles	6 metres 19ft 8in	UO Parallel toll motorway open; heavy traffic; suitable for caravans using toll motorway. Pass road closed to vehicles towing trailers.

* Permitted maximum width of vehicles 7ft 6in + Permitted maximum width of vehicles 8ft 2.5in ++ Maximum length of vehicle 30ft

Pass name, height and country	From and to	Distances from summit and max gradient	Min width of road	Conditions (see page 207 for key to abbreviations)
+Brünig 1007 metres (3304ft) Switzerland	Brienzwiler Station 575 metres (1886ft) Giswil 485 metres (1591ft)	6km 1 in 12 3.7 miles 13km 1 in 12 8.1 miles	6 metres 19ft 8in	UO An easy but winding road, heavy traffic at weekends; suitable for caravans.
Bussang 721 metres (2365ft) France	Thann 340 metres (1115ft) St Maurice-sur-Moselle 549 metres (1801ft)	24km 1 in 14 15 miles 8km 1 in 14 5.0 miles	4 metres 13ft 1in	UO A very easy road over the Vosges; beautiful scenery; suitable for caravans.
Cabre 1180 metres (3871ft) France	Luc-en-Diois 580 metres (1903ft) Aspres sur Buëch 764 metres (2507ft)	24km 1 in 11 15 miles 17km 1 in 14 10.6 miles	5.5 metres 18ft	UO An easy pleasant road; suitable for caravans.
Campolongo 1875 metres (6152ft) Italy	Corvara in Badia 1568 metres (5144ft) Arabba 1602 metres (5256ft)	6km 1 in 8 3.7 miles 4km 1 in 8 2.5 miles	5 metres 16ft 5in	OC Dec–Mar. A winding but easy ascent; long level stretch on summit followed by easy descent; good surface; suitable for caravans.
Cayolle 2326 metres (7631ft) France	Barcelonnette 1132 metres (3714ft) Guillaumes 819 metres (2687ft)	30km 1 in 10 19 miles 33km 1 in 10 20.5 miles	4 metres 13ft 1in	UC early Nov–early Jun. Narrow and winding road with hairpin bends; poor surface and broken edges; steep drops. Long stretches of single-track road with passing places.
Costalunga (Karer) 1753 metres (5751ft) Italy	Cardano 282 metres (925ft) Pozza 1290 metres (4232ft)	24km 1 in 6 14.9 miles 11km 1 in 8 7 miles	5 metres 16ft 5in	OC Dec–Apr. A good well-engineered road but mostly winding; caravans prohibited.
Croix 1778 metres (5833ft) Switzerland	Villars-sur-Ollon 1253 metres (4111ft) Les Diablerets 1155 metres (3789ft)	8km 1 in 7.5 5.0 miles 9km 1 in 11 5.6 miles	3.5 metres 11ft 6in	UC Nov–May. A narrow and winding route but extremely picturesque.
Croix-Haute 1179 metres (3868ft) France	Monestier-de-Clermont 832 metres (2730ft) Aspres-sur-Buëch 764 metres (2507ft)	34km 1 in 14 21 miles 29km 1 in 14 18 miles	5.5 metres 18ft	UO Well engineered; several hairpin bends on the north side; suitable for caravans.
Envalira 2407 metres (7897ft) Andorra	Pas de la Casa 2091 metres (6860ft) Andorra 1029 metres (3376ft)	5km 1 in 10 3.1 miles 25km 1 in 8 16 miles	6 metres 19ft 8in	OC Nov–Apr. A good road with wide bends on ascent and descent; fine views; negotiable by caravans (maximum height vehicles 3.5 metres, 11ft 6in on northern approach near L'Hospitalet).
Falzárego 2117 metres (6945ft) Italy	Cortina d'Ampezzo 1224 metres (4016ft) Andraz 1428 metres (4685ft)	17km 1 in 12 10.6 miles 9km 1 in 12 5.6 miles	5 metres 16ft 5in	OC Dec–Apr. Well engineered bitumen surface; many hairpin bends on both sides; negotiable by caravans.
Faucille 1323 metres (4341ft) France	Gex 628 metres (2060ft) Morez 702 metres (2303ft)	11km 1 in 10 6.8 miles 27km 1 in 12 17miles	5 metres 16ft 5in	UO Fairly wide, winding road across the Jura mountains; negotiable by caravans, but it is probably better to follow La Cure-St-Cergue-Nyon.
Fern 1209 metres (3967ft) Austria	Nassereith 843 metres (2766ft) Lermoos 995 metres (3264ft)	10km 1 in 10 6 miles 10km 1 in 10 6 miles	6 metres 19ft 8in	UO An easy pass, but slippery when wet; heavy traffic at summer weekends; suitable for caravans.

* Permitted maximum width of vehicles 7ft 6in + Permitted maximum width of vehicles 8ft 2.5in ++ Maximum length of vehicle 30ft

Pass name height and country	From and to	Distances from summit and max gradient	Min width of road	Conditions (see page 207 for key to abbreviations)
Flexen 1784 metres (5853ft) Austria	Lech 1447 metres (4747ft) Rauzalpe (near Arlberg Pass) 1628 metres (5341ft)	6.5km 1 in 10 4 miles 3.5km 1 in 10 2.2 miles	5.5 metres 18ft	UO The magnificent 'Flexenstrasse', a well engineered mountain road with tunnels and galleries. The road from Lech to Warth, north of the pass, is usually closed between November and April due to danger of avalanches.
***Flüela** 2383 metres (7818ft) Switzerland	Davos-Dorf 1563 metres (5128ft) Susch 1438 metres (4718ft)	14km 1 in 10 9 miles 14km 1 in 8 9 miles	5 metres 16ft 5in	OC Nov–May. Easy ascent from Davos; some acute hairpin bends on the eastern side; bitumen surface; negotiable by caravans.
+Forclaz 1527 metres (5010ft) Switzerland France	Martigny 476 metres (1562ft) Argentière 1253 metres (4111ft)	13km 1 in 12 8.1 miles 19km 1 in 12 11.8 miles	5 metres 16ft 5in	UO Forclaz; OC Montets Dec–early Apr. A good road over the pass and to the frontier; in France, narrow and rough over Col des Montets (1461 metres, 4793ft); negotiable by caravans.
Foscagno 2291 metres (7516ft) Italy	Bormio 1225 metres (4019ft) Livigno 1816 metres (5958ft)	24km 1 in 8 14.9 miles 14km 1 in 8 8.7 miles	3.3 metres 10ft 10in	OC Nov–May. Narrow and winding through lonely mountains, generally poor surface. Long winding ascent with many blind bends; not always well guarded. The descent includes winding rise and fall over the Passo d'Eira (2200 metres, 7218ft).
Fugazze 1159 metres (3802ft) Italy	Rovereto 201 metres (660ft) Valli del Pasubio 350 metres (1148ft)	27km 1 in 7 16.4 miles 12km 1 in 7 7.4 miles	3.5 metres 11ft 6in	UO Very winding with some narrow sections, particularly on northern side. The many blind bends and several hairpin bends call for extra care.
***Furka** 2431 metres (7976ft) Switzerland	Gletsch 1757 metres (5764ft) Realp 1538 metres (5046ft)	10km 1 in 9 6.2 miles 13km 1 in 10 8.1 miles	4 metres 13ft 1in	UC Oct–Jun. A well graded road, with narrow sections and several sharp hairpin bends on both ascent and descent. Fine views of the Rhône glacier. Alternative rail tunnel available.
Galibier 2645 metres (8678ft) France	Lautaret Pass 2058 metres (6752ft) St-Michel-de-Maurienne 712 metres (2336ft)	7km 1 in 9 4.4 miles 34km 1 in 8 21.1 miles	3 metres 9ft 10in	UC Oct–Jun. Mainly wide, well surfaced but unguarded. Ten hairpin bends on descent then 5km (3.1 miles) narrow and rough. Rise over the Col du Télégraphe (1600 metres, 5249ft), then 11 more hairpin bends. (The tunnel under the Galibier summit is closed.)
Gardena (Grödner-Joch) 2121 metres (6959ft) Italy	Val Gardena 1862 metres (6109ft) Corvara in Badia 1568 metres (5144ft)	6km 1 in 8 3.7 miles 10km 1 in 8 6.2 miles	5 metres 16ft 5in	OC Dec–Jun. A well engineered road, very winding on descent.
Gavia 2621 metres (8599ft) Italy	Bormio 1225 metres (4019ft) Ponte di Legno 1258 metres (4127ft)	25km 1 in 5.5 15.5 miles 18km 1 in 5.5 11 miles	3 metres 9ft 10in	UC Oct–Jul. Steep and narrow, but with frequent passing bays; many hairpin bends and a gravel surface; not for the faint-hearted; extra care necessary. (Maximum width for vehicles 1.8 metres, 5ft 11in.)
Gerlos 1628 metres (5341ft) Austria	Zell am Ziller 575 metres (1886ft) Wald 885 metres (2904ft)	29km 1 in 12 18 miles 15km 1 in 11 9.3 miles	4 metres 13ft 1in	UO Hairpin ascent out of Zell to modern toll road; the old, steep, narrow, and winding route with passing bays and 1-in-7 gradient is not recommended, but is negotiable with care; caravans prohibited.
+Grand St Bernard 2473 metres (8114ft) Switzerland–Italy	Martigny 476 metres (1562ft) Aosta 583 metres (1913ft)	46km 1 in 9 29 miles 34km 1 in 9 21 miles	4 metres 13ft 1in	UC Oct–Jun. Modern road to entrance of road tunnel (usually open; see chapter on Major Road and Rail Tunnels) then narrow over summit to frontier; also good surface in Italy; suitable for caravans using tunnel. Pass road closed to vehicles towing trailers.

* Permitted maximum width of vehicles 7ft 6in + Permitted maximum width of vehicles 8ft 2.5in ++ Maximum length of vehicle 30ft

Pass name, height and country	From and to	Distances from summit and max gradient	Min width of road	Conditions (see page 207 for key to abbreviations)
***Grimsel** 2164 metres (7100ft) Switzerland	Innerkirchen 630 metres (2067ft) Gletsch 1757 metres (5764ft)	26km 1 in 10 16.1 miles 6km 1 in 10 3.7 miles	5 metres 16ft 5in	UC mid Oct–late Jun. A fairly easy road, but heavy traffic weekends. A long winding ascent, finally hairpin bends; then a terraced descent (six hairpins) into the Rhône valley. Negotiable by caravans.
Grossglockner 2503 metres (8212ft) Austria	Bruck an der Glocknerstrasse 755 metres (2477ft) Heiligenblut 1301 metres (4268ft)	34km 1 in 8 21 miles 15m 1 in 8 9.3 miles	5.5 metres 18ft	UC late Oct–early May. Numerous well engineered hairpin bends; moderate but very long ascent, toll road; very fine scenery; heavy tourist traffic; negotiable preferably from south to north, by caravans. Road closed 22.00-05.00.
Hochtannberg 1679 metres (5509ft) Austria	Schröcken 1269 metres(4163ft) Warth (near Lech) 1500 metres (4921ft)	5.5km 1 in 7 3.4 miles 4.5km 1 in 11 2.8 miles	4 metres 13ft 1in	OC Jan–Mar. A reconstructed modern road.
Ibañeta (Roncesvalles) 1057 metres (3468ft) France–Spain	St-Jean-Pied-de-Port 163 metres (535ft) Pamplona 415 metres (1362ft)	27km 1 in 10 17 miles 49km 1 in 10 30 miles	4 metres 13ft 1in	UO A slow and winding, scenic route; negotiable by caravans.
Iseran 2770 metres (9088ft) France	Bourg-St-Maurice 840 metres (2756ft) Lanslebourg 1399 metres (4590ft)	47km 1 in 12 29 miles 33km 1 in 9 20.5 miles	4 metres 13ft 1in	UC mid Oct–late Jun. The second highest pass in the Alps. Well graded with reasonable bends, average surface; several unlit tunnels on northern approach.
Izoard 2360 metres (7743ft) France	Guillestre 1000 metres (3281ft) Briançon 1321 metres (4334ft)	32km 1 in 8 20 miles 22km 1 in 8 14 miles	5 metres 16ft 5in	UC late Oct–mid Jun. A winding and sometimes narrow road with many hairpin bends. Care is required at several unlit tunnels near Guillestre.
***Jaun** 1509 metres (4951ft) Switzerland	Broc 718 metres (2356ft) Reidenbach 845 metres (2772ft)	25km 1 in 10 15.5 miles 8km 1 in 10 5 miles	4 metres 13ft 1in	UO A modernised but generally narrow road; some poor sections on ascent, and several hairpin bends on descent; negotiable by caravans.
+Julier 2284 metres (7493ft) Switzerland	Tiefencastel 851 metres (2792ft) Silvaplana 1815 metres (5955ft)	35km 1 in 10 22miles 7km 1 in 7.5 4.4 miles	4 metres 13ft 1in	UO Well engineered road, approached from Chur by Lenzerheide Pass (1549 metres, 5082ft); negotiable by caravans, preferably from north to south.
Katschberg 1641 metres (5384ft) Austria	Spittal 554 metres (1818ft) St Michael 1068 metres (3504ft)	37km 1 in 5 23 miles 6km 1 in 6 3.7 miles	6 metres 19ft 8in	UO Steep though not particularly difficult, parallel toll motorway, including tunnel available; negotiable by light caravans, using tunnel via Tauern Autobahn.
***Klausen** 1948 metres (6391ft) Switzerland	Altdorf 458 metres (1503ft) Linthal 662 metres (2172ft)	25km 1 in 10 15.5 miles 23km 1 in 11 14.3 miles	5 metres 16ft 5in	UC Late Oct–early Jun. Narrow and winding in places, but generally easy, in spite of a number of sharp bends; no through route for caravans as they are prohibited from using the road between Unterschächen and Linthal.
Larche (della Maddalena) 1994 metres (6542ft) France–Italy	La Condamine-Châtelard 1308 metres (4291ft) Vinadio 910 metres (2986ft)	19km 1 in 12 11.8 miles 32km 1 in 12 19.8 miles	3.5 metres 11ft 6in	OC Dec–Mar. An easy, well graded road; narrow ascent, wider on descent; suitable for caravans

* Permitted maximum width of vehicles 7ft 6in + Permitted maximum width of vehicles 8ft 2.5in ++ Maximum length of vehicle 30f

Mountain passes

Pass name, height and country	From and to	Distances from summit and max gradient	Min width of road	Conditions (see page 207 for key to abbreviations)
Lautaret 2058 metres (6752ft) France	Le Bourg-d'Oisans 719 metres (2359ft) Briançon 1321 metres (4334ft)	38km 1 in 8 23.6 miles 28km 1 in 10 17.4 miles	4 metres 13ft 1in	OC Dec–Mar. Modern, evenly graded, but winding, and unguarded in places; very fine scenery; suitable for caravans.
Loibl (Ljubelj) 1067 metres (3500ft) Austria–Slovenia	Unterloibl 518 metres (1699ft) Kranj 385 metres (1263ft)	10km 1 in 5.5 6.2 miles 26km 1 in 8 16miles	6 metres 19ft 8in	UO Steep rise and fall over Little Loibl pass to tunnel (1.6km, 1 mile long) under summit. The old road over the summit is closed to through traffic.
***Lukmanier (Lucomagno)** 1916 metres (6286ft) Switzerland	Olivone 893 metres (2930ft) Disentis 1133 metres (3717ft)	20km 1 in 11 12 miles 20km 1 in 11 12 miles	5 metres 16ft 5in	UC early Nov–late May. Rebuilt, modern road; suitable for caravans.
+Maloja 1815 metres (5955ft) Switzerland	Silvaplana 1815 metres (5955ft) Chiavenna 333 metres (1093ft)	11km level 6.8 miles 32km 1 in 11 19.8 miles	4 metres 13ft 1in	UO Escarpment facing south; fairly easy, but many hairpin bends on descent; negotiable by caravans, possibly difficult on ascent.
Mauria 1298 metres (4258ft) Italy	Lozzo Cadore 753 metres (2470ft) Ampezzo 560 metres (1837ft)	13km 1 in 14 8 miles 31km 1 in 14 19.2 miles	5 metres 16ft 5in	UO A well designed road with easy, winding ascent and descent; suitable for caravans.
Mendola 1363 metres (4472ft) Italy	Appiano (Eppan) 411 metres (1348ft) Sarnonico 978 metres (3208ft)	15km 1 in 8 9.3 miles 9km 1 in 10 6 miles	5 metres 16ft 5in	UO A fairly straightforward but winding road, well guarded; suitable for caravans.
Mont Cenis 2083 metres (6834ft) France–Italy	Lanslebourg 1399 metres (4590ft) Susa 503 metres (1650ft)	11km 1 in 10 6.8 miles 28km 1 in 8 17.4 miles	5 metres 16ft 5in	UC Nov–May. Approach by industrial valley. An easy highway, with mostly very good surface; spectacular scenery; suitable for caravans. Alternative Fréjus road tunnel.
Monte Croce di Comélico (Kreuzberg) 1636 metres (5368ft) Italy	San Candido 1174 metres (3852ft) Santo Stefano di Cadore 908 metres (2979ft)	15km 1 in 12 9.3 miles 21km 1 in 12 13miles	5 metres 16ft 5in	UO A winding road with moderate gradients, beautiful scenery; suitable for caravans.
Montgenèvre 1850m (6070ft) France–Italy	Briançon 1321 metres (4334ft) Cesana Torinese 1344 metres (4409ft)	12km 1 in 14 7.4 miles 8km 1 in 11 5miles	5 metres 16ft 5in	UO An easy, modern road; suitable for caravans.
Monte Giovo (Jaufen) 2094 metres (6870ft) Italy	Merano 324 metres (1063ft) Vipiteno 948 metres (3110ft)	40km 1 in 8 24.8 miles 19km 1 in 11 11.8 miles	4 metres 13ft 1in	UC Nov–May. Many well engineered hairpin bends; caravans prohibited.
Montets (see Forclaz)				
Morgins 1369 metres (4491ft) France–Switzerland	Abondance 930 metres (3051ft) Monthey 424 metres (1391ft)	14km 1 in 11 8.7 miles 15km 1 in 7 9.3 miles	4 metres 13ft 1in	UO A lesser used route through pleasant, forested countryside crossing the French-Swiss border.

* Permitted maximum width of vehicles 7ft 6in + Permitted maximum width of vehicles 8ft 2.5in ++ Maximum length of vehicle 30ft

Pass name, height and country	From and to	Distances from summit and max gradient	Min width of road	Conditions (see page 207 for key to abbreviations)
***Mosses** 1445m (4740ft) Switzerland	Aigle 417 metres (1368ft) Château d'Oex 958 metres (3143ft)	16km 1 in 12 10 miles 15km 1 in 12 9.3 miles	4 metres 13ft 1in	UO A modern road; suitable for caravans.
Nassfeld (Pramollo) 1530m (5020ft) Austria–Italy	Tröpolach 601 metres (1972ft) Pontebba 568 metres (1864ft)	10km 1 in 5 6.2 miles 10km 1 in 10 6.2 miles	4 metres 13ft 1in	OC late Nov–Mar. The winding descent in Italy has been improved.
***Nufenen (Novena)** 2478 metres (8130ft) Switzerland	Ulrichen 1346 metres (4416ft) Airolo 1142 metres (3747ft)	13km 1 in 10 8.1 miles 24km 1 in 10 14.9 miles	4.0 metres 13ft 1in	UC mid Oct–mid Jun. The approach roads are narrow, with tight bends, but the road over the pass is good; negotiable by caravans.
***Oberalp** 2044 metres (6706ft) Switzerland	Andermatt 1447 metres (4747ft) Disentis 1133 metres (3717ft)	10km 1 in 10 6.2 miles 21km 1 in 10 13miles	5 metres 16ft 5in	UC Nov–late May. A widened road with a modern surface; many hairpin bends, but long level stretch on summit; negotiable by caravans. Alternative rail tunnel for winter.
***Ofen (Fuorn)** 2149 metres (7051ft) Switzerland	Zernez 1474 metres (4836ft) Santa Maria im Münstertal 1375 metres (4511ft)	22km 1 in 10 13.6 miles 14km 1 in 8 8.7 miles	4 metres 13ft 1in	UO Good, fairly easy road through the Swiss National Park; negotiable by caravans.
Petit St Bernard 2188 metres (7178ft) France–Italy	Bourg-St-Maurice 840 metres (2756ft) Pré St-Didier 1000 metres (3281ft)	30km 1 in 16 19 miles 23km 1 in 12 14.3 miles	5 metres 16ft 5in	UC mid Oct–Jun. Outstanding scenery; a fairly easy approach, but poor surface and unguarded broken edges near the summit; good on the descent in Italy; negotiable by light caravans.
Peyresourde 1563 metres (5128ft) France	Arreau 704 metres (2310ft) Luchon 630 metres (2067ft)	18km 1 in 10 11.2 miles 14km 1 in 10 8.7 miles	4 metres 13ft 1in	UO Somewhat narrow with several hairpin bends, though not difficult.
***Pillon** 1546 metres (5072ft) Switzerland	Le Sépey 974 metres (3196ft) Gsteig 1184 metres (3885ft)	15km 1 in 11 9 miles 7km 1 in 11 4.4 miles	4 metres 13ft 1in	OC Jan–Feb. A comparatively easy modern road; suitable for caravans.
Plöcken (Monte Croce-Carnico) 1362 metres (4468ft) Austria–Italy	Kötschach 706 metres (2316ft) Paluzza 600 metres (1968ft)	16km 1 in 7 10 miles 16km 1 in 14 10 miles	5 metres 16ft 5in	OC Dec–Apr. A modern road with long, reconstructed sections; heavy traffic at summer weekends; delay likely at the frontier; negotiable by caravans, best used only by experienced drivers in cars with ample power.
Pordoi 2239 metres (7346ft) Italy	Arabba 1602 metres (5256ft) Canazei 1465 metres (4806ft)	9km 1 in 10 5.6 miles 12km 1 in 10 7.4 miles	5 metres 16ft 5in	OC Dec–Apr. An excellent modern road with numerous hairpin bends; negotiable by caravans.
Port 1249 metres (4098ft) France	Tarascon 474 metres (1555ft) Massat 650 metres (2133ft)	18km 1 in 10 11.2 miles 12km 1 in 10 7.4 miles	4 metres 13ft 1in	OC Nov–Mar. A fairly easy road, but narrow on some bends; negotiable by caravans.

* Permitted maximum width of vehicles 7ft 6in + Permitted maximum width of vehicles 8ft 2.5in ++ Maximum length of vehicle 30ft

Pass name, height and country	From and to	Distances from summit and max gradient	Min width of road	Conditions (see page 207 for key to abbreviations)
Portet-d'Aspet 1069 metres (3507ft) France	Audressein 508 metres (1667ft) Fronsac 472 metres (1548ft)	18km 1 in 7 11.2 miles 29km 1 in 7 18miles	3.5 metres 11ft 6in	UO Approached from the west by the easy Col des Ares (797 metres, 2615ft) and Col de Buret (599 metres, 1965ft); well engineered road, but calls for particular care on hairpin bends; rather narrow.
Pötschen 982 metres (3222ft) Austria	Bad Ischl 469 metres (1539ft) Bad Aussee 659 metres (2162ft)	19km 1 in 11 11.8 miles 9 km 1 in 11 5.6 miles	7 metres 23ft	UO A modern road; suitable for caravans.
Pourtalet 1792 metres (5879ft) France–Spain	Eaux-Chaudes 656 metres (2152ft) Biescas 860 metres (2822ft)	23km 1 in 10 14.3 miles 32km 1 in 10 20 miles	3.5 metres 11ft 6in	UC late Oct–early Jun. A fairly easy, unguarded road, but narrow in places.
Puymorens 1915 metres (6283ft) France	Ax-les-Thermes 720 metres (2362ft) Bourg-Madame 1130 metres (3707ft)	28km 1 in 10 17.4 miles 27km 1 in 10 16.8 miles	5.5 metres 18ft	OC Nov–Apr. A generally easy, modern tarmac road, but narrow, winding and with a poor surface in places; not suitable for night driving; suitable for caravans (max height vehicles 3.5 metres, 11ft 6in). Parallel toll road tunnel available.
Quillane 1714 metres (5623ft) France	Quillan 291 metres (955ft) Mont-Louis 1600 metres (5249ft)	63km 1 in 12 39.1 miles 6 km 1 in 12 3.5 miles	5 metres 16ft 5in	OC Nov–Mar. An easy, straightforward ascent and descent; suitable for caravans.
Radstädter-Tauern 1738 metres (5702ft) Austria	Radstadt 862 metres (2828ft) Mauterndorf 1122 metres (3681ft)	21km 1 in 6 13.0 miles 17km 1 in 7 10.6 miles	5 metres 16ft 5in	OC Jan–Mar. Northern ascent steep, but not difficult otherwise; parallel toll motorway including tunnel; negotiable by light caravans, using tunnel.
Résia (Reschen) 1504 metres (4934ft) Italy–Austria	Spondigna 885 metres (2903ft) Pfunds 970 metres (3182ft)	29km 1 in 10 18 miles 21km 1 in 10 13miles	6 metres 19ft 8in	UO A good, straightforward alternative to the Brenner Pass; suitable for caravans.
Restefond (La Bonette) 2802 metres (9193ft) France	Jausiers (near Barcelonnette) 1220 metres (4003ft) St-Etienne-de-Tinée 1144 metres (3753ft)	23km 1 in 8 14.3 miles 27km 1 in 6 16.8 miles	3 metres 9ft 10in	UC Oct–Jun. The highest pass in the Alps, completed in 1962. Narrow, rough, unguarded ascent with many blind bends, and nine hairpins. Descent easier, winding with 12 hairpin bends. Not for the faint-hearted; extra care required.
Rolle 1970 metres (6463ft) Italy	Predazzo 1018 metres (3340ft) Mezzano 637 metres (2090ft)	21km 1 in 11 13.0 miles 27km 1 in 14 17 miles	5 metres 16ft 5in	OC Dec–Mar. A well engineered road with many hairpin bends on both sides; very beautiful scenery; good surface; negotiable by caravans.
Rombo (see Timmelsjoch)				
Routes des Crêtes 1283 metres (4210ft) France	St-Dié 343 metres (1125ft) Cernay 296 metres (971ft)	- 1 in 8 - 1 in 8	4 metres 13ft 1in	UC Nov–Apr. A renowned scenic route crossing seven ridges, with the highest point at 'Hôtel du Grand Ballon'.
+St Gotthard (San Gottardo) 2108 metres (6916ft) Switzerland	Göschenen 1106 metres (3629ft) Airolo 1142 metres (3747ft)	18km 1 in 10 11miles 15km 1 in 10 9.3 miles	6 metres 19ft 8in	UC mid Oct–early Jun. Modern, fairly easy two to three-lane road. Heavy traffic; negotiable by caravans. Alternative road tunnel.

* Permitted maximum width of vehicles 7ft 6in + Permitted maximum width of vehicles 8ft 2.5in ++ Maximum length of vehicle 30ft

Pass name, height and country	From and to	Distances from summit and max gradient	Min width of road	Conditions (see page 207 for key to abbreviations)
***San Bernardino** 2066 metres (6778ft) Switzerland	Mesocco 790 metres (2592ft) Hinterrhein 1620 metres (5315ft)	21km 1 in 10 13miles 9.5km 1 in 10 5.9 miles	4 metres 13ft 1in	UC Oct–late Jun. Easy, modern roads on northern and southern approaches to tunnel. Narrow and winding over summit, via tunnel suitable for caravans.
Schlucht 1139 metres (3737ft) France	Gérardmer 665 metres (2182ft) Munster 381 metres (1250ft)	15km 1 in 14 9.3 miles 18km 1 in 14 11miles	5 metres 16ft 5in	UO An extremely picturesque route crossing the Vosges mountains, with easy, wide bends on the descent; suitable for caravans.
Seeberg (Jezersko) 1218 metres (3996ft) Austria–Slovenia	Eisenkappel 555 metres (1821ft) Kranj 385 metres (1263ft)	14km 1 in 8 8.7 miles 33km 1 in 10 20.5 miles	5 metres 16ft 5in	UO An alternative to the steeper Loibl and Wurzen passes; moderate climb with winding, hairpin ascent and descent.
Sella 2240 metres (7349ft) Italy	Plan 1606 metres (5269ft) Canazei 1465 metres (4806ft)	9km 1 in 9 5.6 miles 12km 1 in 9 7 miles	5 metres 16ft 5in	OC Dec–Jun. A finely engineered, winding road; exceptional views of the Dolomites.
Semmering 985 metres (3232ft) Austria	Mürzzuschlag im Mürztal 672 metres (2205ft) Gloggnitz 457 metres (1499ft)	14km 1 in 16 8.7 miles 17km 1 in 16 10.6 miles	6 metres 19ft 8in	UO A fine, well engineered highway; suitable for caravans.
Sestriere 2033 metres (6670ft) Italy	Cesana Torinese 1344 metres (4409ft) Pinerolo 376 metres (1234ft)	12km 1 in 10 7.4 miles 55km 1 in 10 34.2 miles	6 metres 19ft 8in	UO Mostly bitumen surface; negotiable by caravans.
Silvretta (Bielerhöhe) 2032 metres (6666ft) Austria	Partenen 1051 metres (3448ft) Galtür 1584 metres (5197ft)	16km 1 in 9 9.9 miles 10km 1 in 9 6.2 miles	5 metres 16ft 5in	UC late Oct–early Jun. For the most part reconstructed; 32 easy hairpin bends on western ascent; eastern side more straightforward. Toll road; caravans prohibited.
+Simplon 2005 metres (6578ft) Switzerland–Italy	Brig 681 metres (2234ft) Domodóssola 280 metres (919ft)	22km 1 in 9 13.6 miles 41km 1 in 11 25.5 miles	7 metres 23ft	OC Nov–Apr. An easy, reconstructed modern road, but 20.8km,13 miles long, continuous ascent to summit; suitable for caravans.
Somport 1632 metres (5354ft) France–Spain	Bedous 416 metres (1365ft) Jaca 820 metres (2690ft)	31km 1 in 10 19.2 miles 32km 1 in 10 20miles	3.5 metres 11ft 6in	UO A favoured, old-established route; generally easy, but in parts narrow and unguarded; fairly well surfaced road; suitable for caravans.
***Splügen** 2113 metres (6932ft) Switzerland–Italy	Splügen 1457 metres (4780ft) Chiavenna 330 metres (1083ft)	9km 1 in 9 5.6 miles 30km 1 in 7.5 18.6 miles	3.5 metres 11ft 6in	UC Nov–Jun. Mostly narrow and winding, with many hairpin bends, and not well guarded; care is also required at many tunnels and galleries (max height vehicles 9ft 2in).
++Stelvio 2757 metres (9045ft) Italy	Bormio 1225 metres (4019ft) Spondigna 885 metres (2903ft)	22km 1 in 8 13.6 miles 28km 1 in 8 12.9 miles	4 metres 13ft 1in	UC Oct–late Jun. The third highest pass in the Alps; the number of acute hairpin bends, all well engineered, is exceptional – from 40 to 50 on either side; the surface is good, the traffic heavy. Hairpin bends are too acute for long vehicles.

* Permitted maximum width of vehicles 7ft 6in + Permitted maximum width of vehicles 8ft 2.5in ++ Maximum length of vehicle 30ft

Pass name, height and country	From and to	Distances from summit and max gradient	Min width of road	Conditions (see page 207 for key to abbreviations)
+Susten 2224 metres (7297ft) Switzerland	Innertkirchen 630 metres (2067ft) Wassen 916 metres (3005ft)	28km 1 in 11 12.9 miles 19km 1 in 11 11.8 miles	6 metres 19ft 8in	UC Nov–Jun. A very scenic and well guarded mountain road; easy gradients and turns; heavy traffic at weekends; negotiable by caravans – extra care required. Not for the faint-hearted.
Tenda (Tende) 1321 metres (4334ft) Italy–France	Borgo S Dalmazzo 641 metres (2103ft) La Giandola 308 metres (1010ft)	24km 1 in 11 14.9 miles 29km 1 in 11 18miles	6 metres 19ft 8in	UO Well guarded, modern road with several hairpin bends; road tunnel at summit; suitable for caravans; but prohibited during the winter.
+Thurn 1274 metres (4180ft) Austria	Kitzbühel 762 metres (2500ft) Mittersill 789 metres (2588ft)	19km 1 in 12 11.8 miles 10km 1 in 16 6.2 miles	5 metres 16ft 5in	UO A good road with narrow stretches; northern approach rebuilt; suitable for caravans.
Timmelsjoch (Rombo) 2509 metres (8232ft) Austria–Italy	Obergurgl 1910 metres (6266ft) Moso 1007 metres (3304ft)	14km 1 in 7 8.7 miles 23km 1 in 8 14miles	3.5 metres 11ft 6in	UC mid Oct–late Jun. Pass open to private cars (without trailers) only as some tunnels on the Italian side are too narrow for larger vehicles; toll road. Border closed 20.00-07.00.
Tonale 1883 metres (6178ft) Italy	Edolo 699 metres (2293ft) Dimaro 766 metres (2513ft)	30km 1 in 12 18.6 miles 27km 1 in 10 16.7 miles	5 metres 16ft 5in	UO A relatively easy road; suitable for caravans.
Toses (Tosas) 1800 metres (5906ft) Spain	Puigcerdá 1152 metres (3780ft) Ribes de Freser 920 metres (3018ft)	26km 1 in 10 16 miles 25km 1 in 10 15.5 miles	5 metres 16ft 5in	UO Now a fairly straightforward, but continuously winding, two-lane road with many sharp bends; negotiable by caravans.
Tourmalet 2114 metres (6936ft) France	Luz 711 metres (2333ft) Ste-Marie-de-Campan 857 metres (2812ft)	18km 1 in 8 11 miles 17km 1 in 8 10.6 miles	4 metres 13ft 1in	UC Oct–mid Jun. The highest of the French Pyrenean routes; the approaches are good, though winding and exacting over summit; sufficiently guarded.
Tre Croci 1809 metres (5935ft) Italy	Cortina d'Ampezzo 1224 metres (4016ft) Auronzo di Cadore 864 metres (2835ft).	7km 1 in 9 4.4 miles 26 km 1 in 9 16 miles	6 metres 19ft 8in	OC Dec–Mar. An easy pass; very fine scenery; suitable for caravans.
Turracher Höhe 1763 metres (5784ft) Austria	Predlitz 922 metres (3024ft) Ebene-Reichenau 1062 metres (3484ft)	20km 1 in 5.5 12.4 miles 8km 1 in 4.5 5 miles	4 metres 13ft 1in	UO Formerly one of the steepest mountain roads in Austria; now much improved. A steep, fairly straightforward ascent is followed by a very steep descent; good surface and mainly two-lane width; fine scenery.
***Umbrail** 2501 metres (8205ft) Switzerland–Italy	Santa Maria im Münstertal 1375 metres (4511ft) Bormio 1225 metres (4019ft)	14km 1 in 11 9 miles 19km 1 in 11 11.8 miles	4.3 metres 14ft 1in	UC early Nov–early Jun. Highest of the Swiss passes; narrow; mostly gravel surfaced with 34 hairpin bends, but not too difficult.
Vars 2109 metres (6919ft) France	St-Paul-sur-Ubaye 1470 metres (4823ft) Guillestre 1000 metres (3281ft)	8km 1 in 10 5 miles 20km 1 in 10 12.4 miles	5 metres 16ft 5in	OC Dec–Mar. Easy winding ascent with seven hairpin bends; gradual winding descent with another seven hairpin bends; good surface; negotiable by caravans.

* Permitted maximum width of vehicles 7ft 6in + Permitted maximum width of vehicles 8ft 2.5in ++ Maximum length of vehicle 30ft

Pass name, height and country	From and to	Distances from summit and max gradient	Min width of road	Conditions (see page 207 for key to abbreviations)
Wurzen (Koren) 1073 metres (3520ft) Austria–Slovenia	Riegersdorf 541 metres (1775ft) Kranjska Gora 810 metres (2657ft)	7km 1 in 5.5 4.5miles 6km 1 in 5.5 3.5 miles	4 metres 13ft 1in	UO A steep two-lane road, which otherwise is not particularly difficult; heavy traffic at summer weekends; delay likely at the frontier; caravans prohibited.
Zirler Berg 1009 metres (3310ft) Austria	Seefeld 1180 metres (3871ft) Zirl 622 metres (2041ft)	6km 1 in 7 3.5 miles 5km 1 in 6 3.1 miles	7 metres 23ft	UO An escarpment facing south, part of the route from Garmisch to Innsbruck; a good, modern road, but heavy tourist traffic and a long steep descent, with one hairpin bend, into the Inn Valley. Steepest section from the hairpin bend down to Zirl; caravans prohibited northbound.

* Permitted maximum width of vehicles 7ft 6in + Permitted maximum width of vehicles 8ft 2.5in ++ Maximum length of vehicle 30ft

Index

Acknowledgements

The Automobile Association would like to thank the following photographers, companies and picture libraries for their assistance in the preparation of this book.

Abbreviations for the picture credits are as follows – (t) top; (b) bottom; (c) centre; (l) left; (r) right; (AA) AA World Travel Library.

4 AA; 8/9 Digitalvision; 11 AA; 12 AA; 13 AA; 14tl AA; 14tr AA; 15 AA; 16/17 AA/R Strange; 18 AA; 19 Digitalvision; 20 AA; 24/25 AA/P Baker, 27 AA/A Baker; 30 AA/A Kouprianoff; 33 Pictures Colour Library; 34 Pictures Colour Library; 36 AA/T Souter; 37 Pictures Colour Library; 39 AA/J Smith; 40tl AA/P Bennett; 41tr AA/P Bennett; 42 AA/M Birkitt; 43t AA/M Birkitt; 43c AA/A Kouprianoff; 45 AA/A Kouprianoff; 46 AA/A Kouprianoff; 49 AA/S McBride; 51 AA/J W Jorgensen; 54 Pictures Colour Library; 55 Pictures Colour Library; 57 Pictures Colour Library; 58 AA; 60 AA/B Smith; 61 AA/I Dawson; 62tl AA/A Baker; 62tr AA/C Sawyer; 67tl AA; 67tr AA/T Souter; 70 AA/D Tarn; 71 AA/S Day; 72tl AA/S Whitehorne; 72tr AA/M Hayward; 75 AA/T Souter; 76 AA/C Sawyer; 77 AA/C Sawyer; 80 AA/K Paterson; 82 AA/C Jones; 83 AA/L Blake; 85 AA/K Paterson; 86 AA/C Sawyer; 87 AA/T Harris; 91 Pictures Colour Library; 94 Pictures Colour Library; 95 Pictures Colour Library; 97 Pictures Colour Library; 98 © David Robertson/Alamy; 100 © isifa Image Service s.r.o./Alamy; 101 © Andrej Crcek/Alamy; 103 © Diomedia/Alamy; 104 Pictures Colour Library; 106 AA/A Kouprianoff; 107 AA/M Jourdan; 109 AA/K Naylor; 110 AA/K Naylor; 114 AA/J Smith; 116 AA/A Mockford & N Bonetti; 117t AA/A Kouprianoff; 117c AA/P Wilson; 120 Pictures Colour Library; 121 Pictures Colour Library; 123 Pictures Colour Library; 124 Pictures Colour Library; 127 AA/J Smith; 130 Pictures Colour Library; 132 AA/M Chaplow; 133 AA/S Watkins; 134tl AA/P Enticknap; 134tr AA/J Edmanson; 137 AA/P Wilson; 138 Pictures Colour Library; 139 Pictures Colour Library; 142tl AA/A Baker; 142tr AA/S Day; 144 AA/P Kenward; 145tl AA/P Bennett; 145tr AA/J F Pin; 147 AA/A Mockford & N Bonetti; 148/149 AA/A Baker; 151 AA/R Moore; 152/153 AA/R Moore; 154 AA/R Moore; 156/157 AA/A Baker; 157r AA/A Baker; 158 AA/A Baker; 159 AA/A Baker; 161 AA/C Jones; 163 AA/N Ray; 165 AA/D Forss; 167 AA/C Coe; 168 AA; 169 AA/J Johnson; 172 AA/C Sawyer; 173 AA/C Sawyer; 176 AA/P Enticknap; 177 AA/P Enticknap; 178 AA/S Watkins; 179 AA/S Watkins; 180/181 AA/A Baker; 197 AA/P Kenward; 198/199 AA/P Bennett; 200/201 AA/P Baker; 202 Digitalvision; 206 AA/R Strange; 207 AA/C Sawyer; 217 AA/A Baker

Every effort has been made to trace the copyright holders, and we apologise in advance for any accidental errors. We would be happy to apply the corrections in the following edition of this publication.

Paris
New York
London
Spain
ITALY
South Africa
galleries

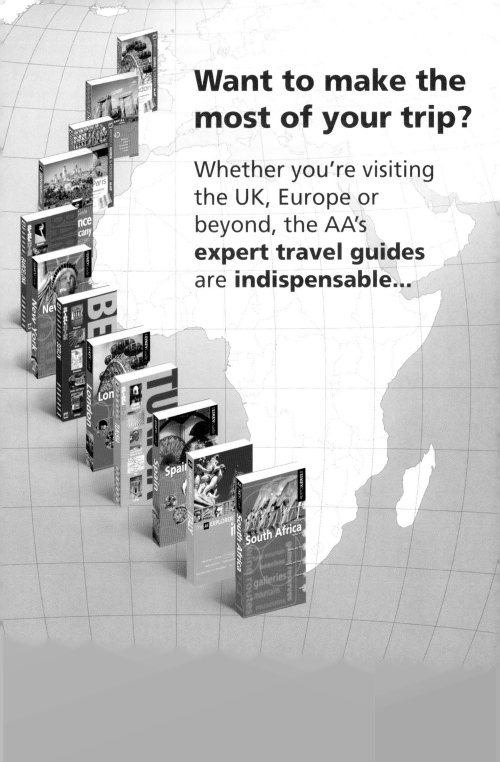

Invaluable travel guides
A little knowledge can take you a long way.
Prague
ENGLAND
PHRASE BOOK
Dutch
The AA Best Spain
Best Drives
SPIRAL GUIDE
MUNICH
The AA EXPLORER Guide
GERMANY
THE AA KEY Guide
Italy